C0-AOF-071

MAN IN EVOLUTION

MAN IN

SECOND AND REVISED EDITION
Edited by Grace F. Knoche

EVOLUTION

G. de Purucker

 THEOSOPHICAL UNIVERSITY PRESS
PASADENA, CALIFORNIA 91109

47657
0250826Y

Second and Revised Edition
Copyright © 1977 by Theosophical University Press

Library of Congress Catalog Card No. 76-45503
Manufactured in the United States of America

CONTENTS

47657

0256264

FOREWORD

SINCE ITS PUBLICATION in 1941, *Man in Evolution* has had a particular appeal for students seeking to relate the theosophic approach to evolution — seen as a cosmic process reflecting itself in the human sphere — to the theories propounded in the main by Charles Darwin and his followers. Today, archaeologists and paleontologists are daring to take a fresh look at fossil findings, so that firmly-established views as to our human origins are undergoing radical change. Those in the vanguard of evolutionary thought no longer look upon man as the descendant of monkey and ape but, on the contrary, as their antecedent, if not their half-parent.

This is calling for a total reversal of psychological outlook for a great many of us, so conditioned have we been from childhood to think of ourselves as having evolved solely through physical mutations which, by some unexplained random leap of consciousness, metamorphosed us from a witless, arboreal creature into the thinking, artistic and creative entity we know as Man.

Not so for the writer of the present volume. Gottfried de Purucker, author and educator, had since youth been a dedicated student of both modern theosophic thought and the traditional wisdom of ancient peoples concerning the origin and destiny of worlds and of the human species — teachings which confirm man as a divine being of immense antiquity, rather than as a recent emergence from lower stocks.

"Man is his own history," says the author, meaning by this that he carries within him the entirety of an aeons-long past. A cosmic entity, he enters earth as a returning pilgrim in process of *becoming*, of bringing into actuality that which is potential, hidden within his inmost essence, and which, given time and the appropriate environment, will flower into fullness. For evolution is no chance happening, but an orderly manifestation of the spiritual-intelligent drive inherent in the universe and therefore intrinsic to all life-particles. Not an atom, cell, human being or sun, could exist unless at the core of each were divinity.

With this as background and foreground of his thought, Dr. de Purucker examines critically one after another the various evolutionary hypotheses, to see where theory merges into fantasy, where concepts still unproven have hardened into "facts" without adequate basis in nature. Rigorous analysis, cogent argumentation, supported by clear-cut testimony of anatomical structure, bring conviction that the human line is of extremely ancient origin, the most primitive of all the mammalian stocks and hence must have preceded, not followed, the more specialized apes and monkeys.

With all his knowledge of biological fact, the author regards man primarily as a god, a divine spark seeking imbodiment in ever-fitter instruments through each of nature's kingdoms. The dignity of humanhood is thus enhanced, giving our lives here on earth majesty and purpose.

The material in the present volume originally stems from a series of lectures titled "Theosophy and Modern Science" given by Dr. de Purucker at the Theosophical Society's headquarters at Point Loma, California, from June through December 1927, and broadcast live over San Diego radio station KFSD. In 1929 these lectures were published, without editing, under the above title. The edition soon sold out, and the book remained out of print for several years.

In 1941 the author issued a somewhat condensed version as *Man in Evolution*, the work of rearrangement having been in large part due to the labors of Helen Savage Todd, whose editorial assistance Dr. de Purucker acknowledged with "grateful and genuine appreciation." For that edition, however, he saw no reason to bring forth "newer and later scientific arguments in favor of the theosophical doctrines," as he regarded those he had drawn upon for his lectures a decade earlier mainly as background for the "theosophical picture" he wanted to portray. To him, the principles upon which theosophy is founded are rooted in the structure of nature herself and therefore are ever-enduring. In an Appendix he did incorporate certain forward-looking statements from noted anthropologists and anatomists of the period (1930-1940), but in view of the greatly extended time span now afforded man by paleoanthropology, reaching back into the millions of years instead of a mere few hundreds of thousands, this material has been replaced in the present volume with two new entries:

Appendix I: "The Antiquity of Man and the Geological Ages" by Charles J. Ryan, which provides a succinct and easily understandable explanation of the geological ages in relation to the "rounds" or cycles and the various "root-races" traversed by humanity. Also included is H. P. Blavatsky's table of approximate time periods placed alongside the contemporary time scale of eras and epochs as generally agreed upon by geologists.

Appendix II: "Theosophy and the New Science" by Blair
A. Moffett, which assembles current findings in physics and
the life sciences, supplying valuable scientific data for comparison with and analysis of Dr. de Purucker's presentation
of man's spiritual and racial origins.

Man in Evolution offers a unique approach: it treats of
evolution from within and above, rather than from without
and below. Instead of relying on missing links among fossil
remains, it provides the one valid missing link in the entire
spectrum of evolutionary theories: that of the spiritual or
dynamic factor, the divinely impulsed intelligent entity at
work in, through and behind all processes of birth, growth,
maturation, decline and death. To the author, man's place
in the cosmos is axiomatic, not something in need of proof.

The editor of the present revision of this important volume acknowledges with gratitude the assistance rendered
by all who helped in its preparation, with a special word of
appreciation due those who undertook the exhaustive research required to check all quotations from original sources.
Where emendations of fact or reference were called for these
have been made; and the works cited by G. de Purucker
are listed in the bibliography.

GRACE F. KNOCHE

November 1976
Pasadena, California

1

AN APPROACH TO TRUTH

It is truly a wonderful universe in which we live! And yet how little we know of it — even of our own mother earth. What brought it into being? What is its past? What is its vital inner and to most of us its invisible structure? What is its destiny? And what of man, its child? Yet there is an answer to these questions, an explanation which by its nature is wholly satisfactory both to the spiritual part of us and to our intellect. It is an explanation of the facts of being not based upon the changing viewpoints of men who, however noble and earnest they may be, are nevertheless researchers only, going ahead warily step by step in their most laudable endeavor to know more of the mysteries of nature. It is an explanation which has been passed on down from immemorial time by great seers, men with wide and profound spiritual vision, who have penetrated behind the many veils of the phenomenal universe, who have sent their spirit with its accompanying consciousness deep into the womb of Being, and have brought back conscious records of what the universe is behind the veils of the outward seeming, and have handed it on through the ages to their disciples, earnest and truth-seeking men, desiring to know the truth at all costs.

This transmitted truth, this coordinated explanation of things, is given to the world today under the name of Theosophy. H. P. Blavatsky, the chief founder of the Theosophical Society of modern times, did not originate, did not invent, the majestic religion-philosophy which passes currently under this name. She was the representative of a certain body of wise and spiritually-minded men, who chose her as their messenger to the world in the nineteenth century, on account of her great spiritual and intellectual gifts. She was to strike the keynote of certain age-old truths which had been forgotten during the passage of many ages; and the aggregate of these teachings which she gave forth in outline in her great work, *The Secret Doctrine,* she called "the Synthesis of Science, Religion, and Philosophy."

It should not be imagined that *The Secret Doctrine* gives all the details of everything that is known. Such a supposition would be an absurdity; but it gives generalizations of the principles and of the lines of thought of the ancient wisdom, and these are illuminating and very helpful.

This school of thought is not based on dogmatic statements. It does not demand of anyone an unquestioning and blind adherence to declaratory assertions made by anybody either now or in the past; but it calls upon everyone to study what he reads or what he hears, and from that earnest and self-revealing study, to draw out for his own benefit, as well as for the benefit of his fellows, for his own self-development and understanding, as well as for the self-development and understanding of his fellows, the truths which those who have advanced beyond the average understanding of men have told us that they have found and experienced in these teachings.

It is for each one of us to test these teachings, to study

them honestly and, above all, to abide by the honest decisions which we ourselves will draw from our study. In thus exercising our inner faculties of will and judgment and intuition, we open within ourselves doors by which the radiant truth may enter our souls. To aspire towards truth is a spiritual exercise of the noblest kind.

There is Truth in the universe. What is that Truth? It is the universe itself, or rather the nature of the universe as manifested in the operations of that universe, which is thus self-expressing itself. Its laws are the courses of action of that universe manifesting itself in cosmic terms; and a true philosophy, a true religion, a true science, attempts to interpret these essentials in formulations of thought. The illuminated human intellect can so interpret these essentials because we, as offsprings of the universe, have all the faculties and powers latent in us that the universe has, expressing themselves in us as our own powers and faculties. Thus we have the organs to understand the universe, and this understanding comes to us through the unwrapping of the enshrouding veils of our nature.

Now the faculty of understanding is something we can evolve. This does not mean that we must build up an organ of understanding much as a man will build a house of wood and bricks. Not at all. Our understanding is within us, not without; and as we grow in self-consciousness, we shall understand ever more clearly the manifesting of the inner light that is at the core of each one of us. Therefore has every teacher said: Look within! Follow the path leading inwards!

Every human being thus becomes the pathway to truth, because in him lies the understanding. Each one of us, each for himself, is a key to all the portals of the universe. By following the pathway which reaches from our own heart and

mentality, along the lines of our spiritual being, always inwards, we attain an ever closer approximation towards that
sublime goal which on account of our expanding consciousness grows ever larger and seems to be ever receding into
some higher and grander truth; literally into that universal
life in whose roots every human being takes his origin, verily
the heart of the universe itself.

Yet, though truth comes ultimately from within, we can
learn much from the fruitage of the mature thought of another mind. Even though it is an importation into our mind
and is not the fruitage of our own inner revelation, we can
learn much from what great and good men may tell us if we
take it into ourselves and honestly ponder over it and seek to
understand it.

What did Paul of the Christians mean when he said to
"prove all things and to hold to that which is good"? Who is
the judge of the good? Is it not the inner faculty of judgment
and understanding? Or are we going to take somebody's say-
so and prove all things that come to us by that? If so, we are
merely testing one dogmatic declaration by another dogmatic
declaration.

Anything we accept from outside, we take either on trust
or on faith, unless we have the faculties developed within
ourselves of judgment, discrimination, intuition, and understanding, these four being fundamentally one. Is it not therefore clear that the process enabling one to prove all things is
the developing of the inner eye? Where else could such an
infallible touchstone be found?

Hence, if we want to prove all things, then we must do it
in the manner of all the great philosophers and thinkers:
cultivate within ourselves the inner faculty of understanding.
This can be done by deep thinking, meditation, refusal to

accept others' say-so, by the exercise of willpower in an inflexible determination to solve questions for ourselves, cost us what it may.

Such mental and spiritual exercise develops the faculties within us; or, to put it more truly, tears down the barriers preventing those faculties from expressing themselves. As we thus exercise ourselves, as surely as the sun deluges the earth with light will we attain to what we are seeking: the faculty of proving all things by knowing them for true or for false. There is the whole philosophy in a nutshell.

Now, the operations of the human consciousness are threefold, if you analyze them carefully; and these have been designated by the words religion, philosophy, and science. Religion comprises the mystical and the devotional (but not the emotional) faculties of man. Philosophy comprises faculties of the human mind which we generally call coordinating; in other words, the intellectual side, that which gathers together and formulates in intellectual fashion the truths which the consciousness intuits in or obtains from nature, often through a study of the outside world. And third is the operation of the human mind which classifies, through and by its inquisitive nature, the facts of the beings surrounding us, which it studies; and that is science.

We cannot separate these three operations of human consciousness and put each in its own thought-tight compartment. They are not fundamentally different, but are like the three sides of a triangle, or like three views or ways of looking at truth, and their unified vision proclaims the recondite facts of Being.

And on what grounds do we say that these three are one and not three radically separate things? Because the supposition that they are separate would be contrary to everything we know of nature and its fundamental unity. It would be contrary to the fact that these three avenues to truth evolve from man himself, who is a child and therefore a part of nature, and who, therefore, expresses all nature's laws and operations in himself, be they in germ or be they more or less developed. Religion, philosophy, and science are the three offsprings of the spirit of man.

As said, they are not three things in themselves, existing so to say in physical or mental space, nor do they represent three intrinsically separate laws of the cosmos. But unless the complete nature of man is brought to bear on these, unless these three facets of the human consciousness cooperate in him completely, there is something wrong, and the mental precipitate will be dogmatism.

There is a tremendous responsibility involved in the giving out of truth, or what purports to be truth. Few people have any realization of the enormous power of ideas over the understanding. The spread of religions, the ready acceptance of philosophical principles, the luxuriant growth of political fads, are all examples of the manner in which men may be torn from their intellectual and moral moorings of principle by the ideas sweeping over their minds and overwhelming both willpower and sense of moral responsibility.

Further, the science of only yesterday has built up barriers of materialistic thinking which have crippled the intuitions, warped the mental faculties, and have left to the men of our time a heritage of soulless dogmas. I have often wondered how many human minds have been ruined, and how many human souls have been emotionally degraded, by the old materialistic teaching of our fathers and grandfathers, that man is nothing but a fortuitous congeries of materials and of something somewhat more subtle, springing from this material, and called force. The idea that there is nothing within or above man intimately connected with him but dead matter, and blind force arising out of dead matter in some perfectly incomprehensible manner, is in itself degrading and unproductive of good.

What is needed is a radical change in the consciousness of men. When this takes place, and if it be directed by the forces of light and heart flowing from within, then the human race need have no fear of anything within or without. But such a change in men's hearts, such a change in men's minds and will, is a matter of long-time education, and comes not overnight.

Yet a very great help towards its coming, and making for the breaking down of the barriers which prevent its coming in order that such a new spirit may enter into our hearts and live there and govern our conduct, is the public promulgation and acceptance by men of the noble ideal of a spirit of reverence for truth so great that nothing will be held of value before it. Henceforth all religious and scientific discoveries would be placed as an impersonal offering upon the altar of truth. What a beautiful ideal, not alone for scientists, religionists, and philosophers, but also for each one of us to follow. There would then be no more enunciations of dogmatic hypotheses or theories, but a reverent placing of a life's work on the altar of that divine ideal, everlasting truth. Great knowledge brings modesty; increasing knowledge brings increasing reverence for truth.

2

THE TRENDS OF MODERN SCIENCE

THERE IS A CLEANSING WIND sweeping over the human mind in our days, a breath, as it were, emanating from the spirit within; and the minds of men are beginning to respond to the messages which this wind is bringing to the understanding.

The ranks of the scientists also are as a matter of course feeling the call of these messages from the inner worlds. They sense the incoming of a new spirit, and in consequence their theories of the cosmos are changing very greatly from what they were some years ago.

In the building up of the scientific theories, which in our days are more or less outworn, the great researchers into the mysteries of physical nature did their best to interpret what they had discovered, in terms and formulae which might appeal to men's understanding; but it was like a putting of new wine into old wineskins, the old wineskins being the prejudices and the ideas which had been inherited by all Europeans from preceding centuries of thought prevailing in the Occident.

These new ideas have been fermenting now for some three hundred years more or less, and are today bursting the old wineskins in which they were confined. Old prejudices and ideas, once thought to be real interpretations of nature, are now cast aside as totally inadequate.

This fermentation of ideas is proceeding today, not only among our scientific researchers, but is being felt by mankind generally. It is significant of the breaking forth of a portion of the mighty powers of the human spirit, and actually signifies a wider opening of the understanding. It is, on the whole, a good thing; and, despite the rather numerous and perhaps regrettable sidelines of action we may be led into, the general line of motion is in advance.

Some of the newer discoveries in physical science are indeed remarkable, and are beyond any possible anticipation that men might have had of the future at the turn of the century. I do not allude merely to material inventions. They in their way are wonderful enough, but I allude here rather to the activity in speculation or theoretic thought which our greater scientists are occupied with; I mean in brief their attempts to find a somewhat adequate explanation of things not within the framework of the old materialistic theories, and thereby to formulate and build a newer and better philosophy in and of life, which really amounts to saying a new religio-philosophical science.

But the giving birth to this newer system of thought is by no means without confusion, and what are, to many, rather severe birthpangs. And there are other difficulties which our scientists encounter, barriers which prevent the free spirit of impartial investigation. These difficulties are not merely in uncovering the secrets of nature and in their interpretation, difficult as this work unquestionably is; they are faced also with difficulties of another kind. Brave men as they are, many of them, often they dare not risk telling the truth about all that they know or suspect, nor in some cases what they have discovered, and the far-reaching conclusions which such discoveries often compel them to draw. Do not think that this is meant as an imputation of moral weakness; conditions sometimes are exceedingly hard and unfair to these earnest men.

Let me quote here the words of Dr. Byron Cummings, professor of archaeology at the University of Arizona, during the course of an address* delivered on New Year's day, 1926, before the convention of the American Association for the Advancement of Science.

Full investigation and careful tabulation of results have too often been retarded by the storm of ridicule and abuse that has been heaped upon the heads of those who brought to light anything unusual. Some of our leading anthropologists have condemned without a hearing facts that are really incontrovertible, and good men have been hounded from the profession by others who happened to hold the center of the stage at the time. A few years ago, some U.S. geologists were making investigations in southern Arizona. . . . [I] suggested to the speaker that it would be fine if he and his associates would continue investigations in this old lake bed until they uncovered some fossil remains of man. The answer came back quick and straight: "Not on your life! If we find any human bones in these fossil beds, we'll bury them instanter, pack our luggage and ask to be transferred to some other locality. We are not going to risk our professional reputation by finding any Pleistocene man."

The Pleistocene epoch is the geologic period which immediately preceded our own or Recent epoch, according to scientific chronology. Dr. Cummings continued as follows:

---

*"Problems of a Scientific Investigator," published in *Science*, vol. 63, Jan.–June 1926; p. 322.

It seems a crime to some to bring to light anything new, anything that contradicts our published theories. Men uncover the bones of Pleistocene animals in California, Arizona, and many other places; and the finds are accepted without question; but if a human bone or implement is encountered in the same or similar strata, its presence must be accounted for in some other way.

And why? For the reason that the minds of our researchers are still under the influence of a dying, if not wholly dead, scheme of theoretic evolution. And that scheme is not true.

Yet despite the difficulties that are encountered, it is a very good thing that this change that I speak of is taking place, because if we are to gain some real knowledge of the things that *are,* some comprehension of reality, we must have a free and untrammeled understanding. Prejudices must be cast aside from us entirely; and the only things that we should hold to are those which have stood the test of time through unnumbered centuries.

What are these things that endure and to which we should hold? They are the fundamental principles of ethics, the fundamental principles of thought and action which the human intellect instinctively recognizes as founded on truth — these never vary. It may be that our understanding or comprehension of them, or rather our interpretation of them, may vary from age to age, but those great ethical principles remain the same forever.

Similarly, the principle, that what can be expressed in a logical category as based upon a fact of nature should be understood as an *intellectual* formulation, is a correct rule to follow. This is vastly different from taking such a fact or facts of the cosmos, and forcing them to fit into preconceived theories or speculations that one or another researcher may have evolved from his own mind, in an attempt — honest doubtless, but an attempt only — at explaining the mysteries of nature.

The scientists themselves are the first to recognize this modern change of spirit; and may we not say that this readiness to recognize and follow the new shows an expanding consciousness, a new life, a new spirit of growth? It is a good thing, for when an idea becomes so fixed, so crystallized, in the mind that almost nothing can displace it, then indeed there is the beginning of a new "church," a new saddling upon the human spirit of still another religious or scientific system. It matters little whether this system or church be a religious or a scientific one, for the human spirit is crippled equally in either case.

We may indeed speak of a scientific church arising under such circumstances. But if such an unfortunate event were to happen, then the scientific ideas ruling such an organized body would make it as dogmatic and as perilous as any dogmatic religion that the world has ever seen, perhaps even more so, because these scientists have stood to us and still stand to the mass of men as the interpreters of the mysteries of the cosmos, and in some vague sense as high priests of truth.

This awakening of the mentality of men to the wonderful secrets of nature dates very largely from the last quarter of the 19th century, from about 1875, when H. P. Blavatsky came to the Western world. She it was who re-enunciated the wondrous philosophy - religion - science — Theosophy — acting as the messenger of those sages or great seers who hold in their keeping a formulation of the truths of nature which they have put together and tested in age after age, searching out the roots of things, and following those roots through trunk and branch and twig, until every detail of what they began to look for was found, every detail as far as our present universe goes.

The theosophist, however, claims no monopoly of truth. No one who knows anything of theosophy could accuse an honest adherent of making any such extravagant claim. But we do claim that there is a formulation of the mysteries of being, which each one of us understands according to his capacities.

It may be of interest to state here that the entire structure of modern scientific thinking, apart from the truths of nature brought to light by research and investigation, is grounded upon ancient thought, mostly that of ancient Greece. The atomic and biological theories of those early thinkers, the metaphysical and philosophical conceptions which those great men of olden times left on record in their different literatures, have come down to us of modern times, and have provided the bases of thought above spoken of.

It was during the awakening from the dark night of the early medieval period that these old conceptions brought into existence new ideas in that benighted epoch, gave thinking men new out-sights and in-sights, new visions into the nature of the universe surrounding them.

It was on these old and inspiring ideas that, for instance, the early European chemists based the theory of their science as being founded on atoms, and the manifold action and interaction of those atoms. They took over the old ideas, sometimes misunderstanding them, but nevertheless they were there — the old vital thoughts — illuminating, constructive, awakening the scientific imagination and the intuitions of those men. They did not have to begin absolutely anew or from the ground up. They took those old thoughts which they knew had been proved good and sound by generations of great ancient thinkers before them, and they constructed around those ideas what have become in our modern times respectively the science of biology, the science of chemistry, the science of physics, and many more such.

The greatest thought of all, however, lying in the background of these old conceptions, has escaped the perception of modern thinkers. And what is this greatest thought of all? It is the absolute unity of the universe, the absolute oneness of being, the full and all-comprehensive nature of the cosmos, as being, every part of it, interlinked with every other part, so that nothing is vagrant or estranged from any other part, but all hang together. And because the universe is obviously such (for we know nothing to the contrary of it), naturally the mentality of man, his intellectual faculties, man being a child of this universe, follow the same course of necessity.

There is but one cosmos. There can be but one fundamental truth about that cosmos; and that truth is itself expressed in the formulation in logical categories of the facts of nature which we know, and the further facts of nature which we learn by investigation and research, and which fit into their proper places in the temple of science, as into niches waiting to receive them. That is the grand conception which comprises the fundamental basis of all theosophical thinking.

There is an immense difference, however, between an established fact of nature, of being, and a hypothesis, a theory, a speculation, a scientific fad. Facts we accept; theories we accept or reject according as we feel, or as we know, that they are true or false, as the case may be. So then when we compare theosophy and modern science, we do it solely on the ground of established facts; because after all, that is what true science is — the classification and the establishment as actualities of the facts of nature.

It is interesting to watch the progress of modern science and see how closely it is approaching to certain truths clearly enunciated or plainly hinted at in the theosophical philosophy. Let me enumerate some of these:

1. That simple materialism, comprising fortuity, chance, and dead matter, as producing life and consciousness, and as an explanation of life and being, is unscientific, unphilosophical, and impossible because contrary to nature and reason.

2. That other planets are inhabited by intelligent beings, or are not so inhabited, as the case may be; a fact that has been generally denied by astronomers, not from knowledge but from ignorance of any such planets — the only planet that we *do* know, our earth, producing living and intelligent beings. A complete denial, therefore, is irrational, purely speculative and theoretical, and based solely on supposedly true facts concerning atmosphere, cold or heat, etc., as these are known on our planet *only*. There have always been, however, eminent astronomers who on the ground both of intuition and scientific probability have not only privately admitted the probable existence of other planets elsewhere which in all likelihood are inhabited as ours is, but have even courageously written of their belief.

3. The unreal nature of the physical universe or sphere; i.e., that all that we see and know with sense perceptions is its purely phenomenal appearance.

This statement, in its philosophical, scientific, and religious reaches, is more or less accepted by the greatest men of science today, at least in principle.

It should be remembered, however, that when we speak of the "unreal nature" of the physical universe, we do not mean that the physical universe does not exist. We mean first, that our understanding of it is unreal, because we do not know it in its essence; and also that considered in its phenomenal aspects it is not a fundamental reality, because it is temporal, changing — effectual, not causal.

4. That force is etherealized matter; or, preferably, that matter is equilibrated or crystallized forces.

These last two items have now been fully admitted by philosophical scientific thinkers and researchers.

5. That electricity and magnetism, twins, are particular, i.e., corpuscular, formed of particles or corpuscles, and therefore are matter. They are the phenomenal effects of noumenal causes — ethereal matter or rather ethereal matters.

Modern science has not yet come to the point where it is willing to acknowledge that magnetism, the alter ego of electricity, is particular or corpuscular, as it now admits electricity is.

6. That the so-called modes of motion, formerly considered as a definition of forces, was a vain and superficial effort to explain forces and energy by ticketing them in a new manner, which explained nothing at all; all forces, in fact, being simply moving and ethereal matters, or vice versa.

7. That all matter is radiant, radioactive, that is, it *radiates* — some forms or states of matter more than others. Note in this connection the work and discoveries of Becquerel, Roentgen, the Curies, Rutherford and Soddy, and the work on similar lines of other great men in other countries.

8. That light is corpuscular (as well as wavelike, adds science) because it is a matter, a substance. Light is a material radiance, in fact.

9. That the transmutation of matters, hence of metals, is a fact in nature, occurring hourly, momently, instantly; and continuously throughout time.

10. That the atom is a divisible body — i.e., the *chemical* or *physical* atom; it is, so to say, merely a smaller molecule.

11. That there is a close analogical resemblance between the operations of the forces and matters working in an atom and those in a solar system; and that each atomic system is in its turn composed of physical infinitesimals or of sub-atoms, or of infra-atoms — called electrons and protons, etc., by science.

12. That the nebular hypothesis as commonly accepted formerly was incomplete, insufficient as a workable hypothesis, although containing certain elements of truth.

13. That the sun is neither burning nor even hot in the ordinary sense (nor is it cold), although it is *glowing* in one sense, superficially; nor does it recuperate its heat, such as it is, and light and other forces as formerly described by astronomers; nor by mere shrinkage of volume, nor by the impact of falling meteors; nor do even the theories of atomic disintegration *fully* account for its vast and ceaseless expenditure of energy.

Much of this is now practically admitted by the scientists, at least in principle. All of it would be fully admitted were there some alternative explanation that they could accept. This they have not yet discovered or evolved from their understanding of the facts before them.

14. That storms — rain, hail, snow, wind — and droughts, likewise most of the earth's heat, are not wholly caused by or derived directly from solar energy, but result from electromagnetic interplay of forces between the earth's mass and the "meteoric masses," or "veil" above our atmosphere —

such phenomena or effects being accompanied partly caus-
ally, partly effectually, by periodic expansion or dilation of
the atmospheric body, and by periodic contractions thereof;
and that the glacial periods of geology, so called, are largely
due to the same cause or causes.

15 and last. That Darwinism and Haeckelism are inadequate to explain and account for the mass of biological
phenomena, from the evolutionary point of view; and that
Darwin's, Haeckel's, Huxley's and Spencer's "natural selection" and "survival of the fittest" are not other than secondary or minor operations of nature, at the very best; that
"transformism" as taught by the speculative scientists is not
evolution, and is both uncertain as a theory, because purely
speculative, and really unscientific likewise because based
on data too few. It is therefore both incomplete and insufficient. Other chapters will indicate to what a large extent
scientists have moved in the direction of theosophy.

I could readily lay before you additional instances of
foreshadowings of other facts of nature and of universal
being, which are now on the highroad of acceptance by the
scientific leaders of our time. However, let me mention just
one more, before passing on. I refer to a statement by
a British scientist, Sir Oliver Lodge, of a new theory of
vision. It was to the effect that vision consisted of two factors: light radiating from an object, which entered the physical eye, and also a ray from within the man himself, which
left the eye and centered upon the object. In other words,
what appears to have been in Sir Oliver's mind was the
existence of a crosscurrent of etheric energy, both together
comprising conscious vision — either one lacking, then vision
failed.

Now this theory is but the old Platonic and Aristotelian

doctrine of vision which was likewise accepted by most Greek and Roman philosophers; and it seems to be very largely the theory of vision as held in other parts of the ancient civilized world.

Much discussion takes place in these days in regard to the work of the scientists — both for and against. Let me quote what was said by the Bishop of Ripon (E. A. Burroughs) in an address given at Leeds, in England (1927), at a meeting of the British Association for the Advancement of Science. Certain ideas in this clergyman's address are very fine in some respects, but on other points we are inevitably compelled to differ from him. He said: *

We could get on very much more happily if aviation, wireless, television and the like were advanced no further than at present.

Dare I even suggest, at the risk of being lynched by some of my hearers, that the sum of human happiness, outside of scientific circles, would not necessarily be reduced if for, say, ten years every physical and chemical laboratory were closed and the patient and resourceful energy displayed in them transferred to recovering the lost art of getting together and finding a formula for making the ends meet in the scale of human life?

It would give 99 per cent. of us who are non-scientific some chance of assimilating the revolutionary knowledge which in the first quarter of this century 1 per cent. of the explorers have acquired. The 1 per cent. would have leisure to read up on one another's work; and all of us might go meanwhile in tardy quest of that wisdom which is other than and greater than knowledge, and without which knowledge may be a curse.

As things stand today, we could get on without further additions for the present to our knowledge of nature. We cannot get on without a change of mind in man.

Let me point out, first of all, that it is not knowledge

---

*As reported in *The Literary Digest,* Oct. 1, 1927.

itself, but the abuse of knowledge, which is wrong; and abuse will inevitably follow when knowledge falls into weak and evil minds. It is not aviation, or television, or the working at full pressure of the physical and chemical laboratories of the scientific men, which is wrong; but the misuse of the knowledge which is given to all and sundry without safeguards or reticences of any kind.

Why try to cripple the soaring of the human spirit, even for ten years? And then the idea that "it would give 99 per cent. of us who are non-scientific some chance of assimilating the revolutionary knowledge which in the first quarter of this century 1 per cent. of the explorers have acquired," seems to me to be entirely arbitrary, because there is no guarantee of any such assimilation of the acquired knowledge so called ever taking place; nor indeed have we any absolute certitude that it is knowledge per se. It may be merely imperfect information based upon the facts of nature more or less inadequately investigated. This ten-year moratorium might give the ninety-nine percent an unfortunate opportunity to accept as dogmatic truths the changing theories which the one percent have collected together or have evolved from their inner consciousness during the past hundred years or more.

In one sense it is the salvation of science from dogmatism that it advances with gigantic strides and without interruptions of any kind, and that the theories of one day, then taught as dogmas and accepted by the people as "religious truths," scientifically speaking, should be shown perhaps in the next five years to be merely theoretical speculations. Nothing so much as this saves science from even greater dogmatism than it now unfortunately has in some respects, as shown by the writings of certain exponents of prevalent scientific theories. Such was the case as regards transformist theories of biology in an attempt to explain progressive development and deriving man from the apes, a theory which is now very largely abandoned by biologists themselves.

The idea, however, that the one percent would have time, during this so-called scientific moratorium of ten years, to read up "on one another's work," is an excellent one, and it is a pity that such does not take place, because in point of fact our scientists today are too largely separated from the work and thoughts of each other.

The fundamental principles in all lines of scientific research today are in question as to whether they represent truths or untruths or half-truths — falsehood or reality. The bases of science itself are called in question, and this is an excellent thing; for nothing is so easy as to slide into dogmatism, from the feeling that we have points of information which are actual realities.

It is an unfortunate tendency of the human mind to insist upon the value of its own understanding and the reality of the theories which it propounds. Hence arise dogmatism, impatience with the views of others and, if the time should be ripe and the mind should be uninformed, the arising of persecution of those who differ from us. The lesson, therefore, that we should draw from it all is that we must ourselves find the key of nature within ourselves, and of our own initiatives accept nothing that is taught to us as authoritative, except that which we inwardly find to be true.

It may be that our knowledge is small and our judgment weak in our present stage of evolution, and that we may reject or pass over some truth by following the noble rule of individual initiative and judgment; but in following that rule, we are cultivating the faculties of our will and discrimination, and of our own understanding. Very soon these faculties will become so strengthened by this exercise that the possibilities of error or of misjudging some truth of nature will, with the passage of time, grow ever more remote, until finally these possibilities of error vanish.

The Bishop of Ripon is right in saying that wisdom is other than and greater than knowledge, and that without wisdom knowledge may be a curse. Wisdom is interior illumination. It is greater than the mere accumulation of scientific facts or the mere evolving of scientific theories. Knowledge in that sense, or a blind following of theories stuffed into our minds by our modern-day methods of instruction, is sterile; also, the ideas floating in the air which enter into our minds and affect us similarly, psychological subjects as we all are, may actually be an automatic curse — not because information or vagrant ideas or any one of various theories are in themselves wrong, but because they did not originate with us. Hence, they are alien to our will and even to our understanding, which fact makes us unfit properly to understand them and to use them aright as masters ourselves rather than as slaves.

Let our laboratories, then, be kept open; let work go ahead. But let there be an end merely to theory-spinning and hypothesis-forming. We do not object to the forming of theories or hypotheses when these are useful in classifying the results of research and in attempting to deduce laws from them. We do not object to the most fervid and continuous use of the scientific imagination when that is helpful to the same ends. On the contrary, that is a laudable pursuit. What we do object to is the postulating of theories and hypotheses as proven facts of the cosmic process, that is, as representing the procedure of the universe itself.

3

THE LAW OF ANALOGY

EVERY THINKING MAN, whether he be of materialistic bent of mind, or mystical or scientific, must realize that because nature proceeds in an orderly manner, its courses can be subjected to categories of logical thinking, if indeed we know those facts of nature. Hence, provided that our method of thinking be based on the established facts of being, there can be no conflict between truth on the one hand and our formulation of truth on the other hand. Theosophy is such a formulation of truth, an aggregate of doctrines dealing with the fundamentals of the cosmos. It is not a new system; it is as old as the ages. If you look back into the literatures of historical periods, you will find it there; and you will recognize also that, in other parts of the world, among nations of men whose literatures have not reached us, there must have been the same method of thinking, the same aspirations towards a universal truth, the same human mentality reducing the facts of being to logical formulation.

It would be an extraordinary fact, inexplicable indeed, if we could imagine a human mind or a body of men, who

could think of something which no one had ever thought of
before, and thus as being out of the cosmic life and procedure. "There is nothing new under the sun," a wise old
Hebrew is reported to have said; and our instinct tells us
that that old saying is true.

Nature moves in cycles, and as these cycles run their
rounds, nations and men rise, reach their maturity, give
forth the flowers of their civilizations; and then, as the wheel
of time whirls on in its unceasing course, they in turn fall,
to give place to men of newer blood who in turn develop
their own systems of thought — originating them, as they
falsely think, but in reality only stating again, albeit in the
manner of their own racial genius, the same old truths that
had been known in former ages. Yet it is true enough that
if we take the larger view of destiny and time, we find that
there is a gradual enlargement of what was known in the
past: what was the child of the mind and spirit and heart
of those who lived in ages long gone by.

Thus we see that the human intelligence operating
through the ages, because based fundamentally on cosmic
factors, must function or operate analogically. What was
regarded as a truth in former ages as based on natural fact,
will be recognized on analogical or similar principles in
a later age; because the fact remains that while human intelligence advances progressively to higher levels of understanding, such development is always on analogical lines
based on the cosmic structure. For the universal organism
operates as a consistent whole, and therefore one general
pattern of action is discernible in all its parts throughout the
entire cycle of manifested life.

Analogy, the much-abused but powerful instrument of
human thinking, is now recognized as one of the master

keys opening nature's portals. One general law and one common system of manifestation rule throughout the universe, and in this fact lies the meaning of that wonderful Hermetic axiom: "As it is above, so is it below; as it is below, so is it above." Or, expressed more fully: As things are above so are they in all intermediate spheres, and below. And as they are here below, or underneath us in planes still more material than ours, so are they above us in planes vastly more spiritual. This does not imply identities in any collection of cases, but states the operation of uniform action in what we call nature; and any such uniform action, consistent always and continuous, having a beginning and proceeding to its cyclic end, we call a "law of nature."

You know that the old Egyptians had some very wonderful books, very few of which have come down to us except by allusion and by quotation, mostly to be found in the Greek and Latin classics. The foremost among these were called the Books of Thoth; and the old Greeks translated the name of this Egyptian god Thoth by using the name of one of their gods, Hermes, the Interpreter, and thence called these books the Hermetic writings — unquestionably with some well-defined suggestion of their being interpretative of hid mysteries.

Most of these Hermetic books have been lost, many doubtless destroyed through the early religious bigotry and fanaticism that followed the downfall of the ancient Mediterranean 'pagan' religious beliefs. In any case one or two have survived, which probably have been more or less touched up by Christian hands; but underneath this retouching there still shines the splendor of the ancient thought. These old books cannot be understood as you run through them; they require earnest meditation and intellectual effort, mental exercise, in order to get at the real meaning which lies not alone in the words, but also behind and within them. It is by realizing this and studying them under this light that we may get the secret of the sense which those words imbody.

In one of these 'books,' a very short one, later called "The Emerald Tablet," we find the ancient and universal teaching of analogy. Its opening words are as follows:

> True, without any error; certain, very true; That which is Above, is as that which is below; and that which is below, is as That which is Above; for achieving the Wonders of the Universe. . . .

This marvelous conception of the uniformity of universal nature within and without, above and below, existed long before it was committed to writing in Egypt and Greece. It is one of the stock-teachings of mysticism of all antiquity and, so far as we know, of the entire ancient world, Eastern and Western. We also find the teaching given in the Upanishads which are among the most noble mystical writings imbodying the theosophy of the Hindus. For instance, in the *Katha-Upanishad,* the teacher is setting forth the absolutely essential identical nature of the universe and the human spirit-soul. The words there are:

> What is here [in the world which our senses cognize] the same is there [in the invisible world of the spirit]; and what is there, the same is here. He who sees any difference here [between these two, between the invisible and the visible] goes from death to death.
>
> It is by the consciousness (manas) that this [the universe we cognize] is to be understood, and then there is no difference at all [the essential identity of all things is recognized]. He passes from death to death who sees any difference here.   — iv, 10–11

The meaning is that he fails to recognize his essential

0250086

identity with the spirit-life of the spaces, and is therefore plunged in illusion or māyā, which means that he is enchained by the attractions of matter, and therefore follows those attractions from birth to birth in physical and ethereal bodies. In other words, he is compelled to follow the ever-turning wheel of life in reincarnation after reincarnation until he learns the oneness of all things visible and invisible, through the developing of his inner self into intellectual understanding: recognizing that the essence of the universe is the heart of his heart, the soul of his soul, and the spirit of his own spirit. Then, having obtained vision, he is freed from the wheel of revolving destiny. He has attained wisdom and freedom; he has become a master of and in life, instead of remaining a slave of the wheel.

What is in the macrocosm or the great universe is in the microcosm or the little universe, whatever that little universe may be, i.e., in one of the smaller parts which compose the whole. What does this mean and imply? That any one of the numberless hosts of little lives or living entities, as a growing and learning thing, has infinity for its playground of progress and evolution, because in itself are contained all forces, latent or active, and all possibilities which inevitably seek their fields of action sooner or later, and therefore require infinity in space and eternity in time for the expression of incomputable possibilities.

There is no absolute gulf separating part from part anywhere; there are no jumping-off places beyond which is nothing, not anywhere. Everything is connected together by unbreakable bonds of law and order, of causation and of effectuation. Everything is expressing its own inherent powers as well as endless capacities for learning, and thereby developing other powers in the latent, learning each time

47657

that it expresses them to unfold them more fully, and thereby to grow larger in comprehension inwardly, and more
powerful in the expression outwardly of the spiritual forces
within.

It is contrary to reason and logic to suppose that one
part of nature operates in contradictory action with any
other part. If there be those so-called laws of nature and
being, they must function equally and consistently everywhere, and function everywhere similarly. It is upon this
one thought, that nature, being a unity in which there is no
fundamental or intrinsic diversity anywhere, but in which
there exists only the diversity of different entities proceeding
towards a larger perfection, from the one fundamental impulse of the one universal life — it is upon this one thought
that the noblest generalization of the ancient outlook was
based. This majestic generalization to one fundamental law
of life is understandable to human beings because we par-
take of that life; and the multitudinous variations that we
see in the phenomenal world are but the ringing of all
possible changes that nature so lavishly provides for our
admiration and utmost reverence.

It is upon such basic thoughts as these that the ancients
reasoned and founded their systems of religion and philosophy, and they are now discovered to have been right, and
their reasoning was, from the above universally accepted
bases, called deductive and analogical. These same bases
are recognized today as fundamental in all philosophical
thinking; and it was merely in order to prove their consequent deductions and analogical discoveries, that they likewise used the inductive method of proceeding from a
multitude of small particles in an attempt to check their
former reasoning.

In the last century it was customary to teach that the deductive system of thinking was that of the ancient times, when men did not know enough about external nature to think inductively; but that now all true thinking is done by induction, reasoning from details to generals; and that all we have to do is to have, mathematically speaking, an infinite number of details, and we shall, by gathering these and correlating them into systems, reach an infinite truth. But how long would it not take to wander from detail to detail, through an infinite time, in order to reach an infinite truth!

Why did they misrepresent the ancient system of thinking? The idea was that these earlier thinkers were so weak in their intellectual capacities, that they merely imagined general truths and reasoned down from them, in an effort to make that reasoning accord with the observed facts of nature. But that was a sheer supposition and a false one, and was based on nothing but the purely human idea, "We are the latest people, and therefore we must be the most advanced. Our method of thinking is better." Perhaps it was for them. But the ancient thinkers, when they reasoned deductively, did not so think as they are alleged to have done. They in their endeavors to read some of the more recondite, more secret truths of nature, began their thinking from postulates considered as *fundamental laws of the human mind.*

As a matter of fact, these very methods of logic, deduction, induction, and analogy, were taken over by us from the Greek thinkers, the first of the European peoples who investigated logical differences by rules and taught them to us, rules which we willfully misapplied in condemnation of our own masters! These historical facts it is well to recall, for the reason that these logical processes lie in the operations of the human consciousness itself, and our recognition of these facts explains a great many things that puzzle students of the old literatures.

It is good to notice that the methods of analogical thinking are again being used in modern scientific circles. I refer particularly to the matter of the structure of the atom. According to recent scientific theories, atoms are now believed to copy analogically the structure and general operations of the forces in the solar system which we know something about. This shows us that one of the finest and most powerful instruments of thought leads us truly on — if we be careful and do not reason by false analogies — to see that nature is built upon a common plan in all its stages from the highest to the lowest, and that it therefore follows similar lines of action everywhere, in the great as in the small.

I might say in passing that had the documents, upon which the Christian religion is said to be founded, been examined in the same spirit of impartiality that is shown today by investigators into the operations of nature, we should know more now about the life of the great Nazarene, about the life of the great Syrian called Jesus, than we do know. But it is one of the weaknesses of the human mind, to wish to establish its own theories as actual truths, in other words to wish to establish its own prejudices as facts.

Let us never forget, then, that the universe is one vast organism. There are no impassable barriers between body and body, between mind and mind, between entity and entity, all of them being children or offspring, that is, coherent parts, of that vast organism of the cosmos; and in consequence having and manifesting in the small all the potencies and powers and energies and forces that exist in that organic

universe. The offspring is a replica, a copy in the minute, of
the great, the microcosm or little world copying in all respects
the macrocosm or great world.

It is along the lines of these forces and energies pouring
forth from the heart of the universe ultimately, that proceed
the psychic, the astral-vital, indeed, in the higher beings
also the intellectual and spiritual powers and qualities which
man and all other entities, great or small, manifest.

This sublime fact of nature, that all beings are inextric-
ably linked together on all the various planes, from the
spiritual to the physical, we express by the term "universal
brotherhood." We might call it the "spiritual or divine oneness" of all that is. Once a man recognizes the working of
this law upon the human plane, he knows that every step
forward that a brother takes, by so much the more is he
himself advanced. More, he knows that by as much as any
spiritual unit, any soul, progresses, by so much does it raise
the entire body of beings to which it belongs.

This spiritual oneness does not mean sheer identity of
consciousness, but oneness in the sense that the innumerable
hosts of thinking beings on this planet, as well as on the
countless other inhabited celestial bodies of the universe, all
spring from one common fountain of life. All are pressing
forward through the innumerable gates of life towards the
same grandiose and ultimate destiny — each such entity pursuing its own individual path, but growing itself greater as
its consciousness evolves and expands; so that it recognizes
in fullness its true oneness in spirit, in sympathy, in destiny,
in origin, with everything else. And part of that destiny is
that each entity must become a fountainhead of innumerable
other entities springing from it, just as a father gives birth
to his child, and as that child gives birth to another, and just

as the human soul gives birth to thoughts; for thoughts after all are ethereal matter, and therefore are things. Thus are the hosts of lives linked together in an endless chain.

A study of the law of analogy brings with it an ever-greater realization of the fact that all things work together towards a common end. There is no real separation or disjunction between thing and thing, or between consciousness and consciousness; therefore none between world and world, and man and man. The farther we go from the heart of Being, the farther we advance outwards from the splendor within, the more are our eyes blinded by the illusions of the phenomenal world, because we lose the faculty of discrimination, of judgment and of intuitive power, for our conscious life is then centered in the multitude of things around us and beneath us, in the atomic world which enshrouds and surrounds us. Our consciousness is, so to say, become diffused and spread over multitudes, instead of being concentrated, as it always is at the heart of our being, in supernal light.

Yet such is the pathway of progress, and it is in this manner that we learn the nature of this universe surrounding us; and such course upwards from the invisible on each new cycle is each time a course of progress on a higher plane.

4

THE ATOMIC WORLD

THE SCIENCE OF chemistry, from the time of its renaissance in modern Europe, was founded upon old Greek thought; but I should like to illustrate, for purposes of future study and in order to avoid confusion, how a true thought may work along very well for a little while, and explain things admirably, and yet in view of new discoveries have to be either modified or even renounced perhaps. In such case the fault lies not in the true thought itself, but in a misunderstanding of its nature and scope. We shall illustrate this by referring to the atomic theory.

The Greeks had what they called their Atomistic philosophy, founded on the work of the philosophers Leucippus, Democritus, and Epicurus, more particularly of the former two. As a matter of fact, Leucippus enunciated a theory of the cosmos, a cosmology, which was later developed by Democritus, who lived some forty or fifty years later.

This Atomistic School had great vogue in ancient times. Lucretius, the noble Roman philosopher and poet, in his didactic poem, *On the Nature of Things,* teaches in splendid fashion the same theory, although he himself was rather a disciple of Epicurus, than directly of Democritus. Epicurus himself was an atomistic philosopher, and whereas he derived the main principle of his theory from Democritus, yet he gave to his own philosophic and scientific ideas a somewhat individualistic turn.

All these thinkers, who taught more or less exactly the same basic thoughts with regard to physiology, as science was called then — the science of *physis* or "nature" — taught that behind all material manifestation, behind all that we can know or sense, and behind those things which we do not yet know or sense, lie *indivisibles,* which were in their view the fundamental units of being. Democritus called them atoms — *atomoi,* a Greek word meaning "indivisibles." They taught further that these indivisibles are practically infinite in number in the cosmos, and that they are incomputable, immeasurable by any method of mensuration in physical nature.

They said also that these "atoms" existed in a "void," which they called *to kenon* or emptiness; and that through their various movements and attractions, through an innate power of self-growth, through magnetic approaches or repulsions, their manifold movements and operations composed the world, the cosmos, which we see around us.

You have there the basis of the atomic theory of modern chemistry; you have there the basis of the nebular hypothesis, and of theories more or less running upon the nebular hypothesis of Laplace and of Herschel and of others. But to these words there have been given meanings quite different from those which Democritus implied in his usage of them.

What did Democritus mean by his *atomoi* and by his *kenon* or emptiness? He meant, first, spiritual monads, full and complete as entities, indivisible particles of substance containing in themselves the potentialities of all possible future development, self-moved, self-driven, as a man is by his character and the forces inherent in his spiritual and intellectual and physical natures.

As a man has his individual character by which he is impelled or motivated or driven to action, so the original meaning of Democritus in these respects was that the universe was composed of an infinite number of what modern philosophy — and Plato and Pythagoras also — calls monads, spiritual indivisible entities, the ultimates of being, self-conscious, spiritual monads.

Nor by his word *kenon,* or void, did he mean an utter emptiness, as we misconstrue that word. He meant the vast expanses of the spatial deeps, Space, in fact, which this infinite host of monads filled. He thus enunciated a theory truly majestic and, I may add, truly theosophical when properly understood.

Look at the notable difference between the misconstruing, on the one side, by modern philosophers, of his atoms and his void: dead, unimpulsed, and acting blindly; and, on the other side, self-living monads, indivisible spiritual entities, living in these spatial deeps, which by their attractions and repulsions and *inwardly* governed movements produce the cosmos which we see around us.

In the last century, chemistry was a science which had reached its ultimate, as was thought, and concerning which nothing more of revolutionary character could be known. Why, I remember, in my youth, that one of the foremost chemists of the day argued that the marvelous discoveries of modern chemical science have proved that there is nothing more to be discovered of a fundamental nature in the entire field of chemical research; all further discoveries will be

simply an amplification of what is already known! Let us
learn a much-needed lesson from this; it is unsafe ever to
say that knowledge has an ultimate, that it has boundaries
that can never be surpassed.

Then, as we all know, came the revolutionary discoveries
in radioactivity, upsetting the whole of science, not indeed
so far as the facts already discovered and proved, but insofar
as the ideas and theories which made the science of that day
are concerned; they indeed were completely upset.

Now it was this very discovery of radioactivity that,
through a misunderstanding of the atomistic theory of
Democritus, put this ancient Greek school of thought into
the discard. When modern chemists discovered something
of the nature of radiant matter, of radioactivity, such as in
the two chemical elements, uranium and thorium, and found
the different generations of so-called disintegrations which
these two elements were shown to follow; and when it was
further discovered that these investigations proved that the
chemical elements were composed of corpuscles which were
neither indestructible nor indivisible, then the name "atom,"
as misapplied by modern science, was indeed recognized as
a misnomer. Perforce, the chemists of today are now seeking, in mind at least, if not in actual practice, for some other
term which will more adequately describe this subtle something, this subtle element, which they feel, which they *know*,
must exist within the confines of the atomic structure, but
which they have not yet been able to demonstrate. And
when they do find it, if they do, they shall then have reached
not only into and beyond the confines of chemistry, as it is
now understood, but will have gone into the very structure,
into the very secrets, of mother nature, and they will have
become true alchemists. Moreover, they will be coming a

step nearer to the original idea in the minds of those ancient Greek philosophers who taught of the "atoms" and the "void."

The teaching of theosophy is that everything actually is more or less radioactive, that is, that everything has at its heart or core an innate force which is its character, a force of a particular kind or quality. It is the pouring forth of these forces, each of its own individual quality, which produces the various phenomena of nature. It is in the radioactivity emanating from the core of the atom that come all the forces and matters which build our physical universe, through the passage from the invisible to the visible, and vice versa — a mystery, wonderful, imagination-provoking, and of the deepest interest to any thoughtful student of the physical structure of the world in which we live. It is these forces, passing from the invisible into the visible, which infill the cosmos with its energies, and which in consequence give our body its life and vitality, which vitalize the cells of which the body is composed, constructed as they are of these radioactive atoms.

The scientists have stumbled, it is true, almost by chance upon a few elements only whose radioactivity can be traced and measured with some degree of approximation of accuracy; but already our chemists and physicists are beginning to realize that there is no easy explanation of the fact that only a few elements in the great body of material compounds should be radioactive.

The theosophical view, it would seem obvious then, is not on all fours with radioactive theories of modern science, which appear to be limited mainly to the phases of explosive and disruptive energy of a certain few chemical elements. To the theosophist radiation is a term of wide and universal application, of which the scientific visioning of radioactivity as a disintegration process is but one small corner.

Today our chemists are talking about the transmutation of elements as well as of metals. Some have already claimed to have transformed one element into another. But nature, when left to herself, has demonstrated in the disintegration products of the two particular metals, uranium and thorium, that by her own alchemical processes she can transmute these two elements into another element — that of lead.

Uranium has a disintegrating genealogy, if we may so call it, of fourteen steps or stages between uranium at the beginning and lead at the end, each such stage formed by the subatomic particles expelled from the nucleus of the uranium atom. The other element, thorium, has also a disintegrating genealogy of twelve steps between thorium at the beginning and lead at the end.

But note here a most interesting fact. Lead derived from uranium has a lower atomic weight than ordinary lead; while the lead derived from thorium has a higher atomic weight than ordinary lead; and it is now supposed that ordinary chemical or commercial lead is actually a product of the mixture of the other two, the lead from the uranium-base and the lead from the thorium-base.

Is not this extremely interesting? All these three varieties of lead are chemically identical, physically identical, spectroscopically identical. By the three main tests known they prove themselves to be lead; and yet we know that they are different — different in atomic weights. Look at the immense scope of thought, the avenues of speculation, that this situation opens up — just this one illustration!

It is now known that the atoms of these elements have an average life of an immensely long period, while some of their so-called disintegration products have an average life of an infinitesimal compass of human time. Take the element uranium, for instance: the uranium atom, it is estimated, has an average life period of eight billion years; while the various disintegration products into which the uranium atom breaks up or rather which it expels from its heart, according to Professor Frederick Soddy,* have widely varying average life periods. One of these disintegration products, called radium c′, has an average life period of one millionth of a second.

It has been discovered in the same way, by the exceedingly delicate methods now followed in alchemical science — which is what our modern science is fast becoming — that the thorium atom has an average life period of twenty-five billion years; while one of its disintegration products, thorium c′, has an average life period of one hundred billionth of a second.

Let us make a few philosophical deductions from these facts. What do we mean by time? We mean by time the expression of the human consciousness's realization of the passage through it of the various procedures which happen around the thinking entity and affect its understanding. Time, in other words, is merely our conception or mental representation of the different stages of duration. Consequently, if we had another order of understanding, if our conception of time belonged to some titanic intellect to whom we on our globe here would seem as infinitesimal entities — much as the inhabitants of an electron of an atom

---

*Formerly professor of chemistry at the universities of Oxford and Aberdeen; retired 1936. See his 4th edition, revised and enlarged, of *The Interpretation of Radium and the Structure of the Atom*, 1922.

appear to us — then, under those circumstances, to such a titanic intellect, the entire life cycle of our solar system would perhaps be a millionth of one of their seconds of time, or a billionth, or even a trillionth of such a second! Time, in brief, is an illusion — an old thought — "illusion" not meaning something that does not exist, but meaning something that is not properly understood by us or reduced to such terms that our consciousness can take it in and understand it.

Our modern scientists talk very much of vibrations, and they give the vibrational rates of various kinds of waves, such as electric waves, and heat waves, and light waves, and ultraviolet rays, and of X rays; and there are multitudes of others. These researchers are now beginning to get a truer knowledge of what these rays really are. They are now more and more, as time passes, inclining towards the ancient theosophical teaching that these "rays" are not mere movements in or of a hypothetical ether. Movement per se is nothing because it is an abstraction. There can be no movement without a thing that moves. It is the moving thing that provides what we call movement. Similarly there can be no vibrations without something which vibrates.

Each one of these so-called waves, according to theosophy, is the activity of some minute entity, some infinitesimal body. Never mind at the moment whether it be a low body or a high, the point is that the moving or vibration is produced by the action of some entity. These minute bodies vibrate or revolve, as the case may be, at a rate which we can estimate, but which is beyond human imagination to conceive or fully to follow with the brain-mind.

For instance, as given by our physicists, the vibrations of electric waves range up to three thousand billions a second. These are the lowest, the grossest, and the most material of the five kinds of vibrating forces given in the list below. In order to facilitate an understanding of these unfigurable numerical quantities, I subjoin them in columnar form:

VIBRATIONS	PER SECOND
Electric Waves	up to 3,000 billions
Heat Waves	3,000 billions to 800,000 billions
Light Waves	400,000 billions to 800,000 billions
Ultraviolet Rays	800,000 billions to 5,000,000 billions
X Rays	400,000,000 billions to 6,000,000,000 billions

The X rays, as you probably know, are chemical light phenomena produced by the γ-rays of uranium and thorium. There are three so-called rays given off by the atoms of these elements in their disintegration. First, there is the α-ray, which is the proton or a part of the proton of the atom. Its penetrating power is but small, yet in it resides most of the radioactivity and most of the chemical and physical properties which the atoms of these two chemical elements exhibit.

The second class of rays are the β-rays, which are electrons or perhaps atomic planets expelled from the atom. Their penetrating power is stronger than is that of the α-rays.

Then come the third class, the γ-rays, which are, or which give off, the X rays. Now, we may, if we follow the chemists' terminology, call these three classes of radiating force "rays"; but, as I have just said, they are — or most of them are — actually particles expelled from the atom, and it is their passage through intervening matter which produces the phenomena of light, which has caused them to be called rays.

These various forces which impel these various matters to action are derived from the monads more or less awak-

ened and dwelling in these various matters as their inspiring
and directing consciousnesses — because that is what matter
is fundamentally, according to the ancient wisdom: sleeping
monads, sleeping consciousness centers, sleeping spiritual
atoms. Each physical atom is the atomic vehicle of its
monad; and each atom is composed of similar monads of
another lower order, evolutionally speaking. The atom thus
forms in its unity the vehicle of the more awakened monad
controlling it, which is, so to say, the god of its little atomic
cosmos.

Throughout all the vast reaches of the cosmic hierarchy
exist these monads in various stages of sleeping and awakening, so that we have the highest, the most awakened (for
that hierarchy), and then the intermediate stages, down to
the lowest steps of that hierarchical scale.

What is man, after all, but a monad more or less awakened? He indeed, in his present stage of evolution, may be
considered as sleeping to monads higher than he; but as
compared with the sleeping monads, the sleeping spiritual
atoms or consciousness centers which form the material
framework and substance of the physical cosmos, he walks
like a god. His impulses, thoughts, and emotions, his ideals,
aspirations, and instinctive reachings out to higher and
nobler things, as well as the vibrations emanating from the
different vehicles of his psychological organism in which he
lives and works, affect not merely the matter of his own
body, but electrically, magnetically, affect likewise the entire
physical, mental, and spiritual sphere surrounding him, as
far as those human vibrations of his can and do reach.

These spiritual consciousness centers in themselves are
absolutely and fully awakened; but those which form the
lowest steps of the cosmic hierarchies are in the present

stage of evolution passing through the 'sleeping' phase of their long developmentary pilgrimage. They themselves, in the core of their being, are always fully awake in their own monadic sphere, but their vehicles, their lowest 'selves,' are not spiritually awakened to and on this our present plane.

Thus you can see why we say that consciousness is matter, and matter is consciousness; not in the old materialistic view but in the meaning of the ancient wisdom — that there is life, or rather that there are lives, everywhere, throughout illimitable space and duration, always working, never inactive or still in the sense of the ceasing of these operations of the universe during the evolutional time periods, cosmic, atomic, or intermediate.

Every minutest speck of even physical matter that surrounds us is built of these sleeping monads, entities of spiritual nature at their core or heart, but spiritually sleeping on this plane, embryos as it were, whose destiny it is to develop into full-grown, self-conscious gods, the inspiring geniuses of future new cosmoi, of universes to follow ours in duration.

It is in the very small that we must seek for the unriddling of the riddle of the origination of life, as well as in the macrocosmic. The physical atom of chemistry has been likened to a miniature solar system, consisting of a protonic center, which is the nucleus or the atomic sun, more minute but vastly more massive than the smaller bodies circling with vertiginous rapidity around that central nucleus, the electrons. And through the open doors of these electrons and protons, we may see still newer and subatomic universes into which our inquiring minds may penetrate, as further knowledge comes to us.

An atom, like everything else, has its life cycle, and at its end follows a course of slow disintegration or decay. We know that this is the case with radioactive bodies, such as uranium and thorium; and that with this disintegration of the structure of the atom, the nature of the atom changes — this process of decay actually being a transmutation of elementary chemical substance.

Now each of these protonic nuclei is a body, a corpuscle of positive electricity, and each of the electrons is a corpuscle or minute body of negative electricity. This means that the entire material framework of the universe is reduced to electrical charges of opposite polarity. When these charges neutralize each other we have material stability, or better, atomic stability. And I might say in passing that it would seem probable that by changing the polarity, not merely of any atom, but of any particular mass of atoms, which is the same as saying of any particular aggregate of electrical charges, thereby you change all the physical and chemical properties of such mass; and if this takes place you may see matters behave in a very extraordinary manner.

Just as the atom has been likened to a miniature solar system, so in its turn may the solar system with its sun and planets be likened to an atom of cosmic dimensions. This seductive idea but repeats an old Hindu teaching concerning the "Atom or Egg of Brahmā."

It is the teaching of theosophy that the universe, being one self-contained organism, follows one line of fundamental action, and that any operation within it is felt throughout its whole; and that as these operations are many, they must affect every particle, every corpuscle, in a similar manner; and therefore that nature repeats herself in the small as in the great — in the atom as in the cosmos.

We see therein the religious, the scientific, and the philosophical rationale of the law of analogy, and why this powerful and ancient instrument of human thought is a true one.

The atom, then, is a miniature of what the solar system is, even as man, in a spiritual and psychological sense, is a miniature spiritual-psychological atom. Now then, atom as well as cosmos, physical atom as well as physical solar system, are alike formed of smaller entities. So numerous are these latter that they are wholly incomputable by any physical or human standards of mensuration. And just as the number of atoms themselves is infinite, so there are innumerable cosmic atoms — other universes outside of ours, formed more or less as ours is, differing among themselves as the leaves of a tree or as men differ, no two being identical and yet all belonging to the same family or order of entities, and thus, in this sense, showing a groundwork of similarity approaching identity.

It is impossible to figurate in imagination the vast numbers of entities both great and small that infill the universe. Speaking of electrons and protons, Professor W. M. Thornton in an article titled: "What is Electricity?" wrote as follows: *

In order to make the electrons in a drop of water just visible to the naked eye it would be necessary to magnify the drop to 100 times the volume of the earth, and it has been said that if we could place all the protons in the earth together so that no hollow cavity existed, they could be packed into a handbag, which would then weigh 6000 trillion tons.   — p. 674

---

*Faraday Lecture given in Glasgow, Scotland on February 7, 1927 and published in full in the *Journal of the Institution of Electrical Engineers*, vol. 65, London; see also *The Pharmaceutical Journal of London*.

Remember that these incomputable hosts of electrons are in reality, small entities; or we may say that there are minute or infinitesimal lives inhabiting the atoms. Why not? Why should not the electrons, the atomic planets circling around their atomic sun, bear sensitive and conscious, thinking and intelligent and self-conscious creatures, even as our planet, one of the cosmic electrons of our solar system, bears us in similar fashion around our own central luminary. Who would dispute the noble conception that even on these atomic electrons there may exist inhabitants or living entities of infinitesimal kind: living, thinking, feeling entities, each of its kind, each of its own genus, so to say, each following its own destiny, its own upward line of evolution, and thereby repeating the law of universal nature.

As we raise our eyes skyward and realize that this so-called dome of space surrounds us on all sides, all that we see seems so great and large to us. But pause a moment, and realize that we judge through and from the nature of our own limited consciousness and interpret only by our own powers of undeveloped understanding.

From such thoughts we may perhaps intuit that to these minute, these infinitesimal, entities which may inhabit the atomic spaces of our bodies, the skyey spaces in their cosmos may be as large and as grand as our own cosmic spaces are to us; and furthermore, that our entire physical galaxy — which is all that is comprised within the bounds of our Milky Way — may be but a molecule of some entity still more incomprehensibly vast and beyond the reaches of our most ambitious imagination. Who dare say that our solar system is not in the mental purview of some entity still more vastly grand, itself but an atom! All is relative.

Our earth is a planet circling around the sun — therefore

one of our solar system's electrons. Our sun is the protonic aggregate of our solar system — a uni-nuclear system because we have but one sun; yet we know from astronomical study that some solar systems evidently have two or perhaps more suns, in each and all cases composed of the protons forming them, and in which reside the mass and the radioactivity of each such system.

Our solar system therefore being a cosmic atom, then the molecule to which it belongs, following analogical reasoning, is all other suns and systems that are encompassed within the encircling zone of the Milky Way; while the other vast universes out in the spaces beyond ours, in their turn are molecules, and thus form the incomparably larger aggregate corpus of some Entity still more incomprehensibly vast!

Consciousness is incommensurable. It cannot be measured by any physical methods of mensuration. We can know consciousness only by consciousness, for it approaches the ultimate mystery of the universe. Hence, size, volume, bulk of physical matters or matter, do not control either its nature or its field of action. It is where it is and it can manifest everywhere.

5

EVOLUTION AND TRANSFORMISM

MAN IS A MYSTERY, a mystery to the inquiring and investigating mind of the researcher into nature; but more so indeed is man a mystery to himself. And because this mystery exists, due to lack of proper research and investigation into his sevenfold constitution, therefore have we the various and the varying ways of looking at man himself, and of his looking at the cosmos, of which he is, on this earth, the most intelligent offspring.

Yet there is a solution of this mystery — a solution which is not new, which is older than the enduring hills, and which again in our age has been given forth through the medium of the theosophical philosophy.

Man, child of the universe, nursling of destiny, stands, so far as his conception of his place in the cosmos is concerned, between two vast spheres, two immense universes, between the cosmos and the atom of physical matter — the one sphere of cosmical, the other of infinitesimal magnitude. He stands thus only because he so sees himself. I mean that it is on account of his having attained his present stage in his long evolutionary journey that he so conceives of himself as holding this intermediate point, and of occupying it, and from these two universes drawing the life springs of the understanding which dignify him as man.

But the majestic philosophy-science-religion of the ages teaches us that there are beings so much greater and higher than man is, and beings so much smaller and less than he, that in reality he himself in turn stands, with his world and his cosmos, as the one or the other of these extremes to such greater or smaller entities.

It is a question of relativity. In order to understand it more clearly we must cleanse our minds of the old ideas instilled into us by false education, both religious and scientific, and philosophic too; also must we understand that man's is not the only mind which can conceive universal things, and that our status in the cosmos is not the only one of supreme importance, as we foolishly but perhaps naturally imagine it to be.

Universal life is infinite in its manifestation in endless forms, and manifested beings are incomputable in number; and no one may say that man, noble thinker as he truly is, is yet the only one in the boundless fields of space who can think clearly and imagine rightly and intuit truth. Such egoistic notions of our uniqueness in the scheme of life are really a form of insanity; but the mere fact that we can understand this egoism and struggle against it, and abandon it, shows that we ourselves are not insane.

Therefore, since both in the very small and in the very great, consciousnesses exist and fill all space, we are their children, their evolving offspring; and, moreover, insofar as the small universe is concerned, the microcosm, within certain frontiers we as individuals are likewise parents of offspring occupying to us the same relative position that we occupy to those greater consciousnesses.

Biologists today compute that in the body of man there are some fifty trillion cells, more or less — living things, physiological engines — out of which his body is built. These cells in their turn are composed of chemical molecules; and these in their turn are composed of still smaller entities called atoms; and these atoms in their turn are composed of things still smaller, today called protons and electrons; and for all we may know, these subatomic particles, supposed to be the ultimate particles of matter, are themselves divisible and composed of entities still more minute! Is this the end, the finish, the jumping-off place? Are there particles or corpuscles still smaller than these? If we are to judge by the past, we are driven to suppose that there is no end.

Where dare one say that consciousness ends or begins? Is it of such a nature that we must suppose that it has a beginning, or reaches an end? If so, what is there beyond it, above it, or below it? The idea seems to me to be fantastic. If consciousness of any kind, man's or any other, have a true limit in itself, then the power of our understanding would not be what it is even in our present relatively undeveloped stage of evolution. We could have no intellectual or spiritual reaches into these wider fields of thought; but we should reach frontiers of consciousness, and we should indeed know them as limits, jumping-off places. In fact, we then could not even conceive of a beyond, because our consciousness would end there.

We sense something of limitations along these lines in our ordinary brain-functioning, because our brain is in itself a limited portion of physical matter; but every thinking individual, if he examine himself carefully and study his own experiences, must realize that there resides in him something which is boundless, something which he has never fathomed, which tells him always, "Come up higher. Reach farther and farther into the beyond. Cast all that has a limit aside, for in such case it does not belong to your higher self."

This consciousness is the working in man of the spiritual self, the operation in his psychological nature of his spiritual monad, the ultimate for him in this our hierarchy of nature only, for that spiritual monad is the center of his being, and in itself knows no limits, no boundaries, no frontiers, for it is pure consciousness.

Evolution — the drive to betterment, the urge to superiority! If we look at it as the old materialists did, then it means superiority over our fellowmen for our own advantage; but if we look at it according to the facts of nature, as we learn them and according to the instincts of our own being, it then means self-superiority in the sense of rising on the ladder of life ever higher, with expanding vision, with expanding faculties and sympathies — not merely in the physical apparatuses of thinking, but growing greater from the spiritual core of our being. In other words, it means opening up for that spiritual essence within us wider doors for it to pass its rays through, down into our personal minds, enlightening and leading us upwards and onwards, illimitably through the various cosmical periods and fields of evolution which the monad follows along the courses of destiny.

Man, as one of the spiritual-psychical-physical corpuscles of the general cosmos — as the microcosm of the macrocosm, the little-world offspring of the great world — merely follows the same operations of nature that the cosmos is impulsed, compelled, to follow: development, growth from within outwards, throwing outwards into manifestation as organic

activity, as expression in organs, so far as his physical body
is concerned, the functions, the impulses within, the drive,
the urge to manifest what is within. That, in a few words,
is the ancient teaching of evolution.

Now let us take up the question of the evolution of
animate beings on this earth more definitely from the theosophical standpoint than we have hitherto done. We use the
word strictly in its etymological sense, as an unwrapping, an
unrolling, or a coming out of that which previously had been
inwrapped or inrolled. Nor do we mean by evolution the
mere adding of physiological or morphological detail to
other similar details, or of variation to variation or, on the
mental plane, of mere experience to other mere experiences;
which would be, as it were, naught but a putting of bricks
upon an inchoate and shapeless pile of other bricks previously so placed together.

No, evolution is the manifestation of the inherent powers
and forces of evolving entities, be those entities what they
may: gods, or the human race, or other races of animate
entities below the human. It is a coming forth of that which
formerly had been involved or inwrapped. It is the striving
of the innate, of the invisible, to express itself in the manifested world commonly called the visible world. It is the
drive of the inner entity to express itself outwardly. It is
a breaking down of barriers in order to permit that self-
expression; the opening of doors, as it were, into temples
still more vast of knowledge and wisdom than those in
which the entity previously had learned certain lessons. It
is this rather than any mere adding of detail to detail, of
variation to variation, be such morphological or physiological. Evolution is a cosmical, a universal, movement to
betterment.

All entities that infill space are following a path to higher things, all are delivering themselves of that which is locked up within them. All are pouring forth the myriad-form lives which they contain — their inner selves and their thought-forms — their vehicles slavishly following the courses that these entities run.

Contrast with this conception the definition of evolution by Professor James Sully,* as a "natural history of the cosmos including organic beings, expressed in physical terms as a mechanical process."

The theosophist rejects that definition; first, because it leaves out the main characteristic of evolution, which is unfolding from the less to the greater. It is not a definition of evolution; it is simply a statement of things we knew before, and it says nothing of development towards higher things. Second, he rejects it on the ground that it is a merely mechanical and purely theoretical explanation of things that should be considered by the different sciences in their own various departments, and it expresses no unification of those sciences or does so only in terms of dead matter, formed of atoms — driven together by fortuitous action.

It matters little, unless we choose to be sticklers over words, whether we say that evolution is the becoming the simple from the complex; or complexity resulting from simplicity. It probably is both, depending upon the way you look at it. The main thought is that at the core or heart of every animate entity, there is a power, an energy, a principle of *self-growth*, which needs but the proper environment to bring forth all that is in it. You may plant a seed in the ground, and unless it has its due amount of water and sun-

---

*Cf. *Encyclopaedia Britannica*, XIth ed., vol. x, p. 22.

shine, it will die. But give it what it needs, let it have the proper environment, and it brings forth its flower and its fruit, which produce others of its own kind. It brings out that which is within it. Yet environment alone cannot produce the flower. *There must be an intelligent entity to act upon environment.*

Thus man, the evolving monad, the inner, spiritual entity, acts upon nature, acts upon environment, upon surroundings and circumstances, which automatically react, strongly or weakly as the case may be. Environment in a sense is an evolutionary stimulus, allowing the expression, as far as its influences can reach, of the latent powers of the entity within the physical body. Herein we find the true secret of evolution.

Therefore theosophy does not teach the growth in progressive development of an evolving entity in the sense that that entity grows or learns through mental or physical accretions; that is, evolution does not consist merely in adding experience to experience, or detail to detail. That idea we completely reject, because it is not what our studies show us to be the facts of nature. Growth — whether physical or mental or spiritual — is not a continuously enlarged pile, either of experiences, or of variation following upon variation in physical structure.

True evolution on the contrary is, as explained, the unfolding and flowing forth of that which is sleeping or latent as seed or as faculty in the entity itself. This works along three lines which are coincident, contemporaneous, and fully connected in all ways: an evolution of the spiritual nature of the developing creature taking place on spiritual planes; an evolution of the intermediate nature of the creature (in man the psychomental part of his constitution); and a vital-astral-physical evolution, resulting in a body or vehicle increasingly fit for the expression of the powers appearing or unfolding in the intermediate and spiritual parts of the developing entity.

Hence, the theosophist of necessity considers the destiny and evolution of the inner parts of the being as by far the most important, because the evolution or perfecting of the physical body has no other purpose or end than to provide a vehicle, progressively more fit to express adequately the powers of the inner nature. Evolution is thus the drive or effort of the inner entity to express itself in vehicles growing gradually and continuously and steadily fitter and fitter for it.

Professor William Bateson, a well-known British scientist, has expressed the idea, somewhat crudely but graphically, by calling it the "unpacking of an original complex." Turn to a flower or to the seed of a tree. The flower unfolds from its bud and finally attains its bloom, charming both by its beauty and perfume; we see here the unwrapping of what was latent in the seed, later in the bud, later in the bloom. Or again, take the seed of a tree: an acorn, for instance, contains in itself all the potentialities of the oak which it will finally produce — the root-system, the trunk, branches and leaves, and the numerous fruits, other acorns, which it is its destiny finally to produce, and which in their turn will produce other oaks.

Evolution is one of the oldest doctrines that man has ever evolved from his spiritual-mental nature; because evolution properly described is merely a formulated expression of the operations of the cosmos. Every one of the six systems of Hindu philosophy is evolutionist in character, or constructed along that line. All the great Greek thinkers, and the Roman thinkers of large intellectual capacity, taught evolutionary doctrines along these lines.

But this ancient doctrine of evolution is not the evolution of modern science, either in its view of man or of the cosmos. What then is the so-called evolutionism so popular today? It is really "transformism" — an adopted French word; and the French very logically and very rightly so call it, because it *is* transformism. Now then, what is the difference between this and evolution?

Reduced to simple language, transformism is the doctrine that an unintelligent, dead, nonvitalized, unimpulsed cosmos, whose particles are driven hither and yon by haphazard chance, can collect itself into the forms of innumerable sub-bodies, not only on our earth, but everywhere else, these sub-bodies on our earth being called animate entities, all of which grow to nobler things, how no one knows, therefore no one can say. It is a theory, an hypothesis. It is, in short, the doctrine that things grow into other things unguided by either innate purpose or inner urge.

How can a haphazard, helter-skelter universe produce law and order, and follow direction, and suffer consequences, results strictly following causes? It is the nightmare of a lunatic. We reject the idea. We reject it because it is unphilosophical, unscientific, and likewise because it is irreligious in the theosophical sense.

Thus theosophists are evolutionists but emphatically are not transformists. We declare that there is development; the slow change through the ages of one being — not into another thing or being, but into an increasingly perfected form *of itself*. That is true evolution. But the idea that one thing can be transformed into another thing is like saying to someone: give me a pile of material — so much wire, so much wood, so much ivory, so much varnish, and a few other things — and just watch that pile evolve into a piano! It never will. That is transformism reduced to simple language.

There is an old Qabbalistic axiom which runs as follows: "The stone becomes a plant; the plant a beast; the beast a man; and the man a god." Verily so it is! But the literal form of these words should not be construed as expressing a perfect Darwinism; not at all.

First, the allusion is to the monad expressing itself through its lowest vehicle, not living in it, but overruling it, working through it, sending a ray down into the pit, as it were, of its lowest body, in this case the stone. The monad provides the invigorating life force, giving to the stone, which is composed of other hosts of infinitesimals, its vital ray. When it is said that the stone becomes a plant, it means that the infinitesimal entities forming and composing the stone have been evolved to express that invigorating ray on a higher plane as a plant; but the inner life and illumination of the monad directing the whole procedure as a unity never abandons its own high plane.

When the saying continues that the plant becomes a beast, this means that the vehicle expressing the invigorating ray from the monad has become fit for that still higher work. The infinitesimal entities forming the plant have become still more evolved or more expressive of the vital ray, and when this occurs they compose and form the beast body, having passed beyond the stage of expressing the plant or the stone.

When the beast becomes a man, it does not imply that man sprang from the beasts, whether from apes or monkeys, or beneath these from the lower mammals. No; it means two things: first, that the inner sun, the inspiriting and invigorating monad — abiding always in its own sphere, but sending its ray, its luminousness, down into matter — thereby gives matter kinetic life and the upward urge, and in this way builds for itself ever fitter vehicles through which to express itself. And second, that each such fitter vehicle was built up — how? By and through the infinitesimal lives which at one period of their existence had lived previously in the beast body which they composed; and before this in the plant which they composed; and before this in the stone which they composed; and lower than the stone these infinitesimal lives manifested the monad in the three worlds of the elementals.

The idea of this progressive development from within outwards is really easy to understand in its first principles. We do not teach that a stone literally metamorphoses itself into a plant and then into a beast at some specified time. Or again, from a beast to a man; or from a man into a god.

The physical body, a congeries of living infinitesimals as it is, itself never becomes a god — which such a literal construction would make it become. It is a transitory and temporal aggregate of these infinitesimals; in reality a form and a name and nothing more — the *nāma-rūpa* of Hindu philosophy. But these infinitesimals which compose the body, being growing and learning and advancing lives, grow ever more fit to express the nobler faculties of the genius overruling and illuminating them, and thus pass by what the ancients called metempsychosis* into the composition of the

---

*Cf. ch. 14, p. 169, "The Rationale of Reincarnation" for a fuller explanation of the term; see also the author's two-volume work, *The Esoteric Tradition*, where the subject of reimbodiment in its several forms is treated in depth.

bodies of the respective higher stages. That genius, in the case of the infinitesimals composing man's body, is man's spiritual nature, for genius and monad are virtually equivalent in the meaning I am using here.

Compare this logical and comprehensive doctrine with the scientific hypothesis of transformism: i.e., that, following various supposed "laws of nature" operating in individuals, one thing is transformed into another thing. Thus stones will become trees through transforming themselves into trees; trees will become beasts by transforming themselves through change into beasts; beasts will become men by transforming themselves through change into men. Now, the biological scientists do not put it in that fashion. Of course not; it is too palpably grotesque. But it illustrates the precise meaning of the word transformism.

Charles Darwin, for instance, thought that man evolved from the beast kingdom by various natural biological factors operating in that kingdom and as expressed in the individual beast or animate entity, as the case may be, or perhaps more primitively in the vegetable kingdom. He specified as operative causes more particularly what he called natural selection, resulting in the survival of the fittest to survive in their particular environment and in the special circumstances which they had to meet.

His ideas were generally based on the speculations — some of them exceedingly fine — of the Frenchman, Lamarck, who taught what has since been called the theory of acquired or favorable characteristics; that is to say, that an animate entity, by acting upon nature and from the reaction of surrounding natural entities and laws upon it, acquired certain favorable characteristics, which were inherited and passed on to the offspring. And as these characteristics were

always for the betterment of the individual acquiring them,
therefore there was a gradual advance and progress of that
particular racial strain.

Let me illustrate this idea of acquired or favorable characteristics by a bit of old doggerel that I once committed to
memory:

> A deer had a neck that was longer by half
> Than the rest of his family's (try not to laugh),
> And by stretching and stretching became a giraffe,
> Which nobody can deny!

But the theosophist does deny it; finds it incomprehensible how any deer, by stretching its neck, even if it be
somewhat longer than the average, in browsing upon the
overhanging branches of trees, should be able to pass on an
elongated neck to its offspring. If we inquire into the nature
of elongate-necked deer, we shall most certainly find that
their offspring are perfectly normal (barring monstrosities)!
And a similar inquiry into the possibility of hereditary transmission of acquired characteristics by an individual would
probably show that they are not transmitted.

Individuals of course are tremendously affected by environment and circumstance, by their action upon nature and
by the reaction of nature upon them; and through long
periods of geologic time it is probably true to say that the
body of the acting individual, or succession of individuals,
would slowly acquire specific modifications. But this would
invariably be along the lines of functional tendencies or
capacities inherent in the germ plasm,* and most certainly

---

*That is to say, in the protoplasm of the germ cells containing the
units of heredity, the chromosomes and genes.

would hardly be classified under the general and rather vague expression "the inheritance of acquired or favorable characteristics."

Hence the theory of the transmission by heredity of acquired favorable characteristics is no longer either popular or widely accepted; although there are yet a few diehards who still hold to it as an explanation of the origination of species.

It is not to be supposed — for the common experience of mankind runs contrary to it — that a living body of vegetable, beast, or man, can pass on to its offspring modifications which it itself acquired or suffered during its lifetime, such as membral change, skill, or muscular development on the one hand, and accidents, such as the loss of a limb, on the other hand. This is obvious, and no one teaches it. But if this living being, or rather all the representatives of any particular phylum, live and die through long generations in some particular environment, do they or do they not acquire characteristics or modifications which become so much a part of their physical being that these modifications are transmitted by heredity? This is precisely the question so warmly disputed.

The general tendency of biological transformist thinkers is to say that this is the very process by which racial strains progress or evolve. But a large number of biological evolutionists, in common with the theosophists, say no; because although the idea, *as stated,* indicates the action or working out of an indwelling drive or urge to higher things, yet these biological evolutionists do not recognize any such inner urge, and therefore discard the theory.

Evolution is a fact. The only question is whether the fortuitous action, through periods of time, of the individuals of a race upon nature, and nature's fortuitous reactions upon those individuals, suffice adequately to explain the process. The idea is steadily growing more and more unfashionable, because the problems of the supposed origination and growth of self-consciousness, and of psychical and intellectual development, are inexplicable by it.

As a matter of fact the real question at issue is this: is there or is there not behind the evolving racial strain, as expressed in its individuals, a vital urge or drive to betterment, working from within outwards? If so, it is true evolution. If the materialistic transformist denies this fact, he has the tremendous *onus probandi* before him, the almost insurmountable difficulty of explaining whence and why and how these marvelous faculties arise and increase in power and expression with the passage of time. No transformist has yet succeeded in meeting this issue.

The Darwinist is fond of talking of the struggle for life, but we claim that this so-called struggle has been greatly overdrawn. It has now become quite popular to believe on proved facts that there is just as much mutual assistance and helpfulness in the animate portion of the cosmos as there is combat and struggle; indeed, more.

It is somewhat like the old theory of the commercial man, who thought the only way to succeed in business was by gaining advantage over his competitors — advantages of all kinds, honest or dishonest, it mattered very little indeed. But the better and the more modern theory is that commercial operations are truly successful when they are cooperative; that it is far wiser and better for men to help each other, to save each other from financial disaster even, than it is to drive one's competitor to the wall. The reason lies in the organic nature of all human activities in which no one can possibly stand alone. There could, in fact, be no such thing as commercial activities unless men worked together, buying and selling to and from each other; and the operation of the same principle of mutual activities and cooperating interests is to be found everywhere.

Now these reflections amount to a recognition of the forces behind the veil working in human nature; and because man is a child of nature, and has in him everything that nature has in herself, in germ or in development, these forces therefore copy or imbody in the small the same operations, the same forces, the same activities, that work in and through the cosmos.

But returning to the doctrines of transformism, as expressed by the hypotheses of natural selection, the struggle for life and the survival of the fittest: do we deny these as factors in evolution? Put in this way, without any collateral implications of theory or hypothesis, the simple answer is no; nobody denies a fact. For instance, it is obvious that of three men, the fittest is certainly the most likely to survive in a given set of adverse circumstances or indeed of favorable circumstances.

There is nothing new whatsover about that idea. It is as old as the ages. The common sense of mankind has recognized that the man fit for a certain career will be more likely to succeed in that career than the man who is fit for another career. In each case it is the survival of the fittest to survive in a particular set of circumstances, but the survival of the fittest is not necessarily the survival of the best. And we likewise know, simply put, that nature itself — using nature in a generalizing sense, not as an entity, but as an expression of the operations of the manifold beings with which the cosmos is filled — certainly does "select" or "favor" certain entities because they are fittest for their environment.

The theosophist's whole philosophy-science-religion is based on nature; not alone on the material physical nature which we know with our physical senses, but on that greater nature, of which the physical nature is actually but the vehicle, the expression, of indwelling forces. By nature we mean the entire framework and course of the cosmos, from the ultraspiritual down to the ultraphysical — limitless in each direction.

But why do certain things survive and certain others fail? Why does nature "make selections"? Or, to put it more specifically and accurately, why does nature seem to favor certain races, certain racial strains, certain individuals, allowing them to survive, while others fail or fall?

We have simply to look at nature to find the answer. Why involve ourselves in imaginary hypotheses, when we have the great cosmos all around us, and within us, to draw upon for truth? Certain entities or races survive because they are growing; they are full of vital forces, of an inner urge, which pushes them steadily ahead. Other entities or things fail or go to the wall, because their time to pass away has come, to make place on the stage of life for others to succeed them. Everything in turn has its chance, lives its life and finally passes off the scene.

Is this a helter-skelter universe, in which entities and things are driven by chance hither and thither, in which no law, no consequences operate, in which the good, the bad, and the indifferent, are so just by chance, and not as the result of cause and effect? Who today believes such nonsense? Everything in its turn occupies its place from an anterior operating cause and as a present effect, or exists in a static effectual relation with other things, which temporarily are stronger, more concordant with circumstances and surroundings, and which are therefore fitter to survive than it.

Everything is alive, but not necessarily animately organized; but being living things they must either progress, retrogress, or temporarily stand still — all three of which processes may at some time take place, though the general movement is progressive and forward for all.

The ancients made this same distinction as regards this question of "animate" entities. Those entities, human or subhuman, which possess an "anima," a vital-astral soul, we call *animate* organisms. In the old Sanskrit they were called *jangamas*, that is, "goers" or "movers," as contrasted with those which did not possess an anima, or at least in whom the anima existed merely in germ. In Sanskrit these latter were referred to as "fixtures" and called *sthāvaras*, meaning "unmoving." The "fixtures" therefore are the minerals and the plant world, while the "goers" or the "movers" are the beasts and men, and in much smaller degree even the entities of the vegetable kingdom.

By all the above picture we can see that to the theosophist evolution extends over far wider fields, and reaches to far greater heights, and we observe it operative in nature in a far more complex manner, than does the relatively simple teaching of modern scientific transformism.

6

THE EVOLUTIONARY STAIRWAY OF LIFE

THE PSYCHOLOGY of the times following the publication of
Darwin's works was so strong that most thinking men could
not then be brought to admit that there were any alternative
explanations of the phenomena of progressive development
in life — human, beast, or plant life — to the scheme of transformism which he set forth. This psychological phenomenon was brought about mainly by the efforts of two men,
men of large culture, but vociferously enthusiastic and more
or less dogmatic in the presentation of their views; and they
ended by convincing the world that the evolutionism, in
reality the transformism, that they taught was the actual
procedure of manifested life in producing development in
all creatures.

These two men were Thomas Henry Huxley and Ernst
Heinrich Haeckel. Both were fervent Darwinists, with modifications, both ardent transformists. Their influence, on the
whole, has not been good upon the mentality of the human
race.

We do not question the bona fides of either of them, but
we do question their influence for good upon thinking and

unthinking minds. They taught things that in many important essentials were not true, and taught them in such fashion that their hearers were led to believe that they were true. This influence was brought to bear upon the minds of the people of those days by means of the great literary and scientific standing which these two men in particular had. We do not accuse them of deliberation in misstatement and in divergence from the facts of nature in order to support their theories; we merely state what we believe to be a fact from an impartial consideration of results.

These two men were exceedingly able; but they spoke with the voice of authority on subjects which they themselves, in many particulars, were merely guessing at. These conclusions are not mine alone. They are also the conclusions of many scientific researchers and thinkers of today — greater scientists of their own class, later men with wider knowledge and deeper insights into nature's workings.

Take, as an instance, Haeckel. In our sense he was the more dangerous of the two, for the reason that he had a vein of mysticism running through him; and when a peculiar type of mysticism is combined with blind, crass materialism, it inevitably produces certain doctrines which actually degrade psychologically those who hear and follow them.

A man who will say that there is nothing but intrinsically lifeless matter in the universe, striving chance-like towards better things; and who in the same breath will talk of "plastidular souls" — the "souls" of cells — these "souls" being explained apparently as the fortuitous offspring of lifeless matter; and who will, in order to complete his schemes of genealogical trees as regards man's developmental past, invent, suggest, and print imaginary stages of development in his books without also calling attention to the fact that they were his own inventions, is not, we submit, truly scientific.

One of these inventions is to be found in Haeckel's book, *The Last Link*, published in 1898. In it he divides the evolutionary history of mankind into twenty-six stages. His twentieth stage he gives as that of the "Lemuravida" (who were placental mammals), which might be translated from its hybrid Latin form as "the grandfathers of the lemurs" — the lemurs being a very primitive type of mammal, supposed to antedate the monkeys in evolutionary time, and often called *Prosimiae.* Now, no one ever heard of these particular "Lemuravida" before, and they have never been found since; and, as Professor Frederic Wood Jones, the eminent British anatomist said, they were simply "invented by Haeckel for the purpose of filling in a gap."*

Huxley was a man of very similar scientific type of mind, but with another psychological bent to his genius. He was psychologized with the idea that there was an end-on or continuous or uniserial evolution in the developmental history of animate beings, *as known to him;* that is, that one type led to another type — the highest of the lower order or family or group passed by degrees into the lowest of the next following or higher group. His whole life work was based on this theory; and all his teachings — backed by much biological research and anatomical knowledge, and other factors that make a man's words carry weight — had immense vogue for these reasons.

With this viewpoint in mind, he was continually trying to find connecting links by considering likenesses between man, for instance, and the various stocks inferior to him; and it must be admitted that in his attempt a great many

---

The Problem of Man's Ancestry, pp. 19–20.

unlikenesses and dissimilarities and fundamental differences, all of extreme importance, were either ignored entirely, or — may I say it? — willfully slurred over.

It was the old, old story, both in Huxley's case and in Haeckel's: what was good for their theories was accepted and pressed home to the limit; and what was contrary to their theories was either ignored or suppressed. We submit that, great as these men were each in his own field, such a procedure is not a truly scientific one. We can excuse their enthusiasm; but an excuse is not by any means an extension of sympathy to the mistake.

The idea which governed and directed the entire life-work of Huxley was not the offspring of his own mind. There is little doubt that he took this idea from the Frenchman, de Buffon, who says, for instance, in speaking of the body of the orangutan, that "he differs less from man than he does from other animals which are still called apes,"* that is to say from the monkeys. And Huxley, writing in 1863, has the following in *Man's Place in Nature:*

> The structural differences which separate man from the gorilla and the chimpanzee are not so great as those which separate the gorilla from the lower apes.   — p. 103

Please note that I refer to end-on or continuous or uni-serial evolution only insofar as Huxley thought it existed in the subhuman beings and their geological progenitors that he knew, or thought must exist in order to conform with his theory. As a matter of fact, end-on, continuous, or uni-serial evolution per se, is also fully taught by theosophy, but not that particular line or course which Huxley took for

---

Histoire naturelle, vol. xiv, p. 30, 1766; quoted by F. Wood Jones, op. cit., p. 21.

granted. He took this for granted without adequate proof that the beings now below man, or in geological times of the past then below the human stock, formed or provided the road of the evolutionary course of the prehuman stock eventuating in modern man.

This the theosophist emphatically denies, for the reason that the ancestors of the simian, and of other mammalian entities now existing, were themselves stocks following their own line of development, even as the human stock now does and then did. In other words, instead of there being one single line representing the ascending scale of evolutionary development passing through the geological progenitors of present-day mammals, towards and into man, there are several, and indeed perhaps many, such genealogical trees.

The theosophical teaching in brief is this: the human stock represents one genealogical tree, the Simiidae another stock, each following its own line of evolution. Yet the latter, the simian stock, originally sprang from the human strain in far past geologic times, and also, indeed, the other genealogical trees of the still lower mammalia; while the classes of the *Aves* or Birds, the *Reptilia* or Reptiles, the *Amphibia* or Amphibians, and the *Pisces* or Fishes, may likewise truly be said to have been in geologic times still more remote, very primitive offsprings from the same prehuman (or man) stock.

Huxley thus assumed, because there are undisputed and indisputable likenesses between man and the anthropoid or manlike ape and the monkeys still lower than the ape, that therefore man sprang at some remote period in the geologic past from some remote (but totally unknown) ancestor of monkey and ape. He had never seen such a missing progenitor; no such missing progenitor has ever yet been discovered.

But he deemed that there must be one because it was necessary for his theory; and he so taught it, and taught it with emphasis and with enthusiasm. His voice rang out over the entire English-speaking world, and his ideas were accepted as established facts in organized knowledge — science.

Unfortunate enthusiasm! — culminating in the teaching to modern man that his ancestry was bestial, beasts whose ancestry again was that of some still lower creature, perhaps a quadruped, whose remote ancestor in its turn still farther back was perhaps a fish, whose still remoter ancestor was a protozoon — some one-celled entity. Huxley's scheme has never been proved true; some of the most brilliant minds in biological research have sought to substantiate it; yet the result of their researches has been entirely contradictory of it.

We must not imagine for a moment that the natural truth of progressive development, modernly called evolution, is something new in our age or in the age of our immediate fathers, nor that it originated in the mind of Charles Darwin, whose great work, *The Origin of Species,* was published in 1859.

The idea of there being a ladder of life, a rising scale of entities, some much more advanced than others, some more retarded in development than others, is a very old one. There have existed in the world among the different races of men, in ages preceding our own, various systems of accounting for what the inquisitive intelligence of man plainly saw exists among the animate entities of earth — a rising scale of beings. Here you have the picture: first man, supposed to be the crowning glory of the evolutionary scale on earth; and underneath him the anthropoid apes, and underneath them the monkeys, the simian stock; and under these latter the lemurs, sometimes called the *prosimiae;* and underneath these have been frequently placed the quadrupedal mammals; and underneath these various classes, orders, genera, and species of vertebrate animals; and underneath these again a very wide range of invertebrates or animals without a backbone; and so forth down the scale.

This idea of a progressive development of all animate entities on earth in present and past geological periods is, indeed, a very old one. Leaving aside for the time being allusions to teachings as to evolutionary development in the archaic writings, such as in the Purānas of India, or in the so-called speculations of Greek and Roman philosophers and thinkers, let us come down to periods more near our own.

For instance, here is a thought taken from Sir Thomas Browne's *Religio Medici* — quite a remarkable book of its kind and published in 1643. He says:

> . . . there is in this Universe a Stair, or manifest Scale, of creatures, rising not disorderly, or in confusion, but with a comely method and proportion.

Just so. There is a stair of life; it is what the Swiss philosopher and biologist, Charles Bonnet, and the French thinkers and biologists, Lamarck, de Buffon, and especially Jean Baptiste René Robinet, called *l'échelle des êtres* — "the ladder of beings." It was the very recognition of this scale of animate life, swaying the minds of these earlier investigators, that led to the culmination in our time of the theory of so-called evolution; and it was Charles Darwin himself who is responsible for having formed a more or less coherent structure of argument, building up a logical outline, as far as he could understand it, of the facts of nature, his theory, or rather his method, attaining almost immediate acceptance.

While we see this ladder of being and must take it into

a full and proper consideration in any attempt to ascertain the rising pathway of evolutionary development, is that a sufficient reason for imagining — and teaching our imaginings as facts of nature — that there has been a progressive development running through these particular and especial discontinuous phyla or stocks, and eventuating in man?

This is one side of our quarrel with modern transformism. The series is obviously discontinuous; none of the steps of this ladder melts into the next higher one, or inversely into the next lower, by imperceptible gradations, as should be the case if the transformist theory were true.

Biologists themselves soon found that this so-called stair or ladder of life was a discontinuous one. They saw, as their knowledge of nature increased, that each of these great groups below man — the backboneless animals or invertebrates, and the vertebrates or backboned animals such as the fishes, amphibians, reptiles, birds and the mammals — did not graduate into each other.

Between these various groups there were vast hiatuses without known connecting links; and researchers hunted long and vainly for "missing links," and found them not. They found them neither in any living entities, nor in those forming the formerly animate record of the geological strata; and those missing links have not yet been discovered. These gaps, therefore, made the biologic series of living entities discontinuous instead of continuous, as Darwin's method required.

Darwin and his followers imagined that they had perceived, by investigating various stages in this presently existing ladder of life, the route, the way, by and through which the human stock had climbed from lower beings to higher — to present-day man. But every attempt to find missing links — that is to say, links binding the highest of one particular phylum or stock to the lowest of the next superior phylum or stock — has always broken down. No such missing links have ever been found. There are wide hiatuses where, according to this transformist theory, these missing links should be.

Now, obviously, any stock supposed to have been evolving through these various groups, could not have made such jumps from one great group to another great group. One of Darwin's maxims was *Natura non facit saltum,* "Nature makes no leaps." Evolution is a steady progression forwards, he said, from the less to the more perfect, from the simpler to the more complex. There is here no ground for dispute between our two otherwise extremely diverse views as to the nature and course of evolution.

What then is the explanation of this discontinuity — of this lack of connections or links between the phyla or stocks? For we find this discontinuity in every instance where we pass from one great stock or phylum to the next. It is not the case of a single instance; it is not a unique situation, explainable perhaps by certain causes, of which we are ignorant; but this discontinuity is repeated between every one of the great stocks.

The fact is that there is not, as regards the beings existent today, or rather as regards their progenitors in geological eras of the past, an end-on evolution or uniserial evolution up to and including man, the supposed crown of that biologic series, *in the manner that we have been taught;* but instead, a number of stocks, each passing through various stages as marked out by their different orders and families and genera and species.

The truth is that instead of there being one genealogical

tree, there are many. Whence came these different genealogical trees? The human stock is one; the anthropoid apes
are another, closely allied with the monkeys; then the quadrupedal mammals again are another stock; the birds are still
another; and so forth. These are all different stocks, though
undoubtedly connected together in various ways by vital
bonds of contemporaneous development both now and in
the past. Otherwise they would not be collected together
on our earth, nor would they show those particular affinities
which these various stocks undoubtedly do show today as
well as in past time. We may contemplate all this and admit
these various facts, and yet say with perfect security that
they do not furnish or form that ascending ladder of life,
through which we as humans passed in order to reach our
present stage, in the degree and in the continuity of continuous gradations from lower to higher, that the true evolutionist must demand.

There has been, I repeat, no end-on evolution *of this
kind or in the manner outlined;* that is to say, man did not
evolve through and in the creatures of all degrees and of all
classes and orders and families and genera existent on the
earth today, or rather as regards their more remote and most
distant ancestors. The specific characters in the various
stocks are all too far evolved along their respective lines, and
have existed too far back in geologic time, for the human
strain to have passed through them on its upward journey.

Research has shown that instead of its being the highest
of any subphylum passing into the lowest of any higher
subphylum, it is almost invariably the lowest representative
in each phylum which are most alike in primitive features —
a most significant fact. It was so with all the groups, particularly so in the case of the vertebrates or animals with back-

bones, that is to say the fishes, amphibians, reptiles, birds and mammals.

The simple reason is that the farther we go back in time the nearer we approach to the junction point or starting point of the various mammalian and premammalian genealogical strains. This is because, springing from one common source, they naturally approximate both in type and character the farther back we can trace them.

Simply stated, the farther we go back towards the origin of any such great group, the nearer we approach to the general and common point of departure — and the nearer those earliest progenitors of each such great group will resemble each other in basal mammalian simplicity; while, on the other hand, the farther we recede from that general and common point of departure, in other words, the nearer we approach our present age, the more widely separate must the representatives of these various great stocks be from each other, on account of the differing natures and the inherent forces evolving through them.

What is this common point of departure? It is the human stock. The human race considered as a whole is the most primitive of all the mammalian stocks on earth today, and always has been so in past time. I mean by this, that it is the primordial stock; it is the originator of the entire mammalian line, in a manner and according to laws of nature which we shall reserve for a future study.

The human stock was the first mammalian line; obviously it is at present the most advanced, and the logical deduction would be that it is likewise the oldest in development. Having started the first, it has gone the farthest along the path. But we will not press that point for the present.

Man is, in fact, the most primitive of *all* stocks on earth.

Remember, however, that in the present great evolutionary period on earth, or what in theosophy is called the present "globe-round," it is the mammals only that trace their origin from the primitive human line. The other vertebrates, as well as the great groups of the invertebrates, likewise were derived from the human stocks, but in the previous globe-round — comprising a vastly long cycle of evolutionary development, which was ended aeons upon aeons ago, and which itself, i.e., the former globe-round or great tidal wave of life, required scores of millions of years for its completion. Evolution as taught by theosophy calls for a time of vastly long duration; indeed, many hundreds of millions of years.

The Darwinists have never been able adequately to prove the thesis of Charles Darwin, considered as a method, because they could not prove an end-on, continuous, or serial developmental growth from any one of the lower great groups into the next higher great group; or, more generally speaking, from the lowest life up to man. There is along *that scale,* let me repeat, no end-on evolution, and none knows this better than modern biologists themselves.

Yet theosophy teaches that evolution, if it exists at all, must be an end-on, continuous, or uninterrupted serial evolution. An evolution of form which consists mainly of jumps from great group to great group is no evolution at all, and presents anew the very riddle which the Darwinian theory was expected to explain. The problem is cleared up when we remember that evolution is continuous for each stock *along its own particular pathway.* Instead of there being one ladder of life, leading up to man who is the crown of that ladder, as it were, there are many such ladders of life, each such being composed of one of the great groups of animate entities. Instead of there being one procession of living entities pursuing an uninterrupted course from the protozoa or one-celled animals up to man, there are various ladders of life along each of which a procession of its own kind climbs. It is essential to understand this idea, because it expresses some of our main points of divergence from the Darwinian theories.

7

PROOF OF MAN'S PRIMITIVE ORIGIN

THE THEOSOPHIST, although he places the body of man square-
ly in the animal world, does not mean by this that man's
physical encasement is evolved from the beasts. He means,
on the contrary, that actually the beast world, and in fact
the worlds below it, were originally derived from man himself in far past ages of the life history of our globe.

This means that man is the most primitive of all the
stocks, and that he is thus the most highly evolved. He has
been able to evolve the inner vehicles, the inner organs,
which give him power to express his inner faculties and
spiritual parts. In the beast, indeed, lie the potencies of
everything in the universe, latent or active, in germ or in
manifestation as the case may be. It has all the possibilities
of evolutionary growth that man has, but the beasts have
not yet evolved the inner organs suitable for the expression
of these inner powers.

It is because of man's superior status, as an *inner* entity,
that we elevate the human stock into a kingdom of its own,

a fourth kingdom — that of man; for man possesses unique intellectual and psychological faculties, which no other creatures known to us possess in anything like so great a degree.

Now what proof have we that the human stock is the most primitive on earth? To answer this question, we shall have to go into a number of technical biological details. I have made notes from various biologic works of a number of exceedingly interesting skeletal and muscular features which man has, in order to show the extreme primitiveness of the human stock, more particularly with relation to his mammalian peculiarities.*

---

*There is a tendency in some modern textbooks on zoology to abandon, albeit with some hesitancy, the placing of man and the other primates at the end of the mammalian series. See, for instance, *College Zoology* by Robert W. Hegner, Ph.D. (Macmillan, 4th edition, pp. 588, 596). The author of this textbook places the primates as the 6th order in a series of 19, i.e., very near the beginning of the mammalian classification, but finds it necessary to defend his unusual arrangement by saying that however strange it may seem to students to depart from the accepted classification, he does so because man and the apes "retain a larger number of primitive characters than do the orders that are placed above them in this classification."

Another significant statement made by Hegner is that whereas the primates excel principally in the development of the nervous system and in the large size of the brain, their bones, muscles, teeth, etc., are comparatively primitive.

Note that it is only those features (brain, nervous system, etc.), which are useful to man for the expression and complete functioning of his *inner* psychological and intellectual nature, which show specialized development. The significance of this is made clearer in a later chapter, "Specialization and Mendelism"; but in connection with the subject of specialization in general, attention is also called here to important statements by Luther C. Snider in his *Earth History* (The Century Co., 1932), especially chapter xxiv, "The Change in Living Things," where the writer gives abundant evidence to show that "the simple, generalized types are thus centers from which others radiate," and that the "generalized types are the most persistent" (p. 476).

1. Let us speak of the human skull. The bones of the human skull articulate at the base of the skull and on the sides of the braincase in a manner which is characteristic of primitive mammalian forms, but they show a contrast, a very marked contrast, with the arrangement of those same bones in the anthropoid apes and the monkeys.

However, the human skull in these respects exactly resembles the same handiwork of nature as is found in the case of the lemurs, a curious group of primitive mammals preceding the monkeys in evolutionary development and time, according to the Darwinists.

Hence the only conclusion that we can draw from this anatomical fact is, that since in the case of monkeys and apes these bones are differently arranged, and that the arrangement in the human skull is very primitive, therefore the anthropoids and other simians show an evolutionary development away from the primitive mammalian base, which man in common with the lemurs far more closely represents.

2. The nasal bones in man are exceedingly primitive in their simplicity. In the case of the monkeys and anthropoid apes, these animals cannot approach man in this respect of primitive simplicity, and we must therefore conclude that in the cases of these particular beasts, the evolutionary development has resulted for them in a wider departure from the original or primitive strain.

3. The primitive architecture of the human skull is likewise shown in a number of features in the face. Professor Wood Jones in *The Problem of Man's Ancestry* (p. 31) says:

The structure of the back wall of the orbit, the "metopic" suture, the form of the jugal bone, the condition of the internal pterygoid plate, the teeth, etc., all tell the same story — that the human skull is built upon remarkably primitive mammalian lines, which have been departed from in some degree by all monkeys and apes.

4. The same anatomist likewise points out:

The human skeleton, especially in its variations, shows exactly the same condition [of primitive mammalian simplicity].

5. Another quote from the same source:

As for muscles, man is wonderfully distinguished by the retention of primitive features lost in the rest of the Primates.

Primates, you will understand, is a scientific term comprising the higher animals of the supposed evolutionary series, and including man, the anthropoid apes, monkeys, lemurs, and perhaps one or two other minor families.

As regards man's primitive muscular features, let me first point out that in skull, in skeleton, and in the arrangement of his muscles, man in a host of respects is an entity of very primitive type, and has not, so far as these particular instances are concerned, the same large and wide specific variations that the monkeys and apes have followed in their respective line.

Let us take the *pectoralis minor* muscle, as an instance. This is a muscle which runs from the ribs towards the arm. It is attached to the coracoid process of the shoulder girdle. In the anthropoids it is attached to the coracoid in part, and in part to a ligament passing downward to the humerus, that is to the bone of the upper arm. In the monkeys it is attached still farther down the same ligament, but also to the humerus; while in many quadrupeds it is attached to the humerus altogether.

Now, as you may know, the usual way of attempting to prove the evolutionary development of man from lower ani-

mals by the transformists of modern times is to make anatomical and physiological research into the bodies of beings
below man. For instance, a favorite course of procedure
followed is the attempt to trace skeletal or muscular identities, variations, or analogies, first in the apes, then in the
monkeys, then in the lemurs, then in the quadrupeds; and if
the researcher find similarities or identities or analogies in
this examination, the conclusion is immediately drawn that
these beasts form a part of the evolutionary road up which
the human stock has climbed in its development. In other
words, that man is the latest in the series of living forms,
and that these and other creatures were his predecessors and
formed the links of the evolutionary chain, the lowest being
the original or primitive form.

But it is an entirely misleading method to follow, because, as we have just shown, the stocks are different; there
are no still existing connecting links between the great phyla.
Last but not least, these lower stocks are far more widely
evolved along their own particular lines in respect to certain
important skeletal and muscular variations than man is, who
is the most primitive of all the stocks.

In our present instance, that of the *pectoralis minor*
muscle, we find that the coracoid process is the primitive
attachment of this muscle, and man and some other exceedingly primitive animals retain today this very ancient type of
insertion. The transformists would say that in its evolutionary development this muscle has climbed up from the
humerus, which according to them is its primitive attachment, and having risen along the ligament has finally reached
the coracoid process in its highest form of development in
man. But this is an exact reversal of the truth as shown by
an anatomical examination.

6. The human tongue is also very primitive in type. The chimpanzee's tongue resembles man's in some degree; yet man's tongue is far more primitive than that of any monkey or anthropoid ape, the nearest to man of the animal entities beneath him in the supposed ascending but yet discontinuous scale of evolution, through which, according to the Darwinists, the human stock evolved.

7. The human vermiform appendix is curiously like that of some of the marsupials or pouched animals of Australia. It is very different in monkeys and in apes.

8. The great arteries arising from the arch of the aorta in man have the same number, are of the same kind, and are arranged in the same order, as is the case in a most curious and exceedingly primitive little animal, some eighteen or twenty inches long, found in Australia and Tasmania, the *Ornithorhynchus anatinus* — which little beast is commonly called the duckbilled platypus, so called because it has a bill closely resembling that of a duck. It is the lowest of all known mammals, because it actually has mammalian glands, which are without nipples; yet it lays eggs. In Australia it is popularly called the watermole. It is not, however, a mole, but it is a mammal of its own peculiar type. As said, the number and kind and order of the great arteries named are the same in man and in these extremely low mammalia, which are primitive in the highest degree. On the other hand, the arrangement of these arteries in the anthropoid apes and the monkeys is quite different.

9. The human premaxilla, or the bone which carries the incisors or chisel-teeth, that is to say the front teeth, no longer exists as a separate element in man, if it ever did so exist; but in all the apes and monkeys and in all other mammals, this premaxillary element is shown on the face by

suture lines, marking the junction with the maxillary bones. Because in man it is not a separate element, but is a separate element in all other mammals, it is, therefore, what would be called in science a specific human character.

With regard to this bone, please mark that it is already established as a distinguishable character in one of the earliest stages of the development of the human embryo, when that embryo is no more than three-fourths or seven-eighths of an inch long; as Professor Wood Jones says, when the embryo is "no longer than ten times the diameter of an ordinary pin's head" (op. cit., p. 37).

Hence, in view of the biogenetic law controlling embryological growth, called the law of embryonic recapitulation, this human character being shown so early in the development of the human embryo, forces us to conclude that it was a specific human character at a very early stage of human evolution, thus again demonstrating that man is an exceedingly primitive being.

According to this process of embryonic recapitulation, the embryo in its growth passes through the various stages which the stock to which it belongs had passed through in preceding biological time periods. It is a sort of rehearsal in brief of former evolutionary stock-history. And the human embryo shows this as a human specific character when the embryo itself is no longer than three-fourths of an inch; indeed, it is already outlined when the future bones of the face are still merely nuclei of cartilage.

Moreover, the earlier a specific character appears in the embryo, the farther back in time must it be searched for in the evolutionary history of the stock to which the embryo belongs; and conversely, those characteristics latest to appear in the embryo are those which appeared latest in the evolution of the biologic stock to which the embryo belongs.

Further, it is said that the embryo repeats in its growth first the grand features of the class to which it belongs; then come the features, as the embryo grows, of the order to which it belongs; then those of the family; then those of the genus; then those of the species — and these specific characters come last of all.

That is the alleged law; hence, if we find any character, any specific feature, which appears in the early stage of embryonic growth, this law says that we must search far back in the evolutionary history of the stock to which the embryo belongs, in order to find its first appearance there.

10. The human foot is another very primitive characteristic or rather character of the human race — of man. Have you ever looked at the foot of an anthropoid ape, or of a monkey? Do you realize that an ape's foot is actually, in some respects, more like the human hand than its own hand is? Instead of being a foot in its function, it is really a hand in function, because it operates like one on account of the great opposability of the big toe, which can be made to diverge or stick out almost at right angles to the digits of the ape's foot.

But turn to the beast's hand, to that of the gorilla, for instance, and you will see that the thumb is but a stump, so to say, as compared with the human thumb; and if you have ever watched an ape or a monkey attempting to pick up a pin or a needle, you could not have done otherwise than have seen the difficulty it has in doing what a man can do instantly, on account of man's opposable thumb.

If you will look at your hand, you will find that the third finger, the third digit, is the longest of the five digits; it is likewise so in the hand of the ape, and in the hand of the monkey. It is likewise so in the foot of the ape, and in the foot of the monkey.

It is for this reason that I prefer the old descriptive term given to the anthropoid apes and the monkeys in 1791 by Blumenbach, who called them *quadrumana,* or four-handed creatures, because the feet of these beasts can be used as hands as readily, or perhaps more so in some respects, than the hands themselves. The hand of the ape or the monkey often functions rather like a hook than in the manner of a grasping prehensile hand. "Quadrumana," therefore, is an extremely graphic descriptive term; and the placing of the monkeys and apes under the more modern term of primates unfortunately tends to hide this extremely specific character of both ape and monkey.

T. H. Huxley in his enthusiastic championing of the Darwinian theory did a great deal to belittle the unique and specific character of the human foot, and this work must be thoroughly undone. Man's foot is, as just said, unique in nature; no other animate entity has a foot that can compare with the typically specific features of the foot of a man.

The typical human foot is arranged so that the big toe is the longest of the five digits; and the other toes usually range in a progressively shorter sequence to the fifth and shortest. It has been said that this specific shape of the human foot is the result of wearing shoes — and I cannot but feel that this rather extravagant guess is a desperate effort to attempt to account for the wide divergence of the human foot from that of the apes and monkeys and of the supposed monkey-ancestors of man. But the attempted explanation is obviously untrue.

A baby's foot shows exactly the same character that I have spoken of; the unshod savage's foot also shows exactly the same character; and while it is true that on some old Greek statues of the gods or of human beings, the second (but not the third) digit is occasionally slightly longer than the big toe, that happens also today in some living individuals. In any case, it is not the third digit of the human foot which is ever the longest of the five, which it invariably is with the apes and with the monkeys.

Let us now turn to the human embryo in search of further proof of our point. An examination of the growing infant *in utero* shows that from the very first period when its foot is outlined in embryonic growth, exactly the same unique character is seen as in the foot of the human adult; and please note further that this fact is seen early in the embryo's development. Hence it must have appeared early in the evolution of the human stock.

Further, the foot of the embryo is never, at any time in its growth, an ape's foot or a monkey's foot; it is typically human from the time of its first appearance, which is an extremely significant fact, for it shows that the human foot is a specific human character, and must have been acquired early, and perhaps very early, in the evolution of the human stock.

Therefore, again according to the biologic law of recapitulation, which is made so much of by the Darwinists themselves — and we feel that they have truth and fact with them in this instance — we must conclude that the human foot in all details of its architecture is an exceedingly primitive character or feature, and that the human stock, early man, must have acquired it in the very beginnings of his evolutionary history.

11. Let us now turn to another example, to the *peroneus tertius* muscle or third peroneal muscle of the leg, leading

down into the fifth metatarsal of the foot, into which its tendon is inserted. This is one of the important muscles which aid a man to stand upright and to walk; but it is found in no other animal whatsoever, not merely not in the apes and in the monkeys, but in no mammal whatsoever. It is purely human. Further, it is found in the human embryo early in its development. Therefore, it, like the foot to which it belongs, must be a specific character evolved early in the growth of the human stock. From this we are again obliged to draw the significant conclusion that man's upright posture must have been his posture from the very origin of the human stock, or nearly so.

The old theory was that man only a relatively short time ago was but an improvement upon his alleged ape-ancestor, which, in its halcyon days of freedom from any moral responsibility whatsoever, ate fruit and insects between intervals of swinging from branch to branch of some primeval forest tree; and which, on the rare occasions when it came down to the ground, ran around on its knuckles as the ape does today.

This picture of the Saturnian Age of man, in late Miocene or in the Pliocene epochs, may be humorous, and interesting as an exercise of human ingenuity; but we search in vain in the geological record, or in the skeleton and muscular system of man himself, for any real proof of it.* There is no foundation in the facts of nature for it, nor in embryonic develop-

---

*In speaking of these different geologic ages, I am here following the example first set in the theosophical world by H. P. Blavatsky in *The Secret Doctrine* (II, 688, 693, 709–16), where she adopted the nomenclature of the system used by Lyell. Modern geologists have increased the length of the geologic periods enormously since H. P. Blavatsky wrote, and it should be clearly understood that throughout this book her time-periods are used. [See Appendix I.]

ment, nor has any such entity — between man and ape —
ever been discovered in the geological strata which have
been explored. It was a theory, a speculation, doubtless
enunciated in good faith by the extremely vocal proponents
of Darwinism in their efforts to trace man's ancestry through
the anthropoids. A man may be very enthusiastic and very
sincere, and yet not be a truthful exponent of the facts of
nature, if he allow his imagination to run before his scientific
caution. Enthusiasm and truth do not necessarily clasp
hands together.

But when we consider the human foot and this particular
muscle of man's leg, both very ancient in his evolutionary
development, and both solely human, what conclusions must
we draw? That man almost from his beginning, perhaps indeed from his beginning, was an entity with upright posture.

12. The human hand and forearm are likewise exceedingly primitive in many features. Professor Wood Jones
further says, concerning the human hand and forearm, that
in their muscles, in their bones, and in the joints, they are
astonishingly primitive, and therefore could not have been
evolved at a late date in man's evolutionary history; and, as
a matter of fact, if you have ever examined the pictures as
given in scientific books, of some of the extinct reptiles,
fossils which are occasionally dug out from the rocks of the
Mesozoic or Secondary Age, you will see that the hand or
the paw, and the forelimb, or whatever you like to call it, of
those exceedingly primitive creatures, bear an amazing resemblance in general appearance to the human hand and
also forearm.

The transformists of the modern school have often told
us that the line of evolutionary development of the human
stock ran back through the apes and the monkeys into the

quadrupedal mammalians, which means that if this theory were true man should even today show, in his forearm and hand, distinct traces of his passage through that alleged line of ancestry. In other words, man's arm and hand should still bear some remnants or traces of his having formerly used his forearm and hand as a support for his body in the times when he is supposed to have been a pronograde mammal like the horse and the dog and the ox, etc.

The fact is, however, that that idea has now been given up entirely by transformists, as far as I know, thus creating another wide hiatus in the supposed ladder of life given in the Darwinian or neo-Darwinian theories setting forth the ascending evolution of man. No anatomist today would do or could do otherwise than reject the idea, for it is impossible of credence, because man's forearm and hand, from the anatomical standpoint, were obviously never built or used as the supporting forelimb of a mammalian quadruped.

Professor Wood Jones, who is a courageous and honest scientist, an anatomist by profession, nevertheless believes that while man never was a quadruped in his past evolutionary history, he was at some very early period of his developmental line an arboreal animal of small size — an insectivorous little beast, I take it for granted, eating insects and fruits, living in the treetops because it was safer to live there than on the ground. Wood Jones further points out that in the forests of Malaysia there is a curious little monkey, which he calls the lowest of the monkeys, the tarsier. This is still a very primitive creature showing small development from the type of its remote ancestors geologically speaking; and is represented in the early Eocene epoch of the Tertiary period by *Anaptomorphus,* a genus of creatures closely resembling the present-day tarsier in all essentials.

Professor Wood Jones, if I understand him aright, seems to think that man originated from some creature, arboreal in habit, closely resembling the tarsier of today, or the *Anaptomorphus* of the Eocene of North America. I fail to see, in view of the facts that he himself has brought forth as regards the primitive features in man, how this can be so. However, such is his argument. He points out (and it is advantageous to our theme) that the tarsier-monkey and man — that is to say the lowest monkey known, and the highest of the Primates, man — are astonishingly alike in a number of primitive features such as the architecture of the skull, the peculiarities of the arteries which arise out of the aortic arch; and also with regard to the kidney of the tarsier which is formed on the same type that the human kidney follows.

When we remember that, as just said, the tarsier type goes back to the very base or beginnings of the Eocene epoch, and that the true anthropoid apes appeared in the next following period or the Miocene, we have a most persuasive suggestion that man himself must have existed in Eocene times — which, indeed, is the teaching of theosophy, which says that even in that remote age man was man in all respects, and had developed one of the most advanced civilizations that the earth has seen, on a continent now sunken beneath the waters of the stormy Atlantic.

We have adduced a significant number of important anatomical instances* in proof of the fact that man is the most primitive mammal on the globe today, and always has so been — and we might as readily have brought forward a

---

*Drawn chiefly from *The Problem of Man's Ancestry* (1918), by Frederic Wood Jones. This subject is more fully handled by the same author in two other works: *Arboreal Man* (1916), and *Man's Place among the Mammals* (1929).

host of others — as is also proved by the facts in the geological record setting forth the fascinating story of the so-called ladder of life, and by the so-called laws of biology as they are enunciated by our greatest biological, that is, zoological and botanical, researchers and thinkers.

Further, we have pointed out that each of the stocks below man — we now take specifically the anthropoid and simian stocks — has wandered far more widely from that original primitive basal simplicity than man has; that man retains more of the basal mammalian features or characters in his body, that is, in his muscles, and in his skeleton, than any other animal now living on earth does; and that the apes and monkeys have wandered far afield in that respect, far more so than man has wandered from the primitive mammalian stock, *which was early man himself.*

With all this evidence before us to prove man's primitive origin, what becomes of the Darwinian "ascending ladder of beings," each stage of which is more complex than the one preceding it, and which is supposed to have eventuated in man as he is today? The two theories cannot exist side by side. One or the other must go by the board; and modern research and deduction is moving, albeit slowly, away from the Darwinian theory, towards the more enlightened conception that man leads in the evolutionary history of the various stocks that this earth has produced.

8

MAN AND ANTHROPOID — I

So far as the ancestral derivation of man is concerned, we assert that he has not one drop of anthropoid or simian blood in his veins, and never had. I wish to emphasize this, because we must free our minds in many important respects from that teaching which so very large a part of the public has unconsciously accepted as a true statement of the facts of man's ancestral tree. We must make our minds receptive of and more concordant with new discoveries, newer truths which the great researchers into nature's mysteries have found out for us.

It is true that theosophy does not teach that primitive man was physically fashioned as he is at present. On the contrary, man himself has evolved from a more primitive to a more perfect form even as other and lower creatures have so evolved. And it is a fact that though he possessed the same general type of physical structure that he now has, he actually was apelike in appearance, but he never was an ape. I repeat, *at no time was man ever an ape,* for the simple reason that the ape appeared in geologic time far later than did physical man, being in part an offspring of an early human stock. The ape in some degree even today resembles in physical appearance his human half-parent of that distant time.

It should be remembered, moreover, that the apes, being of half-animal and half-human origin, are far more beastlike in appearance than man ever was, even in those early ages. Therefore, when we say that man, in early geological periods was "apelike in appearance," we merely mean that the evolving human monad passed through human bodies which at one stage of their evolution had what now would be called certain modified yet apelike looks; but these, as time passed, became more and more refined and human in appearance until they are what they are now.

Professor Wood Jones corroborates this viewpoint:

we may say that not only is he [man] more primitive than the monkeys and apes, having become differentiated specifically in an extremely remote past, but also that he has been a creature which walked upright on his two feet for an astonishingly long period.*

Likewise Professor Boule of Paris concludes, from a close study of the skeleton-fossil of the individual discovered in 1908 at La Chapelle-aux-Saints, that man had

been derived neither from the Anthropoid stem, nor from any other known group, but from a very ancient Primate stock that separated from the main line even before the giving off of the Lemuroids.†

Yes, provided that we add that that "very ancient Pri-

---

*The Problem of Man's Ancestry, p. 38.
†"L'Homme fossile de la Chapelle-aux-Saints," Ann. de Palæontologie, 1912; quoted by Wood Jones, op. cit., p. 34.

mate stock" was man himself — not man as we now know
him, but the man of that geologic period which theosophy
states to have been in the Secondary times; more definitely in
the early Jurassic. Nor did the human stock "separate from
the main line," because man was himself that "main line."

It is very unfortunate that the calm, conservative attitude
of mind which all true scientists should have, has so often
been departed from in former years by enthusiastic proponents of accepted scientific theories. Haeckel, for instance,
the anthropologist, paleontologist, zoologist, and whatnot,
used to teach — and it was accepted as a fact of nature, because the great Haeckel taught it — that in the respective
embryos of man and of ape the differences between them
could not be distinguished until the fourth or fifth month of
pregnancy — a teaching which was not true. As Professor
Wood Jones says, it is a teaching whose results we now must
take time and energy to undo. The differences between the
embryo of the ape and the embryo of man are noticeable far
earlier, embryologically speaking, than the fourth month of
intrauterine life.

I was looking this morning at an interesting picture. It
was the picture of the embryo of a gorilla a short time preceding birth; and this curious little beasty was an ape all
through, as was to be expected. The bestial mouth was
there; the long arms; the unmistakable features and specific
characters of the anthropoid type — all were there. Yet it
was more humanoid in appearance than its parents were,
more humanlike in appearance than it itself would have
been, had it lived and grown to adulthood. The braincase
was relatively larger and more human in shape, the forehead
taller and nobler than the receding forehead of the adult
gorilla. Its foot likewise approximated much more closely to

the normal human foot in appearance; and whereas these are but superficial features of judgment, being mere resemblances, yet they properly can be employed in argument, and the Darwinists and neo-Darwinists and transformists are the last to object to it, because their own theories are so widely based upon resemblances between man and ape.

It is well known that the infant ape appears to be more human in general and in detail than does the adult. As growth proceeds the forehead recedes, the mouth becomes still more bestial, the foot becomes more typically the hand-foot of the anthropoid stock; and in many other respects, as for instance in the protruding jaw, the typical ape-appearance is acquired.

What is the explanation of this problem, and of the larger departure from the humanoid towards the more anthropoid? And also towards the type, now extinct, which furnished the other half-parent of the ape strain?

The theosophist says that the more human appearance of the early ape embryo is a case of reversion to the former type of a far past geologic time, towards the human half-parent of the progenitors of the present ape stock; and because the particular anthropoid strain, indwelling in the germ plasm of the cell which brings the ape individual to grow and to develop into its adulthood — as that cellular strain or potency seeks to express itself, it follows of necessity the only path open to it, its own path. It climbs its own ancestral or genealogical tree.

Nature always follows grooves; it always takes the path of least resistance, the path of the pioneers who have gone before. All forces in universal nature do this: electricity as an example in point. Nowhere in nature do you find a natural force or an evolving entity following the path of greatest resistance. A biologic habit once established will prevail until it is succeeded by the growth and dominance of a succeeding habit; and it is the essential work of evolution to produce ever nobler courses, ever nobler habits, than those which had preceded the newer.

Consequently, the pathway which has once been opened is automatically taken by all evolving entities that are included in any particular group or stock or race or strain coming along behind.

It is the teaching of theosophy that the anthropoid or ape stock in a far remote past, in the Miocene of the Tertiary period, sprang from the human stock on one side and from a quasi-beast — simian — ancestry on the other. This explains why the ape so closely resembles man in some things and shows such immense dissimilarities in other things — in the nobler characters and features which man has.°

Similar was the case with regard to the lower simian stocks, the monkeys; but that event happened at a period still more remote in geologic time, to wit, in the Mesozoic period, during the period of existence of what we call the "mindless" human races. In those far back days, these particular crossings were almost invariably fertile, for the simple reason that matter was then far more plastic than it now is;

°Such is the case with the anthropoid apes. The touch of humanity from their early human half-parent still works within them, but is overshadowed in power, in influence, and therefore in biologic consequences, by the stronger beast evolutionary strain. Nevertheless, because our earth and its entire groups of inhabitants of all kingdoms are even now beginning what in theosophy is called the ascending arc of evolutionary development, the human influence in the ape stock now surviving will become still stronger in power as future ages roll by into the ocean of the past. This means that in distant future time the apes will slowly become more humanlike than now they are.

matter had not yet set into the grooves that it now follows.

Thus the apes and the monkeys have traces of human blood in their veins; the monkeys a single dose, so to say, of the nobler strain, and the apes a double dose of the same. But *no man* has one drop of either simian or anthropoid blood in his veins.

I weigh on this point with emphasis because the other idea, that of the ape ancestry of man, is so difficult to eradicate. Though it is not now accepted by most modern biologists, curiously enough it remains alive. People are averse to changing their minds in relation to what they think are proved facts. Old and worn-out ideas, ideas which are actually behind the knowledge, scientific and other, of the day, still remain in our minds and plague us.

It was Darwin who in his book *The Descent of Man* gives voice to his opinion that the origin of man is to be found in an anthropoid ape living in a remote geological period; and scientists ever since have elaborated the theory. Despite the vastly wider light thrown on the problem of evolution by modern research, this outworn theory is still taught in many of our public schools as being a résumé of the facts of nature, as far as man's evolutionary past is concerned. It sounds incredible, but such is the case.

Let me quote here a few passages from *The Descent of Man* in which this theory is expressly stated. In chapter six, Darwin says:

Now man unquestionably belongs in his dentition, in the structure of his nostrils, and some other respects, to the Catarrhine or Old World division [of monkeys]. . . . There can, consequently, hardly be a doubt that man is an off-shoot from the Old World simian stem. — p. 153

If the anthropomorphous apes be admitted to form a natural subgroup, then as man agrees with them, not only in all those characters

which he possesses in common with the whole Catarrhine group, but in other peculiar characters, such as the absence of a tail and of callosities, and in general appearance, we may infer that some ancient member of the anthropomorphous sub-group gave birth to man.
—p. 154

But we must not fall into the error of supposing that the early progenitor of the whole Simian stock, including man, was identical with, or even closely resembled, any existing ape or monkey.   —p. 155

Obviously not.

We are far from knowing how long ago it was when man first diverged from the Catarrhine stock; but it may have occurred at an epoch as remote as the Eocene period.   —p. 156

And finally, we have this gem:

The Simiadæ [in Darwin's classification, all anthropoid primates] then branched off into two great stems, the New World and Old World monkeys; and from the latter, at a remote period, Man, the wonder and glory of the Universe, proceeded.   —p. 165

The more enlightened theory — that the anthropoid and monkey stocks, the anthropoids in particular, probably sprang from man as their half-parent (theosophy says actually) in a far-gone period of geological time, though not as degenerate men — this theory in differing forms is in greater or less degree hinted at or upheld by a number of very eminent zoologists before and after Darwin, each of course after his own manner. I may mention the Frenchman de Quatrefages, several German biologists, and possibly even the modern author and anatomist Wood Jones, also Klaatsch of Heidelberg University, and apparently Osborn of Columbia University. Some or all of these men uphold the theory that the anthropoid stock may have originated wholly or partly in and from the human stock. These scientists may differ as among themselves, but the root-idea seems to be common to them all.*

Some diehard proponents of the older and now more or less rejected evolutionism also assert that preceding man's evolution through the anthropoid and simian stocks, he even passed through quadrupedal mammalian forms, of which the mammalian quadrupeds on earth today are the modern descendants. But let me remind you of what Professor Klaatsch has to say about that idea — merely echoing, by the way, what many another great man has said to the same point in former years: "Man and his ancestors were never quadrupeds as the dog or the elephant or the horse."

This renowned anthropologist further states emphatically that monkeys and apes are "degenerated branches of the prehuman stock." Such, as far as it goes, is precisely the teaching of theosophy, which, however, claims that this is but half the truth, adding that the primitive human stock was but the half-parent of the original ancestors of the modern anthropoids. This does not mean, however, that monkeys and apes are or were degraded men, but that they were in part human, and in part animal — derived from an early human stock on one side, and from an early animal stock on the other; and that they have since shown a strong tendency to revert to the types of former geologic apes.

The Darwinians and the neo-Darwinians still say that man belongs to the same subphylum or stock that the apes and monkeys do. If he belongs to their subphylum, he is either their descendant or their ascendant. Now if man sprang from the apes, how is it, please, that he has lost the specific characters or features which mark the anthropoid

---

*[See Appendix II for more recent and identical findings.]

and lower simian stocks, and has wandered back in so many respects to an identical basal mammalian simplicity of structure which he must have possessed before, thus violating one of the best known of the biological laws. This is the law of irreversibility, which sets forth that in evolution no entity, losing an organ or a character or a feature, takes that identical organ up again, or regains it; but that if the recurrent conditions of environment are ever similar to what they were before, he then gains new organs suited to these recurrent conditions in the new circumstances in which he finds himself. Louis Dollo, a Belgian paleontologist, has done some remarkable work in proof and in demonstration of this law of irreversibility, which is today accepted by most representative biologists.

Thus if man cannot have been derived from the apes and the monkeys, as is now very generally accepted by biologists, and yet is the most primitive in origin of all the mammals on earth, what is the logical, the inevitable, deduction that we must make? It is this: that belonging to their subphylum or their stock, as they say, and not being their descendant, he must be their ascendant, their progenitor. That is precisely what we say, although we explain the facts in a very different and, we believe, more convincing way.

Darwinism became the favorite scientific evolutionary theory of the time. Nowadays it is more or less moribund, although there are still a number of "won't-give-ins" who cling to the old Darwinian ideas; yet they belong, for all that, rather to what is called the neo-Darwinian scheme, which is Darwinism more or less modified by other natural facts which have been discovered and investigated to some degree since 1859 when Darwin published his important book, *The Origin of Species*.

No one can rightly say that all that Darwin taught wrong, or that all that the neo-Darwinians teach is erroneous. That position would be absurd. On the contrary; for there is some truth in the explanation of the facts of nature which Charles Darwin and his followers investigated and supposed that they had found out. Nor can one say that the theories of Lamarck, Darwin's predecessor whom Darwin so largely followed, are altogether wrong. There is some truth in them both, particularly in Lamarck's idea or intuition of the appetence innate in the organism striving in its environment — i.e., the inward urge of the evolving organism towards action upon that environment. Speaking generally, there is some truth in the larger ideas of all great men. It is indeed great men who have adopted and elaborated the theories of progressive development of the human stock and of the stocks below man, and they have accumulated a large number of natural facts, which in larger or smaller degree furnish some support for those theories.

No one denies an actual fact or any number of actual facts. But it is a vastly different matter when our men of science undertake to raise upon these natural facts various theories or speculations or hypotheses and to pass these off upon a trusting public as established facts of nature. As freethinking men and women we should reserve the right to accept or to reject any hypothesis or theory exactly in the degree that we find it to be true or untrue.

As a matter of fact, what theosophy claims, and what we have been teaching for many decades is this: that the evolution of man and of the beings below him, and of the universe itself, cannot be logically and completely explained on accepted scientific lines, or by the alleged facts of science depending solely upon physical and chemical agencies.

These are not the only factors working in the evolution of beings; and the main divergence (leaving other important facts aside) between the theosophical view of evolution and those theories hitherto current in the world, is that the latter refuse to admit a psycho-vital engine or motor behind and within the running physical machine — or rather engineers, call them spiritual entities if you like.

We claim that there are designers in the world — designers of many degrees, vast hierarchies of them, infilling and, in fact, forming the invisible part of the cosmos itself. They are the origin of the life forces working through the life-atoms of all evolving entities; and it is in these designers that we live, and move, and have our being, even as the cells and atoms of a man's body — those small and elemental lives — live and move and have their being in him; further, that the working of these designers is de facto neither fortuitous nor haphazard, but is essentially the result of the purposive and teleological striving of these designers towards a larger and more perfect expression of their indwelling and native powers.

This again is one of the largest differences between the theosophical and the accepted scientific view of evolutionary development. We assert that natural forces, the indwelling powers in these designers, work towards a definite or purposive end; while, on the other hand, the popular scientific theories avoid or disregard this vitally important question and, usually tacitly, postulate fortuity, chance, or the random origination of species and biological variations.

Charles Darwin himself, in the opening words of the fifth chapter of *The Origin of Species,* explicitly declares that he wrongly uses the word "chance" in connection with the origination of species, saying that it is "a wholly incorrect expression," but that this word "chance" nevertheless suffices to set forth our ignorance of the actual cause of specific variations. Strangely enough, he then immediately proceeds to set forth the cause of which he has just confessed he was completely ignorant — natural selection — resulting in the survival of the fittest.

9

MAN AND ANTHROPOID — II

In the *Scientific American** some years ago there appeared an extremely interesting article called "Dawn-Man or Ape?" by William King Gregory, then professor of vertebrate paleontology at Columbia University. He is apparently of the neo-Darwinian persuasion, and in discussing the question of the evolution of man from the apes, as alleged by the Darwinian theory, he says:

> *In other words, even if we did not have the chimpanzee we should have to infer its existence as a sort of half-way station in the long road of ascent from the primitive Eocene primates.* Darwin's theory that man is a derivative from the anthropoid ape stock, although not from any existing type of ape, accounts for hundreds of such peculiar resemblances between man and ape. And what other scientific hypothesis can do this?

We have here precisely the same spirit of vaulting enthusiasm, of what is to me exuberant imagination, that was

*September 1927, p. 232.

manifest and that wrought such curious work in a biological sense in the cases of Huxley in England and Haeckel in Germany — inventors, these two, of imaginary steps in their evolutionary ladder of life; for does not Gregory say in the same spirit: "Even if we did not have the chimpanzee we should have to infer its existence" — we should have to invent one? Fortunately, the chimpanzee exists; but the idea of substitutive invention is there. Enthusiasm for biological invention is there.

As regards the "hundreds of such peculiar resemblances between man and ape," such resemblances most unquestionably exist, though hundreds seems to be a large number. But this is another example of the Darwinian method, just as Huxley and Haeckel followed it: they emphasized and overemphasized the manifold points of resemblance between man and his younger brothers, the apes — or rather his degenerate half-children, the apes and the monkeys; but they omitted to point out at their full value the host of dissimilarities, the wide divergences, that exist in even greater number between the human stock and the anthropoid and lower simian stocks. They recognized them in some cases, but denigrated their value, underestimated their importance, or slurred them over as things which are so obvious they need scarcely to be mentioned with more than a passing allusion to their existence. I must point out that this method of suggestion of the unimportance of important features or characters differing as between the two stocks, has a direct psychological influence upon those who see or hear them. As I have said before, people take such statements at their face value, without further examination, as established facts of nature, which most emphatically they are not.

In an address to the British Association for the Advancement of Science, Sir Arthur Keith, held by his colleagues to be "the most brilliant anthropologist of the day," said:*

> The evidence of man's evolution from an ape-like being, obtained from a study of fossil remains, is definite and irrefutable, but the process has been infinitely more complex than was suspected in Darwin's time. Our older and discarded conception of man's transformation was depicted in that well-known diagram which showed a single file of skeletons, the gibbon at one end and man at the other.

We all know that picture: it is still in many of our museums, and is still taught in many of our biological books. These also show intermediate stages of bestial or subhuman creatures, which are announced as having actually been the intermediate steps or stages of man's evolution from the ape; yet in no case, please mark well, are these creatures announced as being mere offsprings of the scientific imagination of their reconstructors, reconstructed perhaps from a portion of a fossil skull, or perhaps from a portion of a jaw or from a tooth or two, or one or two or three of these together. From and around these scanty fossil remains have been built up the various pictures of more or less manlike creatures, growing gradually more beastly and apelike as they descend the scale towards the gorilla or the chimpanzee or the gibbon, as they go down the file towards the apes and monkeys.

I may add here that the mistakes and faults of these imaginary reproductions of former men are rarely, or never perhaps, obvious to the trusting student or reader; and yet a striking instance of such false reconstructions may be shown with regard to Neanderthal man, who has always

---

* "The Evidence for Darwin is Summed Up"; for full text see *The New York Times*, September 4, 1927, sec. 8, pp. 1, 10.

been pictured as having had no human nose, but pictured as a being with a flat, squat nose, somewhat like those of the Catarrhine apes of the Old World. Yet we now know that this was not true, as is well illustrated in the case of the fossil skeleton or individual discovered in France in 1908, at La Chapelle-aux-Saints; for the skull of this skeleton had prominent nose bones and, so far as I know, the skeleton belonged by unanimous consent to a Neanderthal man.

Professor H. H. Wilder, the American zoologist, has shown that this individual must have had an eminent nose, a very pronounced nose; and yet for a long, long time we were taught that the physiognomy of this former living man comprised a nose — if a nose at all — which approximated to the nasal apparatus of the ape.

These reconstructions are, by the necessities of the case, in very large part imaginary. It is unfortunate that they should still be exhibited as representations in the direct line of man's ancestry, and that our children should see them and be taught the falsehood that these imaginary reconstructions represent man as he formerly appeared at different stages of his alleged ascent from the anthropoid.

Sir Arthur continues:

> In our original simplicity we expected, as we traced man backward in time, that we should encounter a graded series of fossil forms — a series which would carry him in a straight line toward an anthropoid ancestor.
>
> We should never have made this initial mistake if we had remembered that the guide to the world of the past is the world of the present.

As I have said before, there is no such end-on, uniserial, rectilinear evolution of man from the protozoan upwards, as the Darwinists have stated it. Yet evolution is indeed an end-on progress. It is indeed a uniserial path, but it is not rectilinear or in a straight line; and it does not proceed along the pathway which the Darwinists and the neo-Darwinists have claimed and still claim for it.

In this assertion the theosophists no longer stand alone, for there is a large and growing and important school now teaching pretty much the same thing.

Continuing from Professor Keith's remarks:

> In our time man is represented not by one but by many and diverse races — black, brown, yellow and white. Some of these are rapidly expanding, others are as rapidly disappearing.
>
> Our searches have shown that in remote times the world was peopled, sparsely it is true, with races showing even a greater diversity than those of today and that already the same process of replacement was at work. We have to thread our way, not along the links of a chain, but through the meshes of a complicated network.

Just so! How pleasant it is to read the apologetic acknowledgments of the mistakes formerly so enthusiastically and positively affirmed as facts of nature, especially when these come from an honest antagonist!

A few years ago it was a scientific heresy of the deepest dye to suppose that man had evolved in any other manner than in that outlined in scientific books, and supposedly along the line of ascent set forth in reconstructive work on skeleton and muscle in our museums. Such evolution, we were taught as an axiom, as a scientific dogma, had proceeded along that certain and particular pathway from the protozoan to man which Professor Keith now very rightly and aptly calls a "discarded conception."

To continue the quotation:

> We have made another mistake. Seeing that in our search for man's ancestry we expected to reach an age when the beings we

should have to deal with would be simian rather than human, we ought to have marked the conditions which prevail among living anthropoid apes. We ought to have been prepared to find, as we approached a distant point in the geological horizon, that the forms encountered would be as widely different as are the gorilla, chimpanzee and orang, and confined, as these great anthropoids now are, to limited parts of the earth's surface.

Have we not been pointing out that a theory per se is not a fact of nature, and that inevitably it would in good time be replaced by a theory more closely approximating to natural truth? Yet we draw the sharpest kind of distinction between a theory evolved from some man's mind and the facts of nature. These latter are the ultimate tests in any proof of a system; not theories and hypotheses.

I continue citing from Professor Keith:

> That is what we are now realizing: As we go backward in time we discover that mankind becomes broken up, not into separate races as in the world of today, but into numerous and separate species. When we go into a still more remote past they become so unlike that we have to regard them not as belonging to separate species but different genera. It is among this welter of extinct fossil forms which strew the ancient world that we have to trace the zigzag line of man's descent. Do you wonder we sometimes falter and follow false clues?*

This is good, although at first it sounds like a contradiction of the fundamental theosophical teaching that all stocks originated from the one main stock, the human. But this apparent contradiction can easily be explained. In tracing back from the present the history of the great stocks, it is

---

*Please understand that different "races of men" means men much more like each other than does different "species of men," and that different "species of men" are more like each other than are different "genera of men."

true that they appear more distinctive and differentiated *up to a certain period,* which in theosophy we call the fourth root-race.

At about that time the world was teeming with a large number of evolutionary strains, because at that period material evolution in various directions had reached the acme of its power. The various types of mankind were more widely separated from each other, not only as regards contemporaneity and succession, but likewise in frequent instances as regards type than are the races of today.

But in times *preceding* this great fourth race, the farther back we go in geologic time, the more closely do the stocks begin to approximate towards each other, so far as type is concerned. In other words, they become more and more generalized the nearer we approach their origin at the common point of departure in ages far preceding that of the fourth root-race. It is in those more generalized and far earlier types, having ancient or modern representatives as the case may be, that we find a greater kinship, biologically speaking, among the various stocks.

Professor Keith ends his address:

Was Darwin right when he said that man, under the action of biological forces which can be observed and measured, has been raised from a place among anthropoid apes to that which he now occupies? The answer is yes! and in returning this verdict I speak but as foreman of the jury — a jury which has been empaneled from men who have devoted a lifetime to weighing the evidence.

That declaration sounds extremely convincing. But let us point out that other juries, empaneled from other men who likewise have spent a lifetime in the study of the evidence, tell us a different tale; and the ranks of these latter are growing daily greater.

Dr. Henry Fairfield Osborn, in an address given before the American Philosophical Society in Philadelphia on April 29, 1927, said:*

I regard the ape-human theory as totally false and misleading. It should be banished from our speculations and from our literature not on sentimental grounds but on purely scientific grounds and we should now resolutely set our faces toward the discovery of our actual pro-human ancestors. . . .

The prologue and the opening acts of the human drama occurred way back 16,000,000 years ago† . . . At this period, or before, the family of man sprang from a stock neither human nor ape-like, . . .

In my opinion, the most likely part of the world in which to dis-

---

*"Recent Discoveries relating to the Origin and Antiquity of Man," read by Vice-president Osborn on the occasion of the bicentenary anniversary (April 27–30) of the American Philosophical Society which traces its origins to the Junta formed by Benjamin Franklin in 1727 at age twenty-one. See *Proceedings*, vol. 66, pp. 373–89.

†It is very remarkable that Professor Osborn gives almost the exact length of time stretching backwards into the past — sixteen million years ago — required to reach primitive man, that theosophy teaches as having been the period of the first appearance of truly physical man, who had been preceded by semi-astral man, and before that by astral man. The first truly physical men existed eighteen million years ago.

Professor Osborn further places the age of man, *in his present stage*, at one million years. It is also the theosophical teaching that man, as he now is in his *present evolutionary cycle*, has been so for one million years more or less. It should be noted, however — and the point is of some importance — that this "one million years" applies to our present humanity or fifth root-race in its present evolutionary stage *only since the time when it became a race sui generis*, i.e., a race with its own typical racial characteristics, and more or less separated from the previous or fourth root-race. Actually the origins of our present humanity or fifth root-race extended several million years farther back than this "one million years" mentioned.

Professor Keith says that it is only about one million years since man diverged from the ape stock, or perhaps, rather, from that common ancestor of man and the ape about which so much is said and so

cover these "Dawn Men," as we may now call them, is the high pla-
teau region of Asia embraced within the great prominences of Chinese
Turkestan, of Tibet and of Mongolia.

Could the contradiction between two eminent biologists
be more absolute? Of course, while Professor Osborn speaks
of the ancestors of man as having been neither human nor
ape, he gives utterance merely to the common biologic
theory that these two stocks were derived from some animal
neither human nor anthropoid. He knows of no proof that
the idea is anything else than a theory elaborated in an
attempt to find a common ancestor for the two classes of the
primates most closely resembling each other, man and ape.
But the theosophical teachings tell us very clearly, and the
facts of anthropology and biology seem to prove the case
fully, that that common ancestor was *man himself* — not man
as he now is, of course, but man as he then was; less evolved
than present mankind, as is to be expected, but yet no
animal as we understand that word, and no ape in any sense,
but original, primitive man himself.

You may call him prehuman, if you limit the term "human" to man as he now is. But the strain from which humans
come, from which men are derived, was human to its source

---

exceedingly little is known; and that this separation of the two stocks
occurred, as alleged, in the beginning of the Miocene epoch of the
Tertiary period of geology. Professor Keith is very modest indeed in
his biologic computations of geologic time. Only one million years,
according to Keith, since the beginning of the Miocene! Other authorities, equally great, differ widely from Keith's time period. For instance in *Organic Evolution* by Richard Swan Lull (1921), various
dates are given as estimates of the duration of these various geologic
periods; and the Tertiary, to which belongs the Miocene epoch, is
given by Matthew as of nine million years in duration — while Barrell
is not satisfied with less than sixty million!

on this earth, and its origin was in godlike creatures, who came to our earth in the earliest days of the planet's life; and, as it were, casting the seeds of their lives into the developing germs, originated the human stock. These very developing germs or life-atoms were those with which these godlike creatures were spiritually, psychically, and therefore magnetically connected in a former period of evolution, in times so vastly far-distant that we call it another manvantara or cycle of manifested life.

Osborn continues:

> It is our recent studies of behaviorism of the anthropoid apes as contrasted with the behaviorism of the progenitors of man which compel us to separate the entire ape stock very widely from the human stock.*

So do the theosophical teachings separate the two stocks very widely. Only I do not understand what Professor Osborn means by the "behaviorism of the progenitors of man," because to study behaviorism you must know the living creature, and I do not know any living creatures who are the progenitors of man.

I continue quoting from Dr. Osborn:

> The term "ape-man" has been forced into our language along a number of lines, and even the term "anthropoid" has come to lose its significance. "Ape-man" gained prestige through early explorers and travelers who represented the anthropoid apes as walking on their hind feet. We have since discovered that no anthropoid ape walks upright; the gibbon balances himself awkwardly when he comes down

---

*It is interesting to note that Professor Keith also contrasts the behaviorism of man with the behaviorism of the apes, and attempts to use this to show a kinship between apes and monkeys and man. Professor Osborn draws diametrically opposite conclusions from the same set of ideas and facts.

from the trees, but all the other apes are practically quadrupedal in motion, except possibly in defense, when they rear as a horse would rear. . . .

Of all incomprehensible things in the universe man stands in the front rank, and of all incomprehensible things in man the supreme difficulty centers in the human brain, intelligence, memory, aspirations, and powers of discovery, research and the conquest of obstacles.

This is the language of a genuine seer. But let me ask: why does this most remarkable scientific thinker speak of man as being so entirely "incomprehensible"? As I see it, it is because, great as he is in his line of scientific work, honest and courageous as he obviously is, he nevertheless is still more or less, unknown to himself, under the psychological influence of the old materialistic teaching that there is nothing in man that can be known except his physical body and its "psychologic" activities.

10

THE MORAL ISSUES INVOLVED

THE QUESTION OF evolution has become a burning one, because men and women have come to realize that there is a moral question involved in the teachings concerning even the physical derivation of the human race.

If the derivation of man from an inferior animal stock were true, that is, a fact of nature, knowing as we do that the universe pursues logical courses and that man has in him a directing moral sense, then we should say it is all right; no harm can come from believing in a fact of nature.

But if, on the other hand, the teaching is based, as it is, not wholly on a fundamental truth but very largely on a speculative theory which is inherently lacking in moral power, and which man in following therefore follows in a necessarily immoral manner, then the case is vastly different; and all thinking men and women find that it is time to call a halt, and to investigate the bases upon which this former speculative thinking rested. Investigate them impartially, not from the standpoint of partisanship nor from the standpoint of a *parti pris,* but making a searching investigation into the actuality of the theory itself — whether it is based on nature or whether it is one of those many fads or hypotheses partly based on nature and partly evolved from the speculative imagination of the framers of it.

Let me turn again to Dr. Osborn. Writing in the *Encyclopaedia Britannica,** he speaks forcibly as regards the causes of evolution:

> The net result of observation is not favourable to the essentially Darwinian view that the adaptive arises out of the fortuitous by selection, but is rather favourable to the hypothesis of the existence of some quite unknown intrinsic law of life which we are at present totally unable to comprehend or even conceive. We have shown that the direct observation of the origin of new characters in palaeontology brings them within that domain of natural law and order to which the evolution of the physical universe conforms. The nature of this law, which, upon the whole, appears to be purposive or teleological in its operations, is altogether a mystery which may or may not be illumined by future research. In other words, the origin, or first appearance of new characters, which is the essence of evolution, is an orderly process so far as the vertebrate and invertebrate palaeontologist observes it.

What a change from the scientific views of the last century! I would like to point out in this truly remarkable paragraph the emphasis laid upon the purposive or teleological principle implicated in this unquestionable truth — teleological meaning that which tends to a well-defined end or object.

Professor G. W. Patrick of the University of Iowa, writing on the broader views of twentieth-century ideas of evolution, has this to say:†

---

*Under the heading "Palaeontology," XIth ed., vol. XX, p. 591.

†"The Convergence of Evolution and Fundamentalism," *The Scientific Monthly*, July 1926, pp. 12–13.

Another feature of twentieth-century evolution is the lesser emphasis put upon the notion of nature as a battlefield — as a scene of sanguinary and ruthless struggle in which the fittest survive. This was one of the unhappy ideas associated with the name of Darwin, even until recently made the excuse and vindication of every evil thing in human society. It is unfortunate that a part of this precious twentieth century has got to be spent in "unthinking our convenient Darwinism." Professor Patten, writing as a biologist, says that the altruism and cooperation which we are coming to recognize as the absolutely indispensable condition of further social evolution are basal and primary factors in the grand strategy of evolution in nature itself.

In fact, there seem to be indications that the whole evolutionary nomenclature of the nineteenth century was unfortunate. Perhaps we need a new set of terms all around to describe that great world movement which for seventy-five years has gone by the name of *evolution.* Many biologists are beginning to question the presupposition of the nineteenth century that the concepts of the mechanical sciences have any special prerogative in the interpretation of life and mind and society. Professor Haldane has gone so far as to reverse the order and suggests that "the idea of life is nearer to reality than the idea of matter and energy" . . .

I interrupt a moment. Here we find a reaction against the old idea of matter and energy as lifeless, soulless, unanimated, unimpulsed, dead things, combining helter-skelter, driven about space fortuitously, collecting together without coherent reason or order to form what we call life and men.

To continue the quotation:

and J. Arthur Thomson believes that the formulae of physics and chemistry are no longer adequate for the description of behavior or of development or of evolution. It is generally felt that Herbert Spencer "put something over" on the scientific world when he exalted a certain trio of concepts, namely, matter, motion and force, whose redistribution was to explain the whole world.

Biologists of the present time are largely engaged in patient and persistent investigation in the field of genetics, wisely refraining from speculation as to the causes and meaning of evolution. But it is diffi-cult to refrain from all speculation, and when biologists do enter the field of philosophy and speak of theories of evolution, it is interesting to notice the new terms which they are using. We hear much of creative evolution, not always in the strict Bergsonian sense. We hear of "emergent evolution." We hear evolution described as "a struggle for freedom," or as a process in "self-expression." We hear of the material fabric of nature as being "alert" rather than "inert." We hear of "the grand strategy of evolution." We even hear of evolution as a process of achievement, in which life and mind and moral conduct and social organization and science and art are values which have been won.

Again, what a change from the earlier scientific views!

Professor Louis Trenchard More of the University of Cincinnati, writing on "Man's Nature,"* has the following to say, among other things of interest, on the inadequacy of the mechanistic biologic theory of transformism, usually mis-called evolution, and of the misuse of that theory, such as it is, by most of the popularizers of scientific hypotheses. He writes:

> For many decades the world has been governed by the philosophy of progress and evolution which was established by the work of the biologists of the nineteenth century. To them we owe not only the solid foundations of the science of biology, but also the dogmatic assumption of the Darwinian theory of natural selection and a philos-ophy of monistic naturalism.

Let me interrupt a moment to say that these scientific theories are not proved facts of nature; they are merely speculations, hypotheses, elevated to the rank of truths of being; but now our modern scientific theorists know better. Professor More continues:

----

*The Hibbert Journal, April 1927, pp. 509–10, 522.

In the meanwhile later biologists have proved, by their own experimental work, that the Darwinian theory is entirely inadequate to explain the appearance of new species, and they have found no other satisfactory cause of variations. They are thus reduced to the position of asking us to accept a general theory of evolution on faith.

This seems to imply that there is a scientific church wherein if we wish to be in good standing and popular, and not to be considered as "cranks" by the unthinking, we must accept things on faith. The statement by Professor More we do not believe to be one iota overdrawn or exaggerated. He continues:

While these results are known by all well-informed biologists, they have permitted, without protest, the popularisers of science, the sociologists, and the clergy to present the subject as one founded on positive evidence. And, still worse, students in schools and colleges are taught biology in such a manner that they are convinced that the special theories of evolution are established as indisputable facts, and that the philosophy of naturalism is the logical conclusion of those facts.

We conclude the extract thus:

There is little wonder that the world at large confuses Darwinism with evolution, and atheism with biology and scientific theory in general. Popular accounts of "missing links" are constantly appearing, and they are not contradicted authoritatively by biologists. And yet they know that to look for a "missing link" means that we have not only the two ends of a chain, but also most of the intermediate parts. The truth is, we have one end of a possible chain, ourselves, and we have certain fragments of fossil remains which have some of our characteristics. But biologists do not know what, if any, animal ancestor forms the other end of the chain, or what links connect us with the past. . . .

And since [the biologist] knows neither the cause nor the method of variations, he is unable to predict the characteristics of even the next generation.

Is not this a most remarkable plea of ignorance, and yet

how honest and forthright it is. Evolution is indeed a fact of being. Growth, learning, advancement, progress, is the general law of the universe. That is one thing which any sane man today admits. But the theories, the ideas, the dogmatic assumptions, the teachings, the hypotheses, the fads, of any particular popularizer of science, be he small or great, are another thing; and we, as thinking men and women, have perfect right, and are upheld by the greater biologists themselves, in accepting such ideas or in refusing to accept them.

It is the so-called popularizers of science, many of them nevertheless very earnest and sincere men, with whom theosophists have bones to pick; at any rate, these are the ones with whom we differ, and positively in some cases, because instead of confining themselves to the noble principles of natural research, they are too often given to dogmatic asseverations concerning facts which have not yet been fully understood or explained.

In *The Story of Philosophy*, Dr. Will Durant says:

> With this new orientation, evolution appears to us as something quite different from the blind and dreary mechanism of struggle and destruction which Darwin and Spencer described. We sense duration in evolution, the accumulation of vital powers, the inventiveness of life and mind, . . . We are prepared to understand why the most recent and expert investigators, like Jennings and Maupas, reject the mechanical theory of protozoan behavior, and why Professor E. B. Wilson, dean of contemporary cytologists, concludes his book on the cell with the statement that "the study of the cell has, on the whole, seemed to widen rather than to narrow the enormous gap that separates even the lowest forms of life from the inorganic world." And everywhere, in the world of biology, one hears of the rebellion against Darwin.   — pp. 497–8

Let me here repeat: theosophists do not admit the existence of any so-called inorganic or lifeless matter; everything is living because everything is a focus of force and therefore of life, for life is energy; life is force. What else can it be? Energies and forces are simply manifestations or phenomena of life. Life is the living fountain, and energies and forces are the streams pouring forth from that fountain.

At a joint meeting of biology and chemistry teachers, physics and botany clubs of New York City, Dr. John M. Coulter spoke on the nature and foundation of evolution.* His opening remarks follow:

> The meaning of evolution is probably more misunderstood than any doctrine of science. The reason is that it has been discussed very freely by those who are not informed, and in this way much misinformation has been propagated.
>
> The general meaning of organic evolution is that the plant and animal kingdoms have developed in a continuous, orderly way, under the guidance of natural laws, just as the solar system has evolved in obedience to natural laws.

We agree; only these "natural laws" are merely the manifesting activities of indwelling intelligences, "the gods," if we may use an unfashionable word. These laws are the expression of the activities of their vegetative or vehicular side, as it were, while the kinetic or active side which they possess, is that which manifests on their own higher planes, and is the expression of their high spiritual and sublimely intellectual activities. These latter activities are the root of the harmony, consistency, correlating nature which the universe manifests; while, on the other hand, it is the corporeal or vegetative side of their nature, so to say, which manifests

---

*"The History of Organic Evolution" presented on March 27, 1926, at the request of the science committee of the Board of Education, New York City. For full text see *Science*, vol. LXIII, May 14, 1926; also *Annual Report Smithsonian Institution*, 1926.

the energies and forces which play through the physical universe that we know.

Dr. Coulter then points out that Darwinism is quite a different thing from evolution per se; and further, that Darwinism is only one of the attempted explanations of the evolutionary biologic phenomena of life. Evolution, he says, is an undoubted fact; but it is quite a different thing, he adds, whether any proposed transformist or evolutionary theory is adequate as an explanation of the natural phenomena of growth and progress. Not a single hypothesis so far advanced, he declares, fits or covers all the facts known.

All this is exactly what we point out. But what I wish to lay emphasis on here is the unfortunate moral effect which these transformist teachings have had upon the world. When men believe that they have a common spiritual ancestry, and spring from a common vital-spiritual root, and are journeying on together through vastly long periods of evolutionary development; when they realize that the blood which beats in the veins of each man is similar to, or perhaps almost identical with, the blood which beats in the veins of all men, no matter how great be the differences between the various races; then men have a spiritual conception of life, which functions as a strong anchor by which they can hold the ship of life in times of stress or danger. Inwardly knowing this, they are not swept away from their moral moorings by false biologic teachings, born of physiologic and psychological fallacies and psychoses of various kinds, and eventuating in the conscious or unconscious belief, which is even taught to our little children, that life is a desperate struggle for superiority, in which each man must succeed through selfishness or "go to the wall," and that, among the religious-minded, the devil gets the hindmost — if indeed there be a devil!

Now what has this biologic bogey of the last century eventuated in? In the idea that man, being nothing but a transformed beast, without a directing soul or an overshadowing spirit, is a creature of haphazard chance, without hope of a spiritual future, and ungoverned by any innately moral sanctions found in the operations of nature itself; and that the only restraining forces are those of social conventions or an intangible kind of moral code arising out of opportunism, and the fear of being caught if his innate aberrant selfishness wanders too far from the straight road. Or again, in the idea that if indeed man has a soul, that soul is only some kind of effluvium arising out of chemico-physiologic action in and on the brain — or some similar nonsense.

These nightmares of the imagination — for they are truly that — are largely responsible for the terrible struggle for material supremacy and power which the world is passing through.

Even Professor Frederick Soddy, ardent champion though he is of science as the great benefactor of the world of men, was driven by the logic of facts to voice in no uncertain terms the same conclusions. Knowledge was misused from lack of a restraining moral and spiritual influence.

Does it do any good to our children to go into museums and see brutish creatures painted on the walls, or in picture books, or to gaze at plaster-of-paris casts or statues of absolutely imaginary apelike ancestors of man?

Professor Wood Jones some years ago wrote on the subject of the "missing link" which anthropologists are so fond of constructing:

Any so-called missing link would be very unlike the popular picture of a brutish, slouching creature made more horrible than any gorilla by a dawning touch of humanity. This missing-link picture must be deleted from our minds, and I find no occupation less worthy of the science of anthropology than the not unfashionable business of modeling, painting, or drawing these nightmare products of imagination, and lending them, in the process, an utterly false value of apparent reality.

I have never used words as strong as these from one of the most eminent anatomists of today. This quotation was taken from *The Problem of Man's Ancestry* (pp. 39–40), which he concludes as follows:

Man is no new begot child of the ape, born of a chance variation, bred of a bloody struggle for existence upon pure brutish lines. Such an idea must be dismissed by humanity, and such an idea must cease to exert any influence upon conduct. We did not reach our present level by these means; certainly we shall never attain a higher one by intensifying them. Were man to regard himself as being an extremely ancient type, distinguished now, and differentiated in the past, purely by the qualities of his mind, and were he to regard existing Primates as misguided and degenerated failures of his ancient stock, I think it would be something gained for the ethical outlook of humanity — and it would be a belief consistent with present knowledge.

Verily so. It is a lack of recognition of our essential oneness in our spiritual origin that allows the growth in the human heart of the evil fountain of selfishness, of self-seeking. This is the root of all evil and of all evil-doing, so far as humans are concerned, as it is the cause as well of all individual misery and unhappiness; because from this evil fountain of selfishness, the child of our lower nature, there pour forth, if they can, when released from the benign and restraining influences of the higher nature, all the things which make life dark and sad and unhappy.

It is of ethics I speak, and they are beautiful indeed. Ethics and morals are founded on the laws of the universe, because they are naught else than rules of harmony in human conduct, copying the harmony prevailing in the cosmic spaces. All that we need to do is to understand those laws, to realize them in our hearts, to take them into our consciousness; for then we shall be able consciously to follow the fundamental operations of the universal life, because thus we are in intellectual touch with those harmonies.

We cannot be in touch with these basic universal laws until we banish from our minds utterly the idea that man is merely his physical body, a body unensouled, and evolved in the mechanical and uninspired method taught by the transformists. We have to recognize man as a spiritual entity, a monadic center, whose origin is the heart of universal life. It is this inner spark of light, in man as in all beings, that furnishes and has furnished the evolutionary urge towards producing ever fitter vehicles of self-expression.

11

SPECIALIZATION AND MENDELISM

No ONE HAS EVER succeeded in bridging the gaps separating the great groups or phyla of animal stocks, and therefore no one has been able to find that alleged continuous stairway up which man is supposed to have climbed to his present evolutionary status. Doubtless there have been in the past intermediate beings, or rather intermediate stages of life between these great groups; but the geologic record, so imperfect, has not yet revealed them. Should they ever be discovered, they would no doubt be acclaimed by transformists as the long sought for and always missing links. It is probable that these particular scientists would ignore the more likely possibility that they are simply specimens of specialization of one or more of the great stocks below man; for we already know that all these great stocks have exhibited examples of aberrant evolution or rather of evolutionary specializations.

Thus these findings would in no sense be de facto missing links, but offshoots from one or more of these great stocks, which offshoots have followed certain minor lines of progressive variation. In fact, each one of the great phyla or groups or stocks, as we now see each one of such today, is but the point of evolutionary variation which they have reached at the present time, and by no means precluding still greater specializations in variability in the future. To put the matter in a nutshell, each of these great groups or phyla is simply a large evolutionary development, a specialization, from the elementary zoologic roots.

Evolution and specialization are, in one sense, almost synonymous. If evolution means the unwrapping of that which is dormant or latent or sleeping, so does specialization mean the same thing. One great group, as is well known in zoology, or in botany for that matter, may take on the specialized forms or variations which are typical or type forms of another great group, frequently lower. A mammal, for instance, may take on variations of a bird type or of a fish type, and yet remain a mammal in both cases.

Consider the wide divergent evolution of the whale. The whale is a mammal, and at one time must have been a land animal which for some unknown reason went down to the sea; and yet it looks like a fish and passes its life in the water of the ocean. If you have ever seen a picture of a whale or of a dolphin, which is also a sea mammal, side by side with the picture of a shark, and if you were to place above these a picture of the extinct species *ichthyosaurus*, they at first glance appear so much alike in general characteristics of shape and form, that you would say, if unacquainted with the anatomical features of these creatures, that all three are different kinds of fish. Yet the shark is a fish, and the *ichthyosaurus* of the Mesozoic or Secondary era of geology was a reptile, while the whale or the dolphin is a mammal. Fish, reptile, and mammal: three widely different stocks which have approached each other in general shape and habit through the influence of environment. That influence has been so strong, though reacting against the inner urge or inner vital drive of the evolving entity in each of these three forms, that it has been prepotent in producing the fishlike body and habit. Though radically different anatomically and derivatively, they yet have the superficial likenesses of the marine fish stock. But strip away the flesh and examine the skeleton of each of these three animals, and the three different stocks to which they respectively belong become immediately discernible.

We might also instance the bat. The bat is likewise a mammal, and yet it has all the appearance and many of the habits of a bird; in fact, it is more of a true flier than any bird is, because virtually its sole mode of easy locomotion is flight. Its flight is so swift and silent and so direct that it very probably may be called the most wonderful flier we know.

All birds have legs and in some cases strong and powerful ones, and can stand and walk with ease and in some cases can run; but the bat, as you must have noticed yourself if you have ever watched one, is almost helpless unless it is in flight. Its movements on the ground or on the floor are extremely awkward. What induced the bat to leave the ground and take to the air? What was the cause of this wide divergence of form and habit from the ancestral mammalian stem? Who can say?

Please remember in this connection that "evolved" or "specialized" does not necessarily mean higher or superior, if we use the technical term of scientific books. It merely means the bringing out of that which is seeking expression, a larger degree of "specialization." Such multitudes of forms, diverging ever more from the primitive or root stock, are always instances of type-specializations. Specialization is in all cases a mark of a greater distance from the origin of any such stock.

Let me illustrate what I mean by the elephant, a quadruped. Look at the development that the nose of the elephant has taken, called its trunk. Look at its immense fanlike ears. These are specific characters belonging to it, and they are found early even in the embryological record of that beast, therefore showing that these specific characters go far back in time in the history of that strain.

Let us instance also the foot of the horse. Do you know what a horse's hoof is? It is the highly evolved and specifically developed toenail of the third digit of each of its four feet. That animal walks literally on the highly developed toenail of the elongated third toe of each foot.

Now there is no such specific characteristic as regards man's hands and feet in the evolutionary history of man, as is shown in the development of the human embryo. In fact, the horse's hoof is a far and wide evolution, a highly evoluted development from the primitive progenitor of the equine stock. It is a specific character belonging to the equine race.

Here is a case in point of what we mean when we speak of the far-flung specific evolutionary development of any one of the various stocks, and of the impossibility of the human strain's passing through it on its upward journey.

It is true also that other animals walk or move more or less in this manner. The ape, for example, when it goes on all fours as it usually does, does not walk along plantigrade, or flatfoot fashion; it walks on its fingers, on the nails or on the knuckles of its hands. Somewhat similarly did the ancestors of the horse. All these are instances of specialization.

Specialization is always a side issue. It is the following of a path which does not lead in the main evolutionary direction. It indicates at least a temporary arresting of *inner* evolutionary development, a running off into unessential bypaths — unessential, that is, from the standpoint of spiritual evolution. Thus, in a sense, all developments of the beast stocks away from the primitive human strain may be said to be specializations, as they diverged more and more widely from the main trunk, each following its own genealogical branching. Their opportunity, indeed their capacity, to forge ahead along psychological lines was limited, though there were infinite possibilities in the way of physiological variations for them to pursue.

Meanwhile the human race, most primitive of all, retained its comparative simplicity of bodily structure and function, because it was not solely concerned with mere experimentation and adaptation along physical lines. Once it had built for itself a suitable vehicle, it abandoned that line of evolution *as a distinct line of evolution for its own sake,* in order to bring into outer expression the far more important *inner* psychological, intellectual, and indeed spiritual factors locked within it.

This same principle works out in the sphere of human life itself. Wherever you see a too great specialization in any branch of science, for instance, you may know that there forward progress is likely to be in abeyance; because running off exclusively into bypaths of specialized study cuts one off from the main course of human thinking, that broad stream which has been fed through the ages by all profound thinkers adding their contribution to the forward evolution of human thought.

Remember that evolution proceeds in all cases by means

of two agencies: the inner drive or urge in the evolving entity, acting upon surrounding circumstances or environment, which react against the creature expressing such inner drive or urge. The resultant of these two forces or conditions is the animal, or the human being, or any other entity, at any moment of its developmental course. Thus we mean by evolution the unfolding or rolling out of potentialities or potencies or latent capacities inwrapt in the creature itself. And when the environment permits an outflowing or unwrapping of these latent powers, they immediately flow forth into manifestation, or assert themselves, the resultant in the case of the beast kingdom being a change in some one or more respects in the physical vehicle or body; and in the case of the human kingdom in its present stage, a fuller expression of the inner psychological entity.

Now I have stated that there was no uniserial or end-on evolution of the human stock through and across the great classes of animate entities beneath the human; and that it is the various gaps or lacunae between the stocks that have formed the main stumbling blocks for the transformists in their attempt to prove their hypotheses. Every attempt to bridge these gaps by an appeal to nature's record has broken down of necessity. But fixed ideas die hard; there has been much work, much of it good and brilliant work, in an endeavor to evolve some new hypothesis, to offer some further explanation, by which the accepted transformist theories of evolution could be proved.

Consequently there has arisen a more modern evolutionary school, which we may call the "Saltatory" school, based on the idea that evolution frequently pursues a "leaping" or jumping course, if we may so express the idea. But no satisfactory explanation has been given of the fact that such sudden and large variations do occur, nor why these leaps or saltatory variations take place. Prominent among the proponents of this particular so-called mutationist school are the Netherlander Hugo de Vries, and William Bateson, a British scientist.

These gentlemen have found that certain plants and animals do show in their biological history wide steps from one stage or variation to another stage or variation, and that these stages in variation are so large and the resultant entity is so specifically different from the step preceding it, that they have called such wide steps mutations. Mutation of course means change, in the sense of variation from the preceding condition. Such mutations do in fact exist.

These are caused by the fact that the evolving entity had accumulated — if we may use such an imperfect expression — a habit or set of habits which remain latent for periods more or less indefinite. Such habits or groups of habits we may call recessive or sleeping or latent; but there they are, and when the environmental circumstances are appropriate for their manifestation, as in all other cases of suddenly appearing variations, out they come, and to all appearances a new species has started its evolutionary course.

Obviously then, the law of evolution by slow and graduating stages, one into the other, has not been in any sense violated, for these habits or groups of habits or variations were accumulated and built into the biologic architecture and history of the cell or cellular organism which produced them. Environment provides the path for their manifestation when the barriers hindering their appearance vanish, or are broken down, or for some other reason no longer oppose the outflowing of the inner forces or force hitherto asleep or latent or recessive.

The explanation of this fact of wide and sudden variations lies in the nature of the cellular structure in the body of each such evolving entity. I do not see how evolution can ever be understood if we limit our study of it solely to the variable and changing body; because it should be obvious to any reflective mind that the body can express only that which an inner and spiritual power has ordained in its endeavors at self-expression through the body, when an appropriate environment allows it to show itself.

We have already pointed out that the inner evolution of man, that is to say, the evolution of the inner powers of his being, is by far more important and interesting, because causal, than is the evolution or change in specialization of his physical frame. But we are limiting our present thesis more or less to the evolution of the vehicle or body through which man, or through which the entities below him, respectively evolve and work or express each its own inner drive.

An interesting scientific discovery of recent years has taken the form of what is now called Mendelism. Gregor Mendel was an Austrian peasant boy with a love of nature, which he studied. He was later a monk, and at his death was abbot of Brünn. Outside of his ecclesiastical occupations he evidently had much time, as a lover of nature, to study the things which interested him. And so in the garden of his monastery, this monkish investigator of some of the mysteries of nature experimented with the common garden pea. He made many experiments, extending over a number of years. He collated the results of his studies, and he found several very interesting things; for instance, that heredity expresses itself along mathematical lines, in quantitative relations, which is likewise how the theosophist regards this question of heredity.

Collecting the results of his studies, he printed them in 1865; and they were promptly forgotten, if indeed they ever received any attention at the time. The world then was ringing with quarrels over Darwinism and the natural selection and survival of the fittest theories. And the studies and explanations of this obscure Austrian investigator were completely lost sight of.

But in the year 1900, eighteen years after the death of Mendel, the results of the studies which he had incorporated in formal shape and had printed in 1865 were rediscovered more or less independently by three great botanists, Hugo de Vries, E. Correns, and G. Tschermak. These botanists found that Mendel's work, as set forth in his printed thesis, aided them greatly in explaining their own mutationist hypothesis, that is, the hypothesis of saltatory evolution or evolution by leaps or jumps.

What then is Mendelism? Mendelism is the theory that there exist in the reproductive or germ plasm of plants and of animals certain powers seeking expression, and that they manifest in mathematical or quantitative relationships.

For instance, we shall take the illustration that Mendel himself chose. In his experiments with peas he crossed a dwarf pea with a tall pea, and in the succeeding generation he found that they were all talls. He therefore said that the tall is "dominant," and that the dwarf strain is "recessive" — *sleeping* or *dormant,* or *latent,* the theosophist would say. He allowed this second generation, all talls, to fertilize itself in the natural course, and their offspring were found to segregate themselves or to sift themselves out as follows: one quarter were dwarfs, three quarters were talls.

He found that the quarter of dwarfs invariably produced dwarfs if they were not crossed, thus showing that it was a pure strain or stock. But of the three quarters consisting of talls, one quarter invariably produced talls, thus showing that that quarter of talls was likewise a pure stock; while the other half of the talls brought forth offspring precisely as their parents had done, that is to say, they produced in the next generation one quarter true-strain dwarfs, one quarter true-strain talls, and two fourths of mixed dwarf and tall strain.

How do these quantitative relations come about? What is it that produces these mathematical relationships in the reproductive or germ plasm? Environment of course has something to do with it, because environment provides the stimulus, as it were, enabling the inner urge or potency to express itself; in other words, environment is the field within which and upon which these natural forces, inherent in the stock, work. But we must look into the inner nature of the individual itself under investigation if we wish to trace these secrets of nature to their origin and to explain them. The solution of this problem lies in the cell, that is to say, in the inherent, or indwelling, or innate, or inclosed powers of the cell itself.

All matter — both the living and the so-called inanimate — is ultimately built up from atoms, each one of which possesses vast and incomputable capacities for change, which is evolution towards growth or retrogression, as the case may be; but always evolution, that is, the bringing out of that which is lying in it seeking expression.

In many instances this evolving, this bringing out, of the inner tendency, potency, or capacity, is inhibited by various circumstances; and in such event, the atom or the cell — for the cell copies the general scheme of the atoms of which it is composed — falls under what in theosophy is called the law of retardation, and must bide its time until its own cycle for growth comes. But if its cycle be one under the action of the law of acceleration, it begins to grow in progressive development, always bringing out that which is within itself, lying latent within it, as potency or tendency.*

Evolution therefore actually is self-expression. It does not proceed in a haphazard manner, but according to the inner urge or drive of the more or less conscious invisible entity or soul, which is the factor seeking to manifest itself through its vehicle or vehicles. Its doing this is what we call evolution. It is in the very small that we should seek for the unriddling of this riddle of evolution, for the solving of the problem of what it is that causes growth, and particularly expansive or forward or progressive growth.

Man being a child of the universe, being a part of that universe itself, he has in him everything — every force, every potency, every capacity — that the macrocosm or great universe has. He, as an entity, in his turn is a macrocosm to the cells which compose his body, for they are a part of him and therefore have everything in them which he has in him, albeit latent or dormant, and not yet kinetic.

---

*An interesting and indeed fascinating observation may be ventured here to the effect that these mathematical relationships so prominent in biological story and so effective in the working of the evolutionary scheme, are more or less automatic as concerns the kingdoms of nature below man. But beginning with man and appertaining to the kingdoms above him, as, for example, to the three kingdoms of the dhyāni-chohans, these mathematical relationships, while just as strict in their action upon evolving entities, nevertheless are then expanding into fields of evolving consciousness, or rather consciousnesses, and this brings about in the long courses of evolutionary history constant increments of individuality as appertaining to units or individuals. Individuality thus always tends to modify the details of a general law; but this does not mean that the general law is not operative.

The powers are there, and when the environment be fit and appropriate, when the barriers have been worn down through evolution, or rather cleared away by the working of the inner drive, then these potencies, these capacities, manifest this inner urge for self-expression; and behold! something new is produced — a new variety, a new species; it may be destined indeed to develop a new stock.

It all depends upon two factors in the biologic equation: an inner urge expressing the inherent potency or capacity with a free path and uninhibited by barriers; and, second, an environment fit and appropriate as a field for their expression.

This is what I have meant when I have said that man is the repertory of all the animate entities on earth. Moreover, he has everything in him that he himself can ever in future be; and these potencies await the time and the place for their coming forth into manifestation. The process is "evolution" or self-expression. I meant further when saying that man gave birth to all the animate creatures below him, that in the beginning the roots or seeds of all the animate creatures below him existed in him as latent or dormant or sleeping things.

Please remember that we now are speaking of man's *physical* body. We do not mean that these animate creatures below him formerly existed in his soul or in his spiritual nature; but that they were sleeping elemental entities in his nature and derived from him as their parent. They took the manifold and many forms and shapes they had and have, because these most fitly manifest the particular kind of energy expressing itself in each and every case.

12

MAN THE REPERTORY OF ALL TYPES

"MAN IS HIS OWN HISTORY." This is a profound epigram which covers the entire outline of the evolutionary progress of the human soul. All things reside in man. He is the epitome of all that is — the microcosm or replica, the duplicate, the copy, of the macrocosm. Therefore he has everything in him that the macrocosm has, although not necessarily fully developed. On the contrary, many of the higher forces, qualities, potentialities, as yet but very feebly show through the veils which enshroud his higher nature; nevertheless he possesses all the elements that his Great Mother — the universe — has, either latent or sleeping, or expressing themselves through his self-conscious side.

Man also holds within himself the history of all inferior types. Man is, and has been, and will be, the foremost of the hierarchy of evolving entities on our earth, the foremost in evolutionary development; and as the leading stock, he therefore is the repertory, the storehouse, the magazine, of all future types, even as he has been of all past types. He throws off these types as he evolves through the ages; each of them becomes in its turn a new stock, and follows thereafter its own individual line of evolutionary development.

It was in this manner that were originated all the stocks below man. Every inferior or subordinate stock was originated as the vital off-throwings of man, these off-throwings being composed of cells of man's body. And each one of these cellular organisms, succeeding its derivation or independent origin from the human stock, immediately began to produce its own stock from the forces inherent and latent in the cells which composed it.

It was these buds, these cellular off-throwings of man from his body, which originated all the stocks below the mammalia in the *preceding* globe-round or great tidal wave of life, hundreds of millions of years ago. Those particular classes were the birds, the reptiles, the amphibians, the fishes, and the vast range of biologic life included under the general term of the invertebrates.

The mammalia, however, were the off-throwings from man in the *present* great globe-round or great tidal wave of life, and had their origin from prehuman man in the very early part of the Mesozoic, and very probably in the last part of the preceding or Paleozoic era, when man himself had become a physical from a semi-astral being.*

I do not mean by what I have said above that these types were or are the bodies in which man once lived, or will live. Not at all. The whole matter of the vital off-throwings is a fascinating and mysterious one, mysterious simply because not yet fully understood. The following observations may perhaps give the key to the idea.

The human body is an exceedingly absorbing subject of

---

*The reader is asked to bear in mind that we are consistently using the geologic time-scale which H. P. Blavatsky adapted from Lyell and Lefèvre. [See Appendix I.]

study in any consideration of the manner in which evolution works. Evolution, indeed, deals with it but in a secondary or effectual manner, not in a primary or causal manner. I mean by this, that the human body merely reflects the various changes in progressive development which actually proceed on interior or causal planes. I have already pointed out that evolution, as we use the word, means the unfolding, the unwrapping, of that which previously had been infolded and inwrapped as potencies in the structure of the cells of which the body is composed; for in the infinitesimal lie the seeds of the world we see about us.

The human body on an average is estimated to contain some fifty trillion cells! — an unfigurable number. The cell, we are told, is formed of protoplasm consisting mainly of four chemical elements, carbon, nitrogen, oxygen, and hydrogen, occasionally with some trace of other chemical elements. We are also told that protoplasmic substance contains two general parts; a central part called the nucleus, and a surrounding cytoplasm, which latter is the larger part of the substance of the cell itself.

Yet all this description does not tell us what the cell really is. Each cell is, in fact, a living entity, a physiological organ, with inherent capacities, inherent tendencies, each possessing its own inherent urge or drive towards self-expression. According to theosophy, this inherent urge or drive originates in the invisible entity from which it proceeds; because, unless there were some cohering power, some force of coherence working in the structure of the individual, no such thing as even a simple cell could exist; it could not even come into physical being or manifestation. It is held together and controlled by the invisible entity behind it, which expresses itself through the finer or more ethereal part of these tiny cells, because that finer or more ethereal part is the nearest in ethereality to its own nature.

A cell is, in fact, an infinitesimal focus of cosmic forces, a channel through which they pour forth into manifestation on our physical plane, each possessing an incomputable capacity for change and growth, being in very fact a dynamo of forces. The incarnating entity is a bundle of such forces and, as said, it expresses itself through the finer or more ethereal part of the tiny cells, because that finer part is the nearest in ethereality to the nature of the force or forces that are seeking expression.

These forces working in the ethereal realms of matter are extremely subtle; their rates of vibration are highly individual. Yet with all their subtlety they have tremendous power. Could such a force be focused directly, let us say, upon the outer physical cell, such a cell would vanish, because it would be disintegrated; the atoms of which the cell is composed could not stand the strain of the forces pouring through them, and the structure of the cell would be wrecked, the component parts of the atoms wrenched apart. But it is very rare indeed that a force is so focused in animate entities, although it does happen constantly and continuously in the cosmic labor. The operation of these ethereal substances which we know as forces is, as a rule, more generally diffused.

Now every cell in man's body is man's own child. Every one of the fifty trillions of cells sprang from him, from his inner self. The dominating entity, the inner man, gave birth to them all. As common parent of them all and working through them, he is their "oversoul." He in a very true sense is their god, even as the divine beings who gave us spiritual birth we call our gods; and just as these divine beings in their turn sprang as spiritual atomic corpuscles from entities still more sublime, and so forth, still higher — an endless hierarchy of ascending and descending intelligences and lives.

It can be seen from the above that in a cell, or in the atoms of which a cell is composed, there are uncounted and actually almost innumerable possibilities of development, locked up or latent potentialities, all seeking expression. Many have to bide their time for ages before that opportunity comes, if their opportunities ever do come; and if and when these potentialities find in their environment an open door for expression, out they go, a rushing tide of life.

Therefore, the cells that man once threw off, even as he is now throwing them off, resulted in the lower creatures, who are not at all degenerate men, as might be supposed, but actually lower types, beginning their evolutionary course towards higher things, springing from man, the repertory or magazine of all types beneath him.

Let us remember that the physical encasements of early men were far more loosely coherent than they are now, and of a much more subtle and ethereal matter than that of man's present physical body. This was because the psychical and physical dominance of the human kind over the cells composing those primitive human bodies was far less strong and less developed than now it is. In consequence of this relatively weak control over the physical cells, each one of such cells was more free than now it is to pursue its own particular individual drive or urge.

Hence, when any one of the cells forming part of such early human bodies freed itself from the psychical and physical control that then existed, it was enabled to follow, and instinctively did follow, the path of self-expression. But in our days when the psychical and physical dominance of the human incarnated entity over the human cells composing the human body is so strong, and because the cells have largely lost their power of individual self-expression through the biologic habit of subjecting to that overlordship of the human entity, such an individualized career of a cell in self-development is a virtual impossibility. However, in those early days of the primordial humanity, the case was very different. A cell or an aggregate of cells could separate itself from the then human frame — if "human" is the proper word to use in such connection — and begin an evolutionary career of its own. This in large degree explains the origin of the various stocks now inferior to the human.

Man has been the storehouse (and still is) from which these other stocks originated and towards which, moreover, they are ultimately straining — towards which they are ultimately evolving. These cells which compose his body, had they not been held in the grip of the forces flowing from the inner dominating entity, man himself, for so long a time that their own individual lives, as it were, have been overpowered and bent in his direction and can now follow almost no other path than his; had they not been so dominated they would, by the amputation of a limb for instance, immediately begin to proliferate along their own tendency-line, to build up bodies of their own kind, each one following out that particular line of life force, or progressive development, which each such cell would contain in its cellular structure as a dominant, thus establishing a new ancestral or genealogical tree.

What is the reason that today a free human cell or an amputated human limb or a bit of the human body cut off from the trunk does not grow into another human being or, perhaps, into some inferior entity, as was often the case in the zoological past? This is the reason: in all the vertebrate animals, that is to say, the higher animate beings in the evolutionary scale, the psychic and material grip of the dominant entity over the cells of its body is so strong that these cells obey the more powerful drive communicated to them from the dominant entity working through them, and hence can follow only that dominating drive which they do through the force of the acquired biological habit. They have largely lost the power of self-expression and self-progress along what would be under different circumstances their own individual pathways. But that liberty of action and that free field for self-expression were theirs in greater or less degree in past times.

In some of the lower invertebrate creatures there exists today a faculty of self-repair by which a creature, low in the scale of animate beings, if it lose a limb or a tail, will reproduce for itself a new limb or tail. A certain kind of worm well known to zoologists will, if divided into two, become two complete worms. Here is a case where the faculty of dominance, or the dominant as Mendel called it, is still weak in its control over the entire cellular structure of the body through which it works, and each cell composing that body, if left to itself — even more so if you could take such a cell out of the body and give it appropriate food and environment — would have an exceedingly good chance of starting upon a line of evolution of its own, following its own inherent tendency or potency or urge, and thus bringing forth some new stock. But as this case rarely now or perhaps never arises, the cells are impelled to follow the reproductive tendency of the limb only to which they belong.

This method of the regeneration of lost parts, or of reproduction, prevailed in a past time in the human frame, as much as and as fully as in the cases of the lower creatures to which I here allude. And it was this general method of reproduction which gave rise to the various animate stocks, the highly specialized descendants of which we find on earth today (except those stocks which have become extinct) and which are the various groups of the beasts.

But this cannot happen in our period of evolution, as can be shown more fully by a study of Weismann's remarkable theory. The cellular structure, the inherent tendencies or potencies of the cells belonging to the bodies of the higher creatures, have the possibility of following only that particular line of unfoldment or of growth which the dominant entity, of which these cells form the body, allows them to have.

It is a case where the individual swabhāva, i.e., the individual capacities or latent tendencies of the cell, are submerged by the overlording or dominance, so to say, of the invisible entity which works through those cells. The inherent potencies of those cells have become recessive, to use Mendel's term; the consequence being that the cell's own individual potencies can express themselves, if at all, only when the power of the dominating entity is withdrawn, perhaps not even then if the submergence of the cell or native cellular potencies has been too great. In this last case they die.

Man still remains the storehouse of an incomputable number of vital or zoologic tendencies latent in the cells of his body; and though the old method of their manifestation has ceased, new and different methods will supersede the old. The urge of life working through the tiny lives of man's physical body will nonetheless inevitably find new methods of expression, and these latent or sleeping tendencies will in far distant future ages find appropriate outlets, thus, perhaps, giving origin to new stocks in that far-distant future.

It should not be forgotten, however, that such originations of new stocks will grow fewer and fewer as time goes on towards the end of our globe-round, due to the growing dominance and ever-larger and wider exercise of the innate powers of the evolving human being, swamping and submerging all tendencies of a minor kind and of inferior biologic energy.

This fact that a cell or aggregate of cells is subjected to the dominance of an oversoul, the incarnating and incarnated entity, is simply the manifestation of what the theosophical teachings call the action of the law of acceleration and retardation, one of the subordinate lines, so to speak, of the general operation of karma or the law of consequences. This law of acceleration and retardation simply means this: when a thing occupies a place of authority in the evolutionary scale, or a position of dominant power over other and inferior or subordinate entities, through the operation of its own inherent forces, or indeed through the inertia of its physical being, no other entity under its sway can find a free field for self-expression while so placed. And every entity so constituted — or, what comes to the same thing, every other entity of which that dominating entity is composed — must obey the dominating urge, the dominating impulses of that overlord. The dominant entity pursues an accelerated course; while the inferior entities under its sway or composing its various parts are retarded in their individual courses of development, which they otherwise freely would follow.

I will give you a poor but perhaps graphic illustration of my meaning. When a railway train rushes along the rails, what does it carry with it? All the living entities in the various coaches, each one on its own errand and business ventures bent, it is true, yet all, for the time being, helpless in the grip of the power to which they have subjected themselves. In somewhat similar manner the cells of the human body are subjected to the law of retardation in evolutionary development, so far as they are individually concerned, until the time comes when they shall have reached, through obedience to the dominating power, which in our present instance is man, self-consciousness of their own, and thereafter, in their turn, grow into nobler learners and more individualized evolvers, as we humans ourselves now are.

Evolution is not merely an automatic response to external stimuli, but it is first of all action from within, unceasing attempts in self-expression; and each response to the external stimuli, which the natural environment provides, gives opportunity for a larger and fuller measure of self-expression.

But I feel that I must add, that while the word *evolution* is usually used, and correctly used, of progressive advancement from the less to the more perfect, yet the term likewise includes all orders of manifestation which bring out merely that which is inwrapt; consequently, there is in one sense an order of inverse evolution which the word itself fully covers. This may seem a little irrelevant, perhaps, at the present moment, but it actually is important as being an explanation as to why certain animate stocks persist in life, from generation to generation, without showing any obvious or indeed actual advancement of type. This is another aspect of the law of acceleration and retardation. An entity in accelerated evolution proceeds steadily, serially, step by step, from the less to the more perfect; but a stock under the action of the law of retardation may remain for ages more or less stationary — an interesting and indeed important side issue of our subject.

The law of retardation operates on a stock, or on any individual animate entity, when a more evolved stock appears on the scene. It is somewhat like the submerging of minor men in the individuality of a greater man — an interesting psychological phenomenon which all of us must have noticed in the affairs of ordinary life. The law of acceleration, on the other hand, operates in the cases where an evolving stock finds the field free and without barriers or hindrances to the full expansion of its innate potencies, faculties, powers.

The animate entities below man have descended to our own time, or in some cases their dwarfed representatives* have so descended, though evolving far less fast than the human stock has done because they are under the operation of this law of retardation.

The progenitors of the lowest animate beings sprang from man in the preceding globe-round, as I have already explained. The mammalians, however, came from the human stock in this present globe-round, during the latter part of the second great root-race and the early part of the third root-race. Man is of course himself a mammal, and therefore these other stocks necessarily partook of the nature of their originating strain.

All these various stocks of animate mammalian entities on earth, all following their own especial lines of development, along their own genealogical trees, were the offsprings of the primitive human stock in that immensely distant past — a time when what we call the "mindless races" lived, before godlike entities descended from the spiritual spheres in order to enlighten the waiting human material organisms with their divine rays.

---

*There are, of course, certain groups of animals which now live no more but which once did live on this earth: for instance, the gigantic reptiles of the Mesozoic or Secondary era. We may say, however, that they are represented today by their dwarfed and pygmy descendants still among us, such as the lizards, probably the serpents, frogs, etc.

They were originally buds or offspring from that mind-less and imperfect human stock; but, as the human spiritual entity was not yet then dominant in the human bodies of that time, and could not fully hold in abeyance the vital potencies of the cells which composed those buds which sprang from the bodies of early man, therefore each one of such bud-bodies or aggregates of buds immediately began to grow, following its own evolutionary tendencies or inher-ent urges, each producing only that which it could produce, that which was inherent in itself; evolving, unrolling, un-wrapping, its own inherent character or nature. This was the origin of the mammalia.

The apes and the monkeys sprang from man likewise, but in another manner. The monkeys were born from the mindless human race which, having no self-conscious mind, having but instinct and a vague and diffused physical con-sciousness, in many cases allied themselves with animal beings who also originally had sprung from the human stock, though not manifesting the dominant evolutionary tendencies for growth into humanity. The results of this shameful union were the lower simian stocks, the monkeys, and this occurred during the Mesozoic or Secondary era, probably during the Jurassic period.

Please understand that this occurred by and under the action of races of early man which did not realize what they were doing. They were as irresponsible as little children and had no moral realization of what we now regard, and justly regard, as shameful to the last degree.

At a later date, towards the end of the great fourth stock-race, during the Miocene epoch, when that race had already far passed its climax of evolution and was repre-sented by many degenerate remnants, some of these degenerate Atlantean or fourth-race men repeated "the sin of the mindless" with the lower simian stock then existing; and this second and still more shameful union originated the anthropoid apes. Hence it is small wonder that they resemble man, their half-parent, in so many particulars, even though that human half-parent was at the time degenerate.

Yet even during the late Miocene epoch, and in fact reaching into the Pleistocene, the great fourth root-race was represented still by brilliant local civilizations in various parts of the earth. But these were sporadic afterglows, so to say; for the culmination of fourth race evolution had occurred long before — in the early Miocene.

As pointed out earlier, though there is a resemblance between man and the apes and monkeys, the two latter are more widely and divergently "evolved" along their own line than man is along his. By now, however, their progressive evolution has very largely ceased, because the door into the human kingdom, towards which all the great stocks below man have ever tended, was closed eight or nine million years ago, more or less, while man will continue to progress as long as this planet bears its groups of living entities.

When I say that the lower groups have almost ceased to follow the path of progressive evolution tending towards man as a goal, I do not mean a transformation of body of beast into man; nor do I mean that they are standing perfectly still in an evolutional sense, but only that their rising along the ladder of life has ceased for this globe-round.

Man's destiny, on the other hand, is to draw steadily and progressively, and as time passes ever more rapidly, away from the lower kingdoms. The destiny of these latter is to die out as time passes, to reappear at the proper time in the next great globe-round.

13

CYCLES OF MANIFESTATION

ONE OF THE MOST momentous questions that every thinking man asks himself is this: Whence do we come into this physical world? And another question of intellectual and heart moment to each one of us is this: Who are we, and what are we? Then comes a third question to the mind as it ponders over the other two: Whither do we go at death? We come here on the stage of life as it is on this planet earth. We make a few gestures and movements, suffer somewhat, rejoice somewhat, are ill or well as the case may be; and then we pass off that stage, which apparently knows us no longer, nothing but a memory of us remains, and perhaps not even that. Yet in a universe governed by law and order and progress, the sufferings that we have endured, the joys that we have had, the ideals fulfilled and unfulfilled, must have had their origin somewhere. Where is that beginning? They have a partial fruition perhaps here in earth life; and then we leave the stage of earth life. Is all then ended? How can that be?

All that we were, as well as our sufferings and our joys and our ideals, manifest or unmanifest, were all forces playing through us. They came from somewhere out of the dark, out of the invisible, and played through us a little while. What then has become of them? They played their part on the stage of life, and that very playing was a cause of other effects and effectual relations which in their turn are forces acting as causes of future effects; and these must have their appropriate stage or stages of action somewhere, somewhen.

It is these same questions, mutatis mutandis, that occur to the thinking mind when it reflects upon the nature, origin, and destiny of the worlds which bestrew the spaces of infinitude. Whence came they? What are they? What is their destiny? These questions are at the background of the minds of all thinkers, of all scientists, of all researchers, and of all lookers into the mysteries of the cosmos or universe surrounding us. They are questions which have answers. The mere fact that these things are, shows that there are answers to be had somewhere to the questions concerning them.

What is the method by which worlds, and we men and other beings, their children, evolve? What is the method by which we come from the invisible into the visible, out of the darkness, as it is to us, into the light as it seems to us? — albeit to the spirit within us material existence is death, and existence in its own realms of spirit is life. This life to it is death and darkness and the tomb; while what we call the darkness of the inner worlds is the supernal light of its own realm to the spirit in us.

The method by which these entities, worlds and men and all the rest, seek expression is a cyclical method, that is to say, a procedure in and through cyclical progress. As the great seers of the human race have put it on record for us — seers who were and who are the most fully evolved men that the globe has yet produced, and who have recorded

their experiences and have handed them down to us as the
guide of our life — that method works somewhat as follows:

Beginning as an unself-conscious god-spark, each entity,
each spirit-soul, each monad — for there is a monad at the
heart of every individual entity — seeks self-expression and
the building up of appropriate vehicles through progress,
until finally such method produces a vehicle which can express, more or less fully, the spiritual energies and forces of
the monad within.

When this point of progress has been reached, man then
from an unself-conscious god-spark has become a self-conscious god, a self-conscious spirit, because he self-consciously
manifests the sublime powers and faculties of the monad
within, and he likewise lives in appropriate realms of existence where he builds for himself vehicles capable of expressing somewhat of the sublime inner faculties.

So it is with all the hosts of lives, because the entire
universe is composite of these hosts, each one of which holds
its character and its individuality and its own particular
origin, this last in the spiritual world it is true, yet each
following its own particular pathway of progress.

All come from the central Fire. Yet from the moment of
their issuance therefrom each such spark follows its own
especial line. Why? Because it is a treasury of sleeping faculties particular to itself; in short, because it is ensouled by
its own characteristic force, its own individuality, its own
swabhāva, to use the Sanskrit term. This amounts to saying
that each such god-spark follows a path of self-development
eventuating in self-directed evolution, when a vehicle capable of expressing self-consciousness has finally been built to
enshrine the god-spark working through it.

So again is it with the worlds, the universes. They issue

forth into physical manifestation from the bosom of great
Mother Nature as nebulae which are composed of most
ethereal matter, matter so quasi-spiritual that we cannot see
it as it is, either with our physical eyes or indeed with our
physical instruments as aid to our vision. There are, at the
present time, uncounted hosts of such spiritual universes,
not yet visible to us, because our physical organs have not
developed the subtlety of vision enabling us to see things so
much more subtle and fine and spiritual than the gross physical matter that our eyes may take in and our brain-organ
understand.

In time each such world as it passes on its downward and
cyclical way into the matter worlds, seeking expression and
therefore knowledge on and of these lower planes and in
these lower spheres, undergoes concretion or materialization
of its substance, partly by the gathering into itself of inferior
and smaller lives which help to build it up, even as man
gathers into his body these inferior and smaller lives which
help to make that body; and partly by the outflowing from
its own core of subordinate lives. Each such world thus
takes a form and a quality and a substance which is a mass
of atoms expressing the inner forces of itself. It thus manifests a spiritual or energic side, and a material or vegetative
or body side.

This course of progression of a monadic ray (or of a
world) through the spheres, from higher to lower planes,
is naught else but a succession of states, spiritual, ethereal,
astral, physical, which follow each other continuously, each
being a continuation on a lower plane in the descent from
a preceding higher state. It is like a flow of water. Thus
downwards, from its spiritual origin in any one life cycle,
passing cyclically through various planes, it continues that

flow of successions of states as it progresses forwards, until it reaches the lowest point of matter attainable in that life cycle; then it begins its ascent on its return to more ethereal realms, and finally to those realms which are its original source — spirituality.

At the end of its period of existence on any one plane — our own physical plane for example, which is its most material sphere, and therefore its turning point before it reascends — our universe, any universe, passes into the invisible realms when its life cycle is run in these realms of matter; even as man passes into the invisible realms when his life cycle is run on this earth. That particular life cycle is then ended. It has attained once again its primordial point of departure, but now it is greater, grander, because more evolved. And with it into invisibility have gone all the various organs or spheres or houses of life which composed the universe, each one with its manifold assortment of lives, which are incomputable in number, for there are hosts upon hosts, hierarchies upon hierarchies of them.

After a long, long period of universal repose, a definite time period called a *pralaya*,* our universe follows a new cycle down into newer substances and matters acting according to a preceding cause, which we may call an evolutionary seed, the fruitage of its former self. The vast aggregate of life forces which now reawaken into life, again

---

*The periods of evolutional activity are called in theosophy *manvantaras*, a Sanskrit term which means periods of manifestation when the universe is not "asleep." In the periods of rest or of "sleep" it reposes. These latter are called *pralayas*, another Sanskrit word, meaning "dissolution." Yet if we were to analyze these periods of rest we should find that they are not a state of mere "nothingness" but are made up of condition after condition through a complete cycle, which closes only as the new cycle of activity begins.

inform a nebula, which will be ready waiting for it, and which nebula will be the first manifestation of the stirrings of its own inner life force. Then, passing through various nebular stages of evolution, it will in time settle down anew into stellar or solar and planetary bodies, each one of such bodies, solar or planetary, bringing forth anew what is within itself, its intrinsic and inherent and latent life forces, expressing itself on this plane, which is a somewhat higher one than the plane on which our universe in its preceding period of manvantara had manifested itself on and in.

Yes, these worlds must have their period of repose, even as man must have his, when his cycle is run. When that period comes they rest in the invisible realms with all their freightage or burden of lives, and after that rest return and repeat the cycle of evolutionary manifestation, but at each recurrence on higher planes than the preceding.

Nature repeats herself everywhere. She follows grooves of action that have already been made; she follows the line of least resistance in all cases and everywhere. And it is upon this repetitive action of our Great Mother — universal nature — that is founded the law of cycles, which is the enacting of things that have been before, although each such repetition, as said, is at each new manifestation on a higher plane and with a larger sweep or field of action. Back of all the seeming of nature, behind all the cyclical phenomenal appearances which our senses interpret to us as best they may, lies the universal life in its infinitude of modes of action and expression.

Let us now take another step in advance in the outlining of this doctrine. What is it that causes this materialization or concretion or thickening of the original substance of a world, a universe? The answer is to be found in the teaching that spirit and essential substance are fundamentally one; which is virtually what the greatest scientific physicists believe when they declare that matter and force (or energy) are fundamentally one. This may seem like a dark saying and a hard one at first sight, but it is the current dictum of modern scientific physics, thus re-echoing the age-old philosophy.

At a certain stage of its movement forwards and downwards of progression or evolution, force passes the frontiers of any particular world-sphere and becomes very ethereal matter, because actually force is ethereal matter, so to say; or, to put it more accurately, matter is crystallized force.

What do we mean by matter? Matter as we cognize it is the physical basis of the things which we see around us. But if we try to analyze it, we seem to reach nothing. We do not know what to think. A man may ask himself, "What is matter, after all?" Let him ask the physicist, the chemist, the philosopher, and the chances are that nine times out of ten they will tell him, as honest men, "We do not know. All we know is that it is the substantial basis in and on which what we call force works."

But what is force? And the answer is, "Force is that which works on matter, and matter provides the substantial basis for force"! Yet are we going to cheat ourselves with words? We can so tie ourselves up in intangible abstractions such as these words, force and matter, that literally we go mentally nowhere and understand nothing.

Force is merely moving matter, or matter in movement, subtle matter, flowing matter. Force on the ethereal planes, or rather forces, are substances: on these ethereal planes they actually are solids, fluids and, if you like, "gaseous" matter; but in our more gross and material world, we sense them only as forces. Electricity is a case in point. It is material; we know that. Otherwise, indeed, how could it work in, through, and upon substance or matter, if it were entirely different from matter and had in itself nothing of a substantial nature? These forces working in the ethereal realms of matter are extremely subtle. Their rates of vibration are highly individual.

When an explosion takes place, what happens? A certain portion of matter then is violently converted into gas. Now if we did not know this true explanation of the fact, we should say that the matter had disappeared or vanished into nothingness, and that force had replaced it; that is to say, that matter had become an energy, which indeed is the actual fact. But energy as so used in ignorance of the true explanation would mean what it meant in the 1890s — that some unknown thing, called force, had suddenly appeared in the explosion to which matter had given birth in an unknown way.

My point is this: gas is matter. Hence when an explosion takes place through the conversion of solid into a gaseous matter, it merely means that matter has become etherealized and energic; it does not mean that matter and force are two utterly separate, distinct things. If we could again explode the gas resulting from the first explosion and thus turn it into a matter or substance still more ethereal than that gas, the same process would have taken place, and the gas would have been turned, as just said, into a matter or substance still more energic than the preceding, but it would still be matter.

Reverse the idea and consider a condensation of ethereal substance into a more material or concrete substance, into a crystallized form of that substance, which before we called force or energy. That is all there is to it.

Spirit and substance are fundamentally one. Matter

passes into force or energy, or substance passes into spirit, when the material or substantial cycle of either is completed — that is to say, when the cycle of any particular evolving entity, be it globe or anything else, is ended, when its time of dissolution or vanishing again into the invisible world arrives. Matter is thus metamorphosed into force again.

The eminent English physicist, Sir Oliver Lodge, stated in a lecture a number of years ago, that the universe is composite of something which he called "substantial," but which, he said, we cannot as yet understand or grasp the meaning of; yet this "something" is an old story in the age-old philosophy, and was as familiar to the sages of the past as it is to those of the present. Theosophists call this something "substantial" one of the garments of *mūlaprakriti* ("root-matter"), that garment being the *ākāśa,* a Sanskrit term meaning "luminous" or "brilliant." Indeed, that is exactly what primordial or original physical matter is: that something substantial of which Sir Oliver speaks is the lowest or most material form of ākāśa — and perhaps we might call it ether, though there are many cosmic ethers of many grades of tenuity, ranging from the lowest material through all intermediate stages to the most highly spiritual.

Original physical matter, even as we see it in the heavens at night manifesting as the so-called irresolvable nebulae — that is to say, nebulae which cannot be resolved by the telescope into groups or clusters of separate stars — is supposed to be of a gaseous nature; but, as a matter of fact, if we could put some of it into our test tubes, we should not know it was there, nor would it respond to any physical test or chemical reagent to which we might try to subject it, because it is a matter entirely different from the physical matter that we know. It is original physical matter, as like-

wise is, by the way, the substance of comets, which will
account for the extreme tenuity of the cometary substance
and the curious behavior of a comet's tail when it approaches
and recedes from the sun, apparently defying the laws of
physical astronomy. This subtle matter we often speak of as
mother-substance.

Sir Oliver further said that this substance or 'fluid' is

in a violent state of spinning, and is the seat of an immensity of energy
such as has never been imagined. 'Matter' is a temporary appearance
or effect in the substance, which can vanish entirely in a burst of
energy.°

This is really a wonderful remark for a modern scientific
physicist! This conversion of force into matter and its recon-
version through a "burst of energy" into force again, is
exactly what happens; and it is the age-old teaching of the
wisdom-religion.

In another lecture, Lodge previsions another theosophical
commonplace of philosophy, in his statement that matter
disappears into energy, or rather force, at the consummation
of the vast life cycle of the universe, only to reappear as
matter again at the beginning of a new life cycle of the
universe in some future age.

Yet in spite of the fact that Lodge declares the fundamental identity of spirit and matter, in certain statements he
still makes a sharp distinction between these two. Is this not
because he is still under the influence of the old materialistic
teaching that matter and spirit are two fundamentally different and distinct things, entirely separate, and that in some
wonderful and mysterious way, which no human ingenuity

°"Energy," Citizens' Lecture, Annual Meeting of the British Association for the Advancement of Science, September 6, 1927.

has yet succeeded in explaining, spirit works upon matter? Yet, how can that be? It is contrary to all the teaching of modern scientific knowledge, physics or other. Only that which is material in some degree can work upon and affect other material things; and therefore do we say, quite in line with this last teaching of physical science, that force and matter are one fundamentally, as is proved by the one working upon the other.

This teaching of the ultimate identity of force and matter, or spirit and substance, is important because, among other things, it furnishes a perfect encyclopedia of suggestions and leads us to draw conclusions which will enable us to settle in our own mind many of the problems which have vexed Occidental scholars for many hundreds of years.

But in talking of these things we find that language is inadequate. We of the Occident have no terms by which to express these utterly new thoughts in our mental world. The most that we can do, in order to give some idea of our meanings, is to hint at these meanings, convey the idea by graphic symbol, or by analogy, or suggestion. Therefore do we repeat that matters, substances, are crystallized forces and, on the other hand, that forces are actually immaterialized matters or substances.

We see matter moved or motivated by force or energy, and when we examine it more particularly with an attention still more profound, we then find that this matter is really matters, and that this force is really forces. The word force is an abstraction, a generalizing term, but if we reduce it to the concrete conception which is indeed its real meaning when properly used, as we see it manifested in the cosmos around us, we find that this abstraction is a mental representation of cosmic forces, just in the same manner that the word *man* when used as an abstraction is representative of human beings, in the sense of humanity.

Now what are these forces? We say that they are monads which have reached full development for and in our own particular hierarchy, that is, our cosmical system, both inner and outer; and that it is their life-impulses, their vitality, which furnish the energies with which the cosmos manifests. More simply put, the forces of the cosmos that we know are the life-impulses, the will-impulses, of these fully developed monads of our hierarchy. In ancient times they would have been called gods. Modern scientific thinkers call them forces; but the term really matters nothing.

The universe is composed of units, and the heart or core of each one of such units is what we call a monad. Each one of these monads, then, is a spiritual consciousness-life-center. And as the universe is infinite, and comprises the infinite degrees or stages or steps of which I have spoken, so these stages or steps are formed of the incomputable hosts of the monads in various degrees of self-expression; or to put it more accurately still, are composed of the vehicles or bodies in which each such monad manifests itself as in a garment taken from its own life and substance.

The lowest range of such garments that we humans can cognize is the congeries of material entities around us, or the aggregate of these garments of the monads, manifesting as potential force-substances, potential or sleeping atoms, but not as kinetic or awakened atoms, for these latter are the intermediate nature between the monad per se and these lower garments. Such is force and matter.

We see, then, that these two fundamental elements of the cosmos, because we understand them only in an illusory manner, are obviously illusions *for us*. The forces which

play in and through the cosmos, although themselves substantial, seem unsubstantial and immaterial to the lower
parts of the cosmos in which they all work. We do not
understand them as they are in themselves.

Consciousness therefore is matter; matter is consciousness; for have we not seen that the cosmos is composed of
nothing but an infinite number of spiritual entities, "spiritual
atoms," if we like, self-motivated, self-driven, self-impelled
particles of consciousness?

Locke, the English philosopher and logician of the seventeenth century, gave birth to a thought which is typically
theosophical. In his two-volume work, *An Essay Concerning
Human Understanding,* he conceived of an immense hierarchy of entities — he called them variously, "spiritual beings,"
"species of spirits," "intelligences," the name matters not for
the moment — running from the Deity or Author of all, down
to the beast, and below. He wrote:

And when we consider the infinite power and wisdom of the
Maker, we have reason to think that it is suitable to the magnificent
harmony of the universe, and the great design and infinite goodness
of the Architect, that the species of creatures should also, by gentle
degrees, ascend upward from us toward his infinite perfection, as we
see they gradually descend from us downwards: . . .
                                                  — Book III, ch. vi

Thus, finding in all parts of the creation, that fall under human
observation, that there is *a gradual connexion of one with another,
without any great or discernible gaps between, in all that great variety
of things we see in the world,* which are so closely linked together, . . .
the rule of analogy may make it probable, that it is so also in things
above us and our observation; and that there are several ranks of
intelligent beings, excelling us in several degrees of perfection, ascending upwards towards the infinite perfection of the Creator, by gentle
steps and differences, that are every one at no great distance from the
next to it.   — Book IV, ch. xvi

Leibniz, the great German philosopher, taught the same thing, but elaborated it to vastly greater length. But the theosophist goes much farther and says that this hierarchy of conscious entities, of monads, of spiritual atoms, in almost innumerable grades of progression, from the highest to the lowest, all moving onward and upward, is but one of an infinite number of such hierarchies. He declares also that the hierarch of any such hierarchy is a fully developed monad, a fully developed intelligence, having under its control, whether that control be cosmic or atomic, the inferior entities comprised in its hierarchy.

When an automobile speeds along the road, it carries with it everything of which it is composed. Of necessity, every molecule, and every atom of the hosts forming those molecules, go with it; and every proton and electron in their turn forming the hosts of atoms, of necessity likewise go with it. All the component parts of which such a vehicle is composed of necessity follow the path which the speeding vehicle follows, because they compose it. And so is it with the various bodies or 'vehicles' which enshrine and manifest and express the indwelling powers or energies or forces, whether such body or vehicle be a sun or a planet or a comet or a nebula, or a human body, or an animal body, or any other body.

The directing intelligence sitting at the wheel of the vehicle which we have chosen for our figure of speech, is representative of the directing intelligence sitting at the heart or core of each and every manifesting body in the cosmos. This directing intelligence is the divine hierarch of the hierarchy or cosmos, great or small, which it guides and inspirits.

The same law runs throughout the countless hierarchies

which go to make up the whole universe as a composite entity. Man's body, for instance, is composed of innumerable lives, hierarchies of lives, of various grades; and ruling over these sits man himself in the temple of his soul, the directing intelligence of all. Man is a composite hierarchy.

These teachings of the true nature of force and matter explain the process by which all hierarchies pass through their evolutionary life cycles. The spiritual body of the universe in its inception becomes more grossly material as the substances and energies of which it is composed transform themselves into inferior matter. This grossening, coarsening, materializing, of these forces becoming substance and matter, proceeds apace as the universe runs its course down into what become material realms.

When the materialization has reached its ultimate, or to put it more clearly, when such materialization has reached what for any particular universe is its period of gross physical existence, then such coarsening or materialization stops, and this is the turning point in the evolutionary path of such a universe. When this gross physical nature has thus been acquired through the progressive coarsening of the forces of which the reimbodied entity is composed, there ensues a change in the direction, as it were, that the universe henceforth must follow. Matter begins then to etherealize itself, to re-energize itself, to rebecome energy, but very, very slowly of course. It takes ages and ages and aeons upon aeons for this cosmic work to eventuate in evolutionary perfection; but that work goes on all the time, without intermission and without ceasing at any instant.

Therefore, as this etherealization goes on, as this re-etherealizing of the matter of which the universe consists proceeds, that universe rebecomes the forces of which it was at first composite, but with all the added qualities and characteristics of an evolved cosmic entity; and this takes place furthermore on a higher plane than that which witnessed the evolution of the universe that preceded it.

The passing of matter back into force gradually leads it upward and upward through progressive etherealization and final spiritualization, until ultimately it rebecomes spirit in those cosmic realms whence it originally set forth on its long evolutionary cyclical journey, but greater in quality and of superior texture in all senses is it when it returns to that primordial source. It is these two procedures that take place during the passage of a world from the invisible into the visible, and then from the visible back into the invisible.

14

THE RATIONALE OF REINCARNATION

THE PHILOSOPHICAL principles, or the laws of nature, which lie behind the processes leading to the formation and the eventuation of the human species are a copy in miniature of what takes place in the universe, the cosmos; the reason being that this universe in which we live is guided from within and acts outwards, and this guidance is by law, that is, by perfect consistency in action.

Given definite circumstances, certain operations of nature always follow the same courses; and these being universal laws, they must therefore likewise affect everything in the universe in which they operate, because everything therein is a part of that universe, a part of its composition, a part of its constitution. Hence, since we ourselves are a part of that universe, we have everything in us that the universe contains, either latent or active. We have all capacities and faculties, developed or undeveloped as the case may be, for understanding it; and we follow those same laws because being a part of that universe we cannot do otherwise. From this fact, so simple, so easily understood, depends the doctrine of cycles as carried out in the evolutionary development of the human kingdom — as indeed of all the kingdoms of universal nature.

Let us recapitulate the main points regarding the doctrine of cycles. A thing has its beginning, proceeds along its course to its culmination, and then, as the life forces, as the cosmic forces, as the human forces — or whatever it may be that is at the time subject to this cyclic law — as such forces pass their point of culmination, they begin to recede, they begin to lose the resiliency of their inner parts, the instant response which belongs to childhood and youth; and finally, there come decrepitude, then decay, then death, then rest; and then a beginning anew, but on a higher plane of the universe than before and towards nobler ends.

Why? Because the entity which had gone to its rest and now reappears for a new course of life had learned certain lessons in the former imbodiment, in the former existence, and with this increase of its intellectual and psychic stock it begins its new evolutionary cycle. When it in its turn is ended, then again comes rest, and after the rest then another life anew; and so forth throughout the eternities, throughout endless duration. But each new life cycle following each period of rest is always on planes and in spheres superior — from the evolutionary standpoint — to the preceding. Throughout all periods of past time has any entity so done; forwards into the future will it do so endlessly, for there are no ultimates, no endings.

Have you ever reflected over the idea of nothingness? Have you ever thought of the meaning of the words "an utter end"? Have you ever tried to realize the meaning of the notion that something had a definite beginning somewhere, somewhen, coming out of somewhere, without object

or aim, and vanishing again into an infinite nothingness —
a useless and futile course of life? Something springing out
of the past, no one knows how or when? These ideas are
mere plays of the fancy, nor is there anything real on which
they rest; for everywhere we look around us we see law, so
called, that is, consistent operations of the universe. And if
the universe is a consistent whole, how can something appear in it from nowhere, run for a while a crazy course, and
then vanish into the nothingness whence it came?

It is amazing how thinking men allow their thoughts to
be led astray by the phantasms of the imagination, the reason being that they have no psychological knowledge of
themselves; they have no key to the mysteries of their own
inner life. They have forgotten whence they came; they do
not know why we are here; they in consequence do not
know whither we go at the great change that men call death.
Yet all our common sense, as well as our intuition, tell us
that we are here for purposes, obviously so. We came here
in response to an operation of nature.

The secret of the origin of the making of man lies in the
making of the universe, in the making of the worlds. We,
children of the universe, intrinsic and inseparable parts of it,
must ineluctably follow its course, yet in following the general courses of the universe in which we live, likewise do we
follow, each one for himself, his own particular life cycle.

In man, then, the evolutionary cyclic course is carried on
by means of repeated incarnations. When the period of
death or rest has been achieved and run through, and rest
no more is needed, then we return to this earth in order to
take up again our interrupted work, further to develop, further to evolve. This advancing, this unfolding and pouring
forth of the energies of the inner generating life is what we

mean by evolution. In similar fashion do all things evolve in appropriate spheres and during appropriate time periods.

It is through the lessons which each incarnated entity learns in and on this material earth that evolution actually takes place. I may add that death itself, which follows a hid process, is actually another school of evolutionary progress by which the soul, passing along its pathway of experience, also learns.

Throughout a single lifetime we do certain acts, using the forces innate in us, and reacting against the stimuli of nature around us; and thus we lay by seeds of action in our characters which become modified by such use of the powers within us. These seeds must some time fructify and bring forth their fruit, even as we here today are the fruits of former actions, former thoughts, former aspirations that we followed or did not follow. Either of the two cases is equally important, because our sins of omission are often as serious in their effects upon our character and the lives of others as are our sins of commission, and in both cases we are responsible.

Man expresses through his various vehicles, visible or invisible, through his physical vehicle, for instance, his inner forces, thus following the imperative drive of his character. This is evolution, which as a procedure has two aspects: (1) the unfolding or unwrapping of the inner powers in response to (2) the multitude of stimuli arising out of the world around him. It is thus that man learns, ever going step by step higher and higher, until from his present stage of imperfect development, he will finally reach a state of divinity, each ego becoming a fully self-conscious god, a fully self-expressing god.

But is this the end? Is this the final culmination of his

destiny through evolution, after which there is nothing more, a complete stoppage of operation of all forces and powers and faculties which he unfolds? No, there is no absolute end, no absolute ultimate.

Man is in his essence a spiritual being, a monad, adopting for purposes of illustration the old Pythagorean term meaning a unit, an individual. Hence he is a consciousness center, a life-consciousness-center, eternal in its essence, because it belongs to those parts of the universe — the higher worlds of the cosmos — which die not, nor do they pass away. It is what is called in philosophy pure substance, and is not the composite matter of which our physical universe is built, but belongs to the more ethereal and the invisible parts of our universe which lie within and behind our physical universe of phenomenal appearances. Yet while these inner and invisible worlds are the spheres of its activity, in its own essence it is far higher than these are, for it belongs to the divine in the roots or heart of its being.

Now this monad, this spiritual life-consciousness-center, when the time comes for its reimbodiment after its rest following its preceding life in the lower spheres, is subject to a coarsening or materializing of its outer vestures. Itself remaining always as divinity pure and simple on its own plane, nevertheless it clothes itself in the lower spheres with these vestures of light, as they would seem to our mental and psychical senses. This is not a metaphor, but an actuality, for light is substance, although to us it manifests as an energy merely because it is a substance superior to the matter of our own physical plane.

Thus the real man passes through the spheres intermediate between his physical vestures and the plane of the monad, by means of a ray emanated from the monad. This monadic ray is the ego-self, and it is this ego-self which passes down through these intermediate spheres, and in so doing takes upon itself garments or vestures or vehicles appropriate to these spheres, each to each. These are its intermediate bodies which, using a generalizing term, we may collectively call the "soul"; until finally the moment comes when that soul, as the aggregate activities of these intermediate spheres, is enabled to influence the forces and matters of our physical world. Thus the ray or soul passes into physical incarnation and takes unto itself a physical vehicle or body, much as it took unto itself appropriate vehicles on the intermediate planes through which it passed, each such vehicle or body thus acting as a carrier of the monadic ray or ego-soul.

Think about this outline of the activities of the monad preceding incarnation, and you will marvel at the consistency of the doctrine from beginning to end. There are no lapses of thought, nor anything left for you to imagine as necessary to fill awkward gaps.

It is an obvious truth, is it not, that a purely spiritual being could not live or express itself on a plane of physical matter, for its energies are not appropriate to such a sphere. The monad must have an appropriate vehicle or body in order to manifest itself, and in which it may live and work; in other words, there must be an appropriate temple for the enshrining of our inner god, which the monad is. This is what is meant in the old teaching which, in the combination of two mystical sayings, I make to run as follows: "Know ye not that ye are the temple of Divinity, and that the Divine dwelleth in you?" (1 Cor. 3:16).

When man, as an ego-soul or monadic ray, thus passes into physical incarnation he is born into the physical world as a little child, and beginning his career here in this manner, he runs through his life courses on earth. What causes these courses which a man follows? What is it that is behind the things that he does and the things that he leaves undone, thereby making for himself a character which culminates in a destiny? What are all these forces in man? What is the drive behind him? Collectively speaking, it is what he has built into himself in preceding lives, and which is now finding its outlet, now finding its fruitage-ground, and it is in this manner that man works out his karma.

A farmer sows seed in a certain field and the seed takes root and grows, and produces its crop. Where? In some other field? No, but where it was sown. In similar fashion do our thoughts and actions plant seeds of future activities into ourselves, into our characters through the action of karma, the law of cause and effect, which more accurately is expressed as the law of consequences.

Man likewise is greatly affected by the general karma of the race to which he belongs, and by the general law of consequence appertaining to the universe in which he lives. It is the working out of all these latent potentialities that he has inbuilt into himself that makes his life in any one incarnation. It is the working out of these which directs what a man will call his struggles to betterment and his aspirations to higher things. Then, when his course is run in any one lifetime, he passes to his postmortem rest; and when this repose in its turn is ended then he returns to this sphere in a new cycle of activity, yet in each new incarnation he gains fresh experiences. Always does he more largely develop his inner faculties and power; always, therefore, has he evolved to a point farther along the pathway than where he was before. It may be little, or it may be much.

Some people object to the teaching of reimbodiment, which in the case of human beings is called reincarnation; and they so object because they do not understand it. Yet it is such an old teaching, and has had the common consent of universal humanity. Until the last fifteen hundred years or so, all the nations of the earth believed it and taught it, as was the case in the European world at that time; and the doctrine is still believed in and taught by the greater part of the human race.

Some people say: "I do not like the idea of being reincarnated. My life has been very sad. I have suffered deeply; this earth has been the scene of my sorrows; I don't want to come back here again." Others say: "I like reincarnation as a theory; I recognize it as the most logical explanation ever offered to thinking man of the problems of life; but I don't like the idea of coming back into this world and having to go through all that I have been through; and the thought of making the same mistakes over again repels me." But they do not understand.

These people seem to think that they will come back into the same old body that they had before. Unconsciously in their own minds resides the thought that they will have the same old name, be in the same old station of life, and have the same old troubles, and do the same old work. No.

In the first place, reincarnation before eighteen hundred or two thousand years have passed, as our teachers have taught us, is an exceedingly rare thing — so rare that we may forget the exceptions. So far as that goes, look at the differences in the conditions of life as they exist in our own present world, and what they were around two thousand years ago. Yet few indeed complain of being in this life, and most people seem to cling to it rather fervidly. The objectors forget that the laws of life are not what we at any one particular moment of time may think that they ought to be, or what we in our blindness might wish them to be. We cannot change the courses of existence by our likes and dislikes.

We do not come back into the same old body. We have a new body, obviously. We do not come back into the same old house, which by the time of our return will have become forgotten dust. Our condition in life may, in our next incarnation, be very much better, or it may be very much worse than the present; for if we do not behave ourselves now when we have the chance of bettering conditions, we certainly will have to take the consequences.

This is the meaning of karma, the doctrine of consequence. We reap what we sow, and where we have sown; and if we have sown seeds of good and evil in this life and on this earth, it is only in another life on this earth that we can reap what we have sown. Would not a farmer be considered a lunatic did he sow a field in one part of the county where he lived, and some months later travel to another part of the county, far from where he sowed his seed, in order to reap his crop? So it is with man. He sows seeds of thought and action, and he reaps that crop where he sowed them, which is in himself and in this physical world.

Our universe is ruled by law and order; and this word karma expresses that fact of universal harmony and consistency manifesting as what we call law and order. Everything that we do, everything that we think, is a productive cause, affecting us and those around us, yet leaving the seeds and the fruits of such thoughts and actions in ourself. This is common knowledge. We have laid up for ourself in past lives treasures for happiness; but we may have also laid

up for ourself a treasure house of another kind, and we are
doing similarly in our present life. We are going to have
a body and a character in our next incarnation which will
be the exact fruitage or consequence of the entire sum total
of what we have thought and done in this life, as modified
only by the as yet unexpressed and by the as yet unworked-
out consequences of previous lives.

I have heard an objection of another kind, running in the
contrary direction, and it is this: "I do not like the idea that
I am going to come back and be another person. I want to
be myself. I do not want a new body: I am satisfied with
this body of mine. It has treated me well, and I have tried
to treat it well, and I want this body and not a new one."
Those who make this objection also do not understand. As
a matter of fact, they are going to keep that same body.
Now this sounds like a contradiction of what I have just
said, but it is not; it is a paradox. What is a body after all?
It is a form, a name, and nothing more. The ancient Sanskrit
writings, as outlined in the noble Vedānta philosophy, called
it *nāma-rūpa,* meaning a "name-form."

The fact is that our body is composed of hosts of lives, of
smaller and inferior entities, which are nevertheless learning
entities just as we are. And I may add in passing that we too
are hosts of smaller lives, smaller and inferior to cosmic
entities far greater than we are. But these hosts of lives
inferior to us and which compose our bodies — what are
they? Are they for all eternity just standing still as they
now are? No, they are evolving even as we are evolving.
They came from us originally; they are our own children;
they are what we call our life-atoms. They sprang from us;
we sent them forth, and we shall have to meet them again
when they return to us at our next incarnation, through and

by the action of psychomagnetic attraction. They will provide for us when they reaggregate themselves into a physical form for our next incarnation; and we shall have a body consisting of just what we have impressed upon them today and in past lives by our thoughts, by our acts, and by the consequences of our thoughts and acts.

So that the next body that we shall get will be — not the same old body that we had before; not the same John Smith or Mary Brown, not at all; for John Smith and Mary Brown are but a name and a form. But our new body will be composed of those same life-atoms in which we lived and worked and expressed ourself in the preceding incarnation, which is our present life. And remember that these life-atoms exist not merely on this physical plane where our physical body is, but they exist likewise on the intermediate planes; that is to say, on the astral and emotional planes, as well as on the intellectual and spiritual planes.

It is by means of these life-atoms on all the different planes that the ego-self, emanated from the monad, is able to build for itself new bodies, inner and outer, in the new incarnation. It passes through all the intermediate planes, building up for itself from the same old life-atoms that it before had — its own children, waiting for it there — a vehicle or body appropriate to each such plane. Similarly is it on the physical plane where the physical body is. Here we have the original and correct explanation of the much misunderstood Christian doctrine called the Resurrection of the Dead.

Now there are three methods, we are told, by which reimbodiment proceeds, and these three work together in strict harmony. One method is what we commonly call reincarnation, which the mystics among the ancient Greeks spoke of as *metensomatosis,* that is to say, coming again into body after body, "re-imbodying." This word was taken over from the Greek Mysteries by Clement of Alexandria, one of the earliest of the Christian Fathers, although with certain modifications due to his Christian bias.

The second method is the procedure called *metempsychosis,* that is to say, coming again into a soul, or psyche — "re-ensouling."

The third method, which the Greeks kept secret in their Mysteries, but which certain of their philosophers such as Pythagoras, Plato, Empedocles, and later the Neoplatonists more or less openly hinted at or taught, is the activity of the monad, the spiritual fire at the core or heart of each one of us. This monad manifests our spiritual self, because it is that spiritual self, a consciousness center which is the fountain of our being, whence issue in flooding streams all the nobler energies and faculties of its own character, and which, considered as a unit, furnish the urge or drive or impulse behind all evolutionary progress.

First, then, there is the activity of the monad, the highest. During the process of incarnation the activities of this monad develop the intermediate nature which ensouls soul after soul, and this is the real meaning of this old Greek word metempsychosis; and these souls thus invigorated, inspired, and driven by the ensouling monad, ensoul body after body, which is metensomatosis, or reincarnation, as the word is commonly and properly used.

Hence, evolution proceeds on three general lines: the spiritual, the mental-emotional, and the astral-vital; and the physical body is the channel through which all these inwrapped capacities, tendencies, and powers, express themselves on the physical plane, if the environment at any particular moment or at any particular passage of time be appropriate and fit for the expression of this or that or of some other such attribute, power, or faculty. The combination of these two — the inner urge, the drive, and a fit and appropriate environment or field — means the evolving, the coming out into manifestation, the expression, of those inner forces or powers.

As is evident, this includes a far wider and vaster conception of evolution than any that has hitherto been entertained in the ranks of the scientific researchers — the Darwinists for instance.

The strength of the doctrine of reincarnation lies in itself, in its appeal to our intellectual and logical faculties, in its own persuasiveness, in the manner in which it answers problems, in the hope that it gives, in the light that it sheds upon collateral questions of human life, and indirectly upon the problems of the physical world surrounding us. It is through and by reincarnation as a natural fact, that we learn the beauty of the inner life and thereby grow, developing a larger comprehension, not only of ourselves, but of the loveliness inherent in the harmony of the universal laws. For there is back of all things beauty, and bliss, and truth.

What men call evil and misfortune and accidents, and the disastrous phenomena of the physical world which sometimes occur, arise out of the conflicts of the wills and powers of the various hosts of imperfect but evolving entities, one of such hosts being what we collectively call humanity.

Reimbodiment is a universal fact because it is a law, that is to say, a continuous and consistent operation of nature, running throughout all being. The universe reimbodies itself when its course has been run, and after its period of rest which thereupon follows. Men do likewise; not because reincarnation is for them alone, but because it is the same fundamental law of cyclic beginnings and endings, and in the case of man it means only that he returns to pick up again the threads which he had dropped at a certain turn of that cycle which we call death.

Its procedure is strictly lawful, there is in its working no haphazard chance, no fortuity, no favor; it is merely the succession of state following upon state in strict accordance with cause and subsequent effect. Nobody and nothing operates it. It simply is; and its working is set in motion in every individual case by the action of the will of the entity upon the nature surrounding it. No god created the law of our reimbodiment. It is an intrinsic function of nature, and it acts in that way only because it can act in no other way, being simply a statement of the doctrine of consequences — of consequences following upon originating causes.

15

MAN'S BODY IN EVOLUTION

THE THEOSOPHIST, a thoroughgoing evolutionist or, perhaps more accurately speaking, emanationist, looks upon the evolution or the perfection of the physical body of man with profound interest. But with a far more profound and wide-reaching searching of his heart does he study the evolution of the inner evolving monad which expresses itself through its physical vehicle, the body, and which on that account furnishes the drive, the urge, the impulse, ever upwards and forwards, causing that body to change its form slowly as the ages roll by, becoming with every new era, with every new aeon, a more fit vehicle to express the indwelling intellectual and spiritual forces and potencies of that monad.

These spiritual forces or potencies seeking an outlet, seeking to express themselves, work through the infinitesimal particles of man's inner constitution, the life-atoms, which exist on many planes, on at least four below the intellectual part of that monad.

In the physical body these life-atoms are enshrined within the cells of that body, working through the atoms of which those cells are composed. Thus is it that the evolutionary drive finds its outlet; it comes from within, expresses itself through the intermediate nature of man, then finds an expression through the physical vehicle, in order that the thinking entity may see this world of matter even as we do see it, and draw such lessons from companionship with it — as a master, if you please, not as a slave — which it may and can draw.

It is to the thoughtful mind a palpable absurdity to suppose that all thinking entities must have a physical encasement in all respects, or indeed necessarily in any respect, identic with the human physical body today. This would be equivalent to saying that no entity could have consciousness or intelligence or the power of consecutive thinking, or the moral sense, unless his physical frame were in all respects identic with our own.

Intelligence and consciousness and the moral sense could live and express themselves quite as easily in physical bodies of an entirely different type from ours. Indeed, it is the theosophical teaching that self-conscious, intellectual, and even *spiritually* self-conscious beings live and follow the courses of their respective lives and destinies on certain other globes of our solar system.

On this earth, self-conscious beings, or what we call humans, currently have the bodies they have as the fruitage of a long evolutionary ancestry, as the necessary resultant, evolutionally speaking, of bygone workings of the inner urge or drive inherent in man's inner constitution and working thence through the physical matter existent at our present epoch. The same thing applies, historically speaking, to all preceding geologic periods and to all zoologic periods which are destined to follow our present one.

For instance, man might have a tail. Would he be less human, if he had a tail? Not at all. A tail neither makes nor unmakes a beast, nor would it make or unmake a man. What is man? Man is the inner consciousness, a thinking entity, the source of the moral sense, the source of the intellectual power, the center of the spiritual aspirations which we all have. Man's body, on the other hand, is but the physical encasement in and around which he lives, self-expressing himself through it; and the manner of that self-expression through this physical body forms a part of the subject of our study.

As a matter of fact, hundreds of millions of years ago, during the third globe-round, i.e., during the preceding great planetary period, the earth bore its appropriate and characteristic fruitage of lives, and many and various were the classes and groups of evolving beings in different degrees of development.

At that remote time man did indeed possess a physical body or encasement of which a tail was then a more or less useful appendage. All record of that zoologic fact is at the present time completely passed from human memory; nevertheless our teaching is that the physical men of that period hundreds of millions of years ago, did have a tail, albeit a short one.

The old Hindu legends and mythoi relate how the gods and the men of a past age associated with intelligent beings who are described as monkey tribes, who spoke and constructed dwelling-houses and built cities, and whatnot. These myths, based upon half-forgotten memories of a geological past and handed down from generation to generation through the ages, acquired in far later times the legendary form in which we now possess them, as for instance in the very ancient and extremely interesting epic tale, the *Rāmāyana,* detailing the adventures and loves of Rāma and his delightfully feminine companion and wife Sītā.

Indeed, if the mere lack of a tail as an appendage to man's physical body were the sole test of evolutionary progress, then the tailless gorilla — one of the anthropoid apes, and considered by some zoologists and anatomists to be man's most immediate beast ancestor — stands higher than man along the pathway of evolution, because the gorilla has but three coccygeal bones or caudal vertebrae, i.e., the bones at the end of his spine; but man has four and sometimes five.

In addition to this interesting fact, we may point out in passing that it is well known that babies are sometimes born with a rudimentary tail. Nature makes no mistakes in her productions of physical beings, and such things could not happen merely by chance, or otherwise than as the result of what we might call an automatic reversion to a former condition.

What is man, I ask again? Man is the inner entity, the thinking energy, the consciousness — all that bundle or aggregate of forces which is consciousness, which thinks, which has a moral sense, and which aspires. The beasts have all these spiritual and psychological potentialities in them also, but they have them latent; they have not developed a proper vehicle for the self-expression of these noble powers and faculties. But in man those fine inner faculties have indeed possibilities of self-unfoldment through a vehicle which has been evolved and trained to manifest them. Hence man is what he now is both physically and psychologically.

The truth of this matter is that man's physical or corporeal encasement exhibits at any period of evolution exactly the state of self-expression on this plane which the indwell-

ing monad has attained. Consequently, his evolution proceeds in stages that his power or facility in self-expression
creates, from the smaller to the greater, the expressing vehicle in consequence following step by step and line by line
the urge or drive of the inner impelling power.

Thus faculty always precedes organ; the organ is its representative, built up by the inner faculty for purposes of self-
manifestation; otherwise, how could it exist? Whence could
it come into being? What use would it have were there no
preceding faculty which had built it for self-evolutionary
purposes? Things do not just arise in the universe in haphazard fashion nor without a well-defined and expressing
cause behind them. Hence, anything that appears or is
manifest is an obvious proof of a forcible urge behind it that
is thus showing itself. In other words, a phenomenon is a
proof of a causal noumenon in the background which manifests itself through a phenomenon, which is thus its organ
of self-expression.

It is a natural consequence of this that the physical body
or encasement or vehicle must take on at different periods of
evolution widely different and varying forms or shapes. Our
bodies have not always been as they are now. What would
you say to the statement that the original "human" corporeal
sheath or body in the early ages of this planetary round on
our globe was of a quasi-spherical shape, of an egglike or
ovoid form, in the center of which the entity resided?

Further, it was not exactly luminous but luminescent and
translucent, starlike, we might say highly phosphorescent.
It is for this reason that we speak of that particular grade of
matter as "astral," because such matter resembled the luminous nebulae that we discern in the blue dome of night; for
astral means "starlike."

Since that far remote epoch of geological time, the bodily shape of the physical encasement has varied and changed step by step according to the calls of evolutionary necessities and progress, before attaining the form that it now has; and this change will continue progressively throughout future time, following faithfully — as the wheel follows the feet of the ox which drags the cart — every increase in power for self-expression that the inner entity acquires.

In the future, man's body will be far different in shape, in texture, and power of expressing the inner faculties, from what it is now. In the distant aeons of the future, our body will change equivalently with the passage of time, responding accurately to new needs, to new calls for self-development, and to new stimuli from the outer environment to which the inner man automatically answers; and, further, that outer environment itself will slowly change to a much more ethereal and refined condition.

Aeons upon aeons hence, during the last part of the seventh globe-round, the outermost covering of the entity which man shall have become will have returned to an ovoid or egglike form and will be, for the far more refined and spiritual matter of those future times, the physical or corporeal — if such words can be used — encasement of the self-expressing divinity at the heart of each such ovoid body. Of course in those days, instead of being composed of gross, coarse, physical substance such as our bodies now are, this ovoid outer form will be a garment of dazzling light, sunlike, glorious, resplendent, and the entity at its heart will be that godlike inner man which man will then have become through self-evolving the spiritual powers which he is in his inmost self.

Thus it cannot be too emphatically reiterated that the

physical body springs from, is a result of, the spiritual and invisible forces inherent within. It is these forces which make that body and control it and govern it, and give it shape and hold it together. This force of coherence, and all the other physical energic phenomena which the body manifests, have sprung from the inner fountain; for it is within the individual that lie the springs of energy or force, and therefore of all action.

Each man ensouls his own body. He is the oversoul, so to speak, of each one of the molecules or cells or atoms composing that body. In like manner do we originate from our spiritual root, because our inmost self reaches back into the heart of the universe. It is, in fact, this self of us which is at the heart of the atoms themselves. It actually forms these atoms, and then casts them forth, excretes them as it were, and thereupon lives in them. Thus does man build up his body from his own interior life forces, and works through it and manifests his various life fires in it.

Medical investigators into the mysteries of the human body used to search in it for an immortal soul, some tangible proof of human immortality. In the name of all conscience, what did they expect to find? An immortal body? A dead body, so called, neither speaks, nor breathes, laughs, thinks, or sighs. What then is death? What has happened when the body dies? Something did so act and manifest itself when the body was alive; that something once manifested all those powers which the living man shows, faculties transcendent with spiritual aspirations. What has become of them? The truth is they could not see the working of the inner entity on account of the manifold phenomena which it expresses in the living body. Consequently they passed over with unseeing eyes and uninterpreting minds the very proofs before them.

How did such ideas arise among Western European thinkers when science began to gather to itself some knowledge of the physical world, and the mind of man found itself more free to embark upon nobler thinking? Did these extremely limited ideas arise out of the fact that pictures and teachings which in the early days of Christianity were symbolic, finally came to be taken as literal facts — such for instance as the pictures that you may so often see in European Mediterranean countries of angels with human bodies, but possessing wings like gigantic birds; or beings with no bodies, and nothing but a head and a pair of bird's wings; or beings depicted as arising out of the corpse in the grave in the shape of a human form more or less outlined; or, as sometimes shown, of a mannikin issuing from the mouth of the expiring one with the last breath?

These very materialistic reproductions of the so-called human soul were originally purely symbolic, and never were intended, when first used, to be taken in their literal form. They were copied from the so-called pagan, Greek and Roman symbolic reproductions of the passing of the inner entity at the beginning of the long sleep which they called and we also call death.

It is true enough that the inner entity, as compared with its gross physical vehicle, is an energy, a force, to our eyes invisible, intangible to our touch, and manifests in the living body as such an energy or force or power, the faculties which it shows during such manifestation being its intrinsic character. Is not this exactly what takes place as shown by the phenomena of the living, conscious, thinking, aspiring, emotional, psychical, passional, intuitive entity as it works through the body? Strange composite of heaven and earth, a compound energy, a bundle of forces, which death separates out and lets go, each of these along its own especial pathway.

Yet when we call the inner entity an energy, a bundle of forces, we likewise mean that it is substantially material in a nobler sense. And in this, the latest discoveries of physical science unknowingly corroborate the archaic teachings, for the scientists today teach that force and matter, or energy and matter, are fundamentally one, matter being, so to say, crystallized energy, or force; and energy or force being, so to say, subtle and moving matter. There are, as has been shown, many degrees or grades or stages of substance. There is, first, the physical; then what we call the astral, or ethereal; then the more ethereal; then the still more ethereal; then the intellectual, if you like so to call it; and then the spiritual; and at the acme, forming the summit of the hierarchical progression, is the divine substance. Even so is man built throughout his hierarchical inner and outer constitution.

This body of ours, though truly wonderful if we look at it from one viewpoint, from another viewpoint is a most imperfect vehicle for the self-expression of the reincarnating and reincarnated entity. It cannot manifest a thousandth part, not even a millionth, a billionth, part of what there is seeking self-expression in the inner man, the invisible human entity.

It is through the senses mostly that we seek to self-express ourselves; and everyone knows how imperfectly they receive impressions from the outside, to say nothing of their feeble power in unfolding the locked-up powers and faculties and feelings which are within.

There are five senses as we now have them. Each one is the fruit of long evolutionary labor; imperfect as they are, yet how well they serve us. But how much better will they not serve us as time passes, in the aeons of the far future when they shall have become much more perfected, much fitter instruments for the self-expression of the inner entity.

This entity, when it seeks incarnation, is essentially an aggregate of forces: spiritual, intellectual, psychical, emotional and astral-vital. When it finds its time for assuming (or reassuming) a new physical body, it is magnetically or perhaps electrically drawn into that family, more particularly into that mother cell, which closest presents in its own cell sphere the lowest rate of vibration of the reincarnating being. In this respect the attraction is magnetic and the incarnating entity is thereby drawn to the cell having a corresponding vibrational rate. Thereafter the rates of vibration coincide and become one in period. In this way developing life in the fertilized cell begins.

The atoms themselves are naught but equilibrated forces, and therefore the cells which they compose are essentially equilibrated forces. Thus it is easy to see how the communication between the visible and the invisible is naught but a question of similar or differing vibrational rates. It is all a matter of vibrational synchrony. You can make a piano wire sing if you strike its keynote on another instrument. You can break a glass, shiver it, by sounding its keynote on a violin or horn, as is well known, if you can catch and sound the vibrational rate that the glass is built on. I believe that in time to come physicians will discover and utilize the marvelous curative powers lying in sound, let us say in music which, after all, is in its physical sense harmonious sounds.

As the body grows, that is to say, as the growing aggregate of daughter cells forming the body of the individual-to-be receives in ever-larger quantity, and in ever-more specialized forms, the different forces of the entity coming into physical life once again from its long rest after its preceding life on earth; or, to put it in other words, as the growing body answers in continuously increasing perfection to the combined rate of vibration of the principles composing the entity then reincarnating, the individual characteristics of that reincarnating entity grow progressively more manifest.

While these rates of vibration are more or less diffused through the physical body when it attains adulthood, nevertheless there are foci in and through and by which the incarnating entity expresses itself, the channels, as it were, the open doors, through which it pours its lower aspects, thus self-expressing itself in that aggregated body of cells which is now in process of building and forming its physical encasement or body.

What are these foci? Generally speaking they are the various organs of the physical body. More specifically pointing out their location, we may say there are seven main foci or centers in the human body, each one fit and built for the purpose of expressing one of the six general principles — the physical body apart — of which man is composite, ranging from the spiritual to the vital-astral, the lowest.

Where are these foci? First, please understand that an ethereal force, a subtle and delicate force, however tremendous its power may be, does not of necessity need a large physical organ for self-expression. If there be in the human frame, in the physical body of man, a point as large as the point of a pin, it may be enough. What we may see with our physical eyes as so small a part of physical matter, from the atomic standpoint may contain heaven knows how many atoms.

These foci, then, these centers of etheric transmission in the human body, in the Sanskrit philosophical and other writings are called *chakras,* a word meaning "wheels" or "circles," and therefore what we might translate in this connection as ganglia or glands, perhaps. Of the seven, I will mention here only the two highest which are within the skull: the pineal gland, and the pituitary gland. These two little glands or bodies enable two different and yet co-working and interlocking forces of the man, that is the real man, to self-express themselves through the body. They were built for that purpose through aeons upon aeons of evolutionary labor, and in time to come they will be still more perfected than they are now, and therefore better able to express those spiritual and intellectual and mental and emotional and psychic and ethereal powers which in their aggregate are man.

It is through the seven chakras, foci, channels, openings, doors — call them what you like — that the incarnating and incarnated entity expresses itself; and through them that the forces of which man is composed are diffused through the entire body, which is his physical being.

Evolution is the breaking down of barriers, and co-incidently the building of the vehicle ever more fit for expressing the interior faculties and powers of the inner entity. It is in part this breaking down of barriers, and in part the refining and building of the vehicle, which enable that inner entity to manifest its faculties proportionately. Evolution is not the adding of stone to stone, of experience to experience — not that alone; it is much more the building up of the vehicle, becoming constantly more fit and ready to express or manifest some part of the transcendent faculties of the human spirit. A highly evolved man has a vehicle more fit and more ready than has a man less highly evolved; and this applies not only physically, but even more strongly on the mental and psychical planes. The inferior man in evolutionary development has not so fit a vehicle, and consequently can express those powers but poorly.

Let us cleanse our minds of crystallized ideas that because things are as they now are, they always have been so, always will be, and always must be; for such would be the reasoning of a child. It is obvious that if things grow, they change; and change is always for betterment in the evolutionary journey — leaving aside all sidelines of growth, such as degeneration. We are now speaking solely of the general course of evolution.

We are all children of the earth in one very true sense, and at the same time we are the offsprings of heaven. Our earth has not produced that wonder-thing within us which directs and governs our lives, which gives us thinking and feeling and aspirations and longings for better things. No, that part which the earth produces is the physical vehicle; but the wonder-thing is we ourselves, and is native in the realms of spirit and ineffable light.

Therefore, while we definitely place man's body in the animal world, we do so because man's primeval physical form was the originant, the primitive source of that entire animal world — an earth product. But is this body of ours man? Man's physical body is but the poor shell enclosing and crippling the powers of a spiritual luminary.

Yet it is a wonderful instrument, if we look at it from another standpoint; but in comparison with the glory of the god which man inwardly is, the beast which is his body and through which this inner splendor seeks to shine, is as nothing. It is but an enshrouding veil, a limiting encasement. Still, it must be a fit vehicle, one appropriate to express those indwelling powers of a spiritual, intellectual, mental, psychic, and astral-vital nature, which in the aggregate are man. It is thoughts such as these which teach us to see the value of ethical rules in life — those fine and noble instincts of the inner being, whose collective mandate is one which we dare not disobey.

Slowly and very gradually do the various vehicles or garments or sheaths, in which the inner nature of man, as of all entities, lives and works, become more refined, more capable of expressing the inner powers and faculties. Behind all there is the general cosmic urge which commingles in action with the individual drive of the entity, always forwards and outwards in self-expression — for the general as well as the individual impetus is always forwards.

And what is this engine whence flow this general urge and the particular drive? It is a spiritual engine. It is, in fact, the monad — the divine root within us, taking its general life force from the universal life of which it is an intrinsic and inseparable part, and which at the same time is the fountain of the individual drive. Back of man, back of the animate entities on earth today, back of the many various stems of animate organisms, there is in each case the vital drive of a living monad. These monads are not soiled by the matter with which they work, and in and through which they work — not more so than the rays from the glorious sun are soiled or spoiled or lose their innate brilliancy by the water and scum and ooze and mud in the fetid swamp through which they may penetrate to some degree, cleansing and purifying all they touch.

It is this inner ray or spark of light in beings which furnishes the urge, the driving force, the innate impulse, to higher things. This light comes from the ocean of universal life; and from that universal life in the beginning of our evolutionary course we issued as unself-conscious god-sparks, so to say; passing through innumerably varied stages along the pathway of evolutionary progress. We learn in each stage lessons appropriate thereto, thus garnering understanding of any such stage of our cosmic journey. Passing thence forwards or, what comes to the same thing in the present instance, farther downwards into matter, we enter the human stage and there attain self-consciousness — a self-consciousness which grows and broadens ever more and more as time goes on; because with every step forwards, with every new lesson learned, our capacities have a larger field for self-expression; and evolution is nothing but progressive self-expression.

When self-consciousness has been won, each new step thereafter we can take with a more confident and stronger stride ahead; and thus at every step forwards we learn more than we knew during the last stage. It is thus that self-consciousness broadens into universal consciousness again, when we pass the turning point of grossest physical matter, and turn our faces ahead for the long, long upward ascent. So it is at the end of our planetary period that human consciousness rebecomes universal consciousness, returning after having reached the culmination of our evolutionary course back to the Source whence we originally came, no longer as unself-conscious god-sparks but as fully self-conscious gods.

16

THE PINEAL AND PITUITARY GLANDS

THE SPIRITUAL BEING that is the real man plays on the physical body as the master musician plays on a wondrous lute or harp. The strings of this instrument, this marvelously constructed physical frame, run from the coarsest catgut, which can produce heavy, sensual sounds, to the silver and gold, and finally to the intangible strings of the spirit; and the musician plays on these strings with masterly sweep of will when we allow it. Mostly we human beings refrain from playing on the nobler and higher strings, and play on the coarse catgut only.

As a matter of fact, this body of ours is one of the marvels of the universe. We at present have no realization of what it contains, of its powers to be developed in the future as evolving time will bring them forth, but which we can hasten in their growth now. These powers of the human being function through the seven main centers of energies in the body: seven organs or glands, sometimes called chakras.*

---

*Strictly speaking, the chakras are the astral organs or functions, and their specific allocations to physical organs are surrounded in exoteric literature with mystery and uncertainty. They have been known and studied, however, in certain schools since time immemorial.

To enumerate these generally, from the lowest up: the genital, the liver and spleen, the cardiac, the brain as a whole, the pituitary gland and the pineal gland. There are others subordinate to these, but the above are the most important. And strangely enough, they are as it were paired: the heart and the brain; the pineal and the pituitary; the liver and spleen; and the pair of the lowest couple, as a matter of fact, is the solar plexus — but this is a story by itself.

Every one of these organs or glands has its own appropriate function, activity, purpose, and work in the human frame. By our will, by proper study, by living the life, we can make the higher, the incomparably more powerful ones within us, active far more than they presently are, and thus become gods among men. Most of us do not do that. We live in the world below the human diaphragm as it were. And yet, despite our worst efforts to kill the god within us, to destroy its holy work, the pineal gland and the pituitary gland, and the heart, continue functioning just the same. We are protected against our own foolishness.

The lowest of these chakras can be made one of the noblest by changing its functional direction for creative spirituality. Waste brings loss; that particular organ in the human frame can be made the organ for the production of the mightiest and noblest works of genius. It has a spiritual as well as a physical side, as all these organs and glands have. But how many remember the holiness of spiritual creation, so to say?

The liver is the seat of the personal man, the kāma-mānasic individual; and the spleen, the lieutenant of the former, is the seat of the astral body, the linga-śarīra. Even at séances — which I would not advise anyone to frequent unless he goes there knowing more than the average man does — it has been shown how the astral body of the medium oozes out, first as a slender thread, and then becomes, when the manifestation is *genuine,* what is now called "ectoplasm," really thickened astral stuff; and it is from the spleen that this astral body comes forth.

Then the heart, the organ of the god within us, of the divine-spiritual: here in the physical heart considered now as a spiritual organ — and not merely as a vital pump, which it is also — is the god within; not in person, but its ray touches the heart and fills it as it were with its auric presence — a holy of holies. Out of the heart come all the great issues of life. Here is where conscience abides, and love and peace and perfect self-confidence, and hope, and divine wisdom. Their seat is in the mystic heart of which the physical organ is the physical vital instrument.

The brain *as a whole* is the organ of the brain-mind, the field of activity of our ordinary reasoning, ratiocinative mentation by which we think ordinary and even higher thoughts, and by which also we go about our daily tasks. But connected with the brain are the two wonderful glands, the pineal and the pituitary, already mentioned. The pineal gland is as a casement opening out into infinite seas and horizons of light, for it is the organ that in us receives the direct *māhatic* ray, the ray direct from the cosmic intellect or *mahat.* It is the organ of inspiration, of intuition, of vision.

The heart is higher, because it is the organ of the individual's spiritual nature, including the higher manas or spiritual intellect. When the heart inflames the pineal gland and sets it vibrating rapidly, then so strong is the inflow of spiritual force that the man experiencing this has his very body clothed in an aureole of glory. A nimbus is behind his head, for as the pineal gland vibrates rapidly the inner eye is opened and sees infinity; and the aureole or nimbus is the energic outflow from this activity of the pineal gland.

The pituitary gland is the lieutenant of the pineal. It is the organ of will and hence also of automatic growth; the organ of will and urge and growth and impulse. But when the pineal sets the pituitary vibrating in synchrony with its own vibration, we have a god-man, for there is the intellect envisaging infinity. Then the divinity in the heart speaks and vibrates synchronously with the pineal gland, and the pituitary thus inspired to action of will, works through the other chakras or organs and makes the entire man a harmony of higher energies — relatively godlike!

All great spiritual leaders and teachers the world over, the great men-gods of the human race, have told us how to increase the vibration of the pineal gland in the skull. The first rule is to live as a true man. It is as simple as that. Do everything you have to do, and do it in accordance with your best. Your ideas of what is best will grow and improve. The next rule is to cultivate *specifically as units* the higher qualities which will make you superiorly human as contrasted with inferiorly human. Be just, be gentle, be forgiving, be compassionate and pitiful. Learn the wondrous beauty of self-sacrifice for others; there is something grandly heroic about it. Keep these things in your heart; believe that you have intuition; live in your higher being. When this can be kept up continuously so that it becomes your life, habitual to you, then the time approaches when you will become a man made perfect, a glorious Buddha. You will manifest the Immanent Christ within you, you will imbody it. There is the spiritual physiology of the whole matter.

The pineal gland was in earliest mankind an exterior organ of physical vision, and of spiritual and psychic sight.

But due to the evolutionary course that the human frame followed, as time passed on and our present two optics began to show themselves, the pineal gland or the "third eye," the "Eye of Śiva," the "Eye of Dangma," began to recede within the skull, which latter finally covered it with bone and hair. It then lost its function as an organ of *physical* vision, but has never ceased to continue its functions even now as an organ of spiritual sight and insight. When a man has a hunch, the pineal gland is commencing to vibrate gently. When a man has an intuition, or an inspiration, or a sudden flash of understanding, the pineal gland is beginning to vibrate still more strongly, albeit softly, gently. It functions still, and can be cultivated to function more, if we believe in ourselves and in our innate spiritual power.

As a matter of fact the pineal gland is connected with what will in time come to be our seventh sense. There are, according to the ancient wisdom, two more senses to be developed, making seven in all. It is a difficult thing to describe just what these senses will be, because as they are not yet existent and working in and through us as manifested activities, we have no names for these virtually nonexistent powers. The sixth sense might be described as psychic or psycho-spiritual sensitivity; just as touch is sensitivity of the skin. This psychic sensitivity does not mean knowing what everyone is thinking. It means impressionability, being subject to psychic impressions of many and various kinds, a sense therefore which can be very valuable, but likewise very treacherous and clothed with peril unless we be eternally on guard.

I think it is due to the infinite kindness of the gods above us that the sixth sense has not yet been developed. It is coming even now slowly into activity, very feebly as yet, but beginning to show itself; and this accounts for the large number of so-called psychics in the world, who are *as a rule,* because of the lack of common human moral development, unsteady people. Thus, if that sense were to come to us now in its fullness, it would be a gift such as that given to Hercules. It might burn us to death like the robe of the centaur Nessus. We are not yet sufficiently developed ethically to carry a sense like that with safety to us, to our sanity, to our health, and highest of all, to our duty to our fellow human beings.

The seventh sense I would call the development of interior, instant, spiritual cognition, intuition, as far as it can be developed in us human beings in this round on this globe. Its organ, the Eye of Śiva, or "third eye," should more correctly be called the "first eye," because it preceded the other two, and should not be spoken of as though it came in as a lame and limping third. It is, as said, even today partially functional, but it has very hard going, mainly due to the work of the two eyes which overcame it. As time passes the two eyes will grow slowly more perfect in function, but will recede in importance; and the "first eye" will come again into its own. It did function in other rounds, during the third and even the second, weakly during the first; because during the first round the monads which we call egos now were then spiritual and semi-spiritual beings, as it were in a samādhic condition on this plane, practically unconscious; but — strange paradox — because of the functioning of this direct consciousness from within in those earliest beings, they had thoughts which embraced infinitude, with scarcely any exterior consciousness of the outside world. This same condition of the first round was repeated in the first race of this fourth round.

It is this Eye of Śiva which will function again one day as the organ of our seventh and highest sense. And when that time comes to pass it will unite in function with the heart; and when these two unite their fluids and energies, we have a perfected man.

17

THE WEISMANN THEORY

EVERY HUMAN BEING — and we are speaking now of the physical body — was in its origin a little cell, a living cell of microscopic size. As we all know, a cell is composed of two main parts, both formed of protoplasm, but differing in function: the general or larger body of the cell, the cytoplasm, and the smaller corpuscle within the cytoplasm, which is, so to say, its heart, called the nucleus, in which resides more particularly the plasm that initiates growth and development, and which August Weismann, of the University of Freiburg in Germany, called the germ plasm.

Weismann's theories had great vogue for some thirty or thirty-five years. When his doctrines are properly understood, we have some approximation to what the theosophical philosophy teaches insofar as the origination of evolutionary stocks is concerned, as well as of the origin of specific variation, which our modern biologists say is the real method or mechanical procedure, if we can use that term, of the working of evolution. Dr. Peter Chalmers Mitchell of Oxford, Cambridge, and London, considers Weismann's theory of the continuity of the germ plasm to be "among the most luminous and most fertile contributions of the 19th century to biological thought, . . ."*

I am going to take Weismann's theory and supplement it with a very important factor which he has omitted because he knew nothing about it, and with this factor added we will have a fairly accurate picture of what theosophy teaches on this subject.

A cell is a house of life. Everything that you now are was, physically speaking, in that original cell. Your physical body is the growth of that cell. It has grown into being you, each such cell into one of you. How did it grow? It grew by division, by self-multiplication and, above everything else, by cell specialization. It is precisely and especially on this ground of cell specialization that rests the main foundation of what I am going to say.

Weismann taught that the vital portion of the nucleus of a cell resided in what the cytologists or cell specialists call chromatin. This substance, said Weismann, was the vital fountain of the nucleus of a cell, and given favorable circumstances starts its course of developmental growth after a particular manner.

Please understand that the cell which we are now discussing is the microscopic fertilized human ovum. When the ovum is fertilized then the cell begins to grow. This growth

---

*Encyclopaedia Britannica, XIth ed., p. 350.

Weismann was at one time a fervent Darwinist. Later he became an equally fervent anti-Darwinist. He had learned more than he knew in his younger days when he elaborated his germ plasm theory, and as he was an honest and courageous man, he risked even the ridicule and the derision and obloquy that scientific men of necessity have to face if they dare to take any stand different in large degree from the popular theories — in his case, of biological or evolutionary development — of the times in which they live.

proceeds in the following manner: a cell divides into two cells, following the initial proceeding of the division of its nucleus. These two cells then proceed to follow precisely the same course that the original cell did, each one of the two divides into two; and this course of division and self-multiplication continues indefinitely, at least until full growth of the entity to be has been attained.

Thus then, we have the original ovum, which is one cell, the original cell; then two cells; then four, eight, sixteen cells, and so forth — the division and self-multiplication proceeding coincidentally with cell specializations, until the body has reached its full growth, containing cells to the number of many trillions.

It would seem to be likewise the truth that even after the body has attained full growth, the cells continue their divisions and self-multiplications in order to keep the body around a certain normal of form and weight, circumstances being propitious; but this division after full maturity would seem to be somewhat different in results from those divisions which took place when the body was in process of developing into adulthood.

As already said, in each such cell lie all the potentialities of the human to be in the future; yet what is it which governs or controls the labor of the protoplasmic substance of the entire aggregate of cells as it grows into the various organs of the body to be? What is it in that original cell which makes it divide itself in particular ways as growth proceeds; that makes it specialize itself, so that of the trillions of daughter cells some become the cells of the heart, some the cells of the brain, some the cells of the spleen, or the skin, the bones, the muscles, or whatnot? To this wonderful question no confident answer has ever been returned.

Biologists know only this: that we are built of cells and that these cells always follow the same course, given favorable circumstances.

The human species produces children of the human species; the cells belonging to the body of any particular beast produce offspring identic with that particular variety or species of beast. In each case, there is the same amazing division of the cell life of the daughter cells into separate organs; there is the same marvelous specializing of the cell life into this, that, or the other part of the body. What is the directing power behind all this that guides the working out of such a marvel as we see the human body to be?

Weismann observed that the chromatin granules which form the vital part of a cell resolve themselves during cellular division into what he called *idants,* which he identified with the chromosomes; and of these chromosomes it is now well known that there are a definite number for each species. In this connection, he further taught that the *idants* are in turn a collection or aggregate of what he called *ids,* and each of these *ids* again is a veritable microcosm, determining the characters both specific and generic, as well as individual, of the entity to be. The class, the order, the family, the genus, the species, the variety, the individual, were all wrapped up in potency, as potentialities, in each one of these *ids.*

Further, these *ids* in their turn had each one a particular "historic architecture," he said; or, what amounts to the same thing, a particular biologic group of impulses or urges or characteristics which were the fruitage of past evolutionary activity. That is to say, its powers and function had been built into the form and type that they possess by the vast numbers of generations preceding the individual cell of the present day, in which these *ids* live.

Next, taught Weismann, each such *id* or microcosm in its turn consisted of minor or subordinate vital units, which he called *determinants,* because these are the particular parts of the *id* or microcosm which determine all parts of the body subject to variation — determining, indeed, or perhaps evolving or governing, the evolution of the specific organs of the future body, i.e., all the organs which in their turn are subject to variation, such as the heart, liver, spleen, etc. These *determinants* again, he said, were built up of hypothetical corpuscles still more minute which he called *biophores,* a Greek compound word meaning "life carriers."

Now, as is well known, each individual to be begins its career as a nucleated fertilized cell, a portion of the germ plasm of one parent — or of the two parents in the case of the present method of reproduction among humans and most of the lower creatures as well. The nucleus of this cell contains the essential germ plasm, composed of chromatin, which in turn is formed into idants (chromosomes), which are collections of ids, the ids in their turn formed of determinants and the determinants of biophores. As growth by food absorption and other means takes place, as multiplication proceeds, each one of the energies resident in and forming the particular characteristic of each one of these things, ids, determinants, and biophores, springs into action and begins its own particular labor.

As the body grows, it is the determinants that from the beginning outline and finally form the various organs, each such determinant assembling or marshaling to its appropriate organ, or organs, of the entity into which the cell is growing, the appropriate portion of the germ plasm which is itself.

Weismann further taught that man's body is composed of

two kinds or varieties of living plasm: a somatic plasm or body plasm, and a germ plasm. A part of the germ plasm which originates all the activities which follow its fertilization, is passed on unchanged and undeveloped from parent to offspring, lying latent, as it were, until the call for a similar activity of entities to be. This amounts to saying that a certain portion of the germ plasm is passed from the parent to offspring in a state of latency, and is not used in the building of the body of the parent nor of the offspring to be, which in turn transmits it to *its* offspring. Otherwise stated, we have in our body as germ plasm the identical substance that was in the bodies of our remotest ancestors, which has come down to us in this fashion and which provides the material for the growth of each generation, as called for according to the theoretic outline of cellular activity which Weismann has set forth.

This carrying on of the germ plasm from parent to offspring through numberless generations is a most interesting and fertile subject of thought. It means that in our bodies exists the very germ plasm that existed in the most distant of our progenitors; so that, for instance, our first race, physically speaking, even yet lives in us, because the plasm of its body has come down through the vast multitudes of our progenitors to our own bodies. We carry in our bodies today the very germ plasm which first came into being from the astral realms, and which lived in that first race, and which has been transmitted down to our own time through all the races to the fifth, our present one.

This immortality of the germ plasm, as it has been frequently called, descends through the ages from parent to offspring, the determinants in each generation marshaling to each appropriate organ of the body that part of the living plasm which goes to form it. The germinal or reproductive part of the germ plasm is assembled or marshaled to the reproductive organs of the new individual. A portion of this plasm is unutilized in each generation, and is marshaled as the body grows to the proper organs of the new generation; and a portion of this springs into activity when the time comes for it so to do — the portion thus springing into activity originating anew the same cycle of activities already described.

That portion of the germ plasm of the cell, that portion of the nucleus, which is not carried over to the offspring in a state of dormancy — i.e., all the rest of the germ plasm remaining in the cell — springs into activity and proceeds to build by multiplication and specialization the body of the individual to be. We see here two portions of the cell: the sleeping or dormant portion of the germ plasm carried over through generation to generation; and the kinetic or active part of the germ plasm which proceeds to form the body of the individual into whom the cell will develop.

So far we have been speaking of the nucleus or the germ plasm; but the protoplasm of the other part of the cell, which Weismann calls the somatic plasm, is used in part as food by the reproductive germ, and in part for the building up of the general body. This constructive work of the somatic plasm proceeds coincidently with the disintegration of the ids which are left over and are not used in the manner aforesaid. Each one of the other ids of the kinetic portion of the germ plasm, as the cell proceeds in its division, no longer forms an aggregated reproductive corpuscle, but disintegrates in that respect. This does not mean that they disintegrate in the sense of going to pieces, or becoming inferior, or in the sense of decay or death; but in the sense of their breaking up their unity and losing the particular faculty of *self*-development. Instead of that line of labor, they become a simpler protoplasm, the somatic plasm, and their energies are turned to building the body.

To restate the principal points: each id is an aggregate of determinants, and when any such id disintegrates in the manner outlined above, the individual development or reproductive faculty of it is thereby lost; the individual determinants then spring into activity and, as growth proceeds, the particular determinants in each id are marshaled to their proper place and organ of the growing body. The heart receives all the heart-determinants, the liver all the liver-determinants, the brain all the brain-determinants, and so forth; each receives the aggregate of determinants from all the daughter cells which belong to it. Thus is the physical body built.

This explains more explicitly than the general remarks made earlier* why it is that a part amputated from the body of the higher creatures will no longer grow into a new individual, as happens in the cases of certain of the lower creatures. The respective ids in the human body as at present developed have lost their individual reproductive faculty of self-development and remain, as it were, but a collection of determinants.

As another eminent German biologist points out, we should not believe that it is the mere aggregation or collection of cells which, through their absorption of food and by their division and growth and multiplication, originate and make the body. It is rather the individual body which forms and makes the cells; and this is precisely the teaching of theosophy.

---

*Cf. ch. 12, p. 140, "Man the Repertory of All Types."

The first or originating cell is the root of the body. As it grows, the latent powers and potencies of the entity seeking incarnation begin to work upon the plasmic substances, and it is that inner entity which governs and controls the growth of the cells which form its body to be.

This teaching of Weismann is in some sense a partial reversion to the biological thought of the eighteenth and seventeenth centuries, but it is so much more comprehensive, it appeals so much more to our logical faculties, that we see it as a truly constructive theory of growth. And although we cannot accept it in all details, the general principles that he enunciated are singularly close to the theosophic doctrine.

Let me point out further that while Weismann's theory is a returning, in some respects, to the biologic thought of the eighteenth and seventeenth centuries, this does not mean that the extravagances which those earlier theories involved and which were taught by Charles Bonnet and Robinet, otherwise great men, are endorsed in any manner, either by Weismann or by theosophists.

These men taught the doctrine of encasement or incapsulation, meaning that all future offspring were carried in the reproductive plasm of man's earliest ancestor or ancestors. Those who taught that all future generations were carried in the substance of the ovum of the mother were called Ovulists; while those who thought on the contrary that all the future generations were carried in the cells of the male parent, called themselves Animalculists. These theories are all more or less extravagant, and in some instances took rather curious forms.

Hartsoeker taught that there was a mannikin seated in the head of the male cell, and that when it fertilized the ovum, the mannikin gradually grew to human size. This of course is wrong, in some respects truly grotesque; but incorrect as the conception is, it is a very remarkable intuition of the fact of the inner incarnating being striving to incarnate through its overshadowing of the cellular potencies, striving to express itself — not a mannikin sitting in the head of the cell, and growing to human size, which is absurd, but the outward flowing of the inner life forces derived from the reincarnating entity, through the cell substance.

To return to the Weismann theory: why is it that one portion of the cell should lie dormant and be carried over to the offspring, and another portion of the cell should proceed to build from its protoplasmic contents the body of the individual which it is destined to form? So far as I know, biologic science has no answer at all to this; but theosophy offers as reason the action of the law of acceleration and retardation, which means that when any dominant power appears, all subordinate parts become subservient to it, or sleeping. The dominant or active parts move into accelerated action; while the dormant parts are retarded.

The reason again why the X-portion of the germ plasm should be carried over dormant, and the Y-portion should proceed to form the body, lies in the great fact — unknown to Weismann — of the activity of the astral fluid of the dhyān-chohan. The actual truth is that any cell, although destined to grow into one individual, is, like that individual, composite of a host of inferior lives, and that particular unit-life of the host which is the dominant in the aggregate, due to the influence of the incarnating astral fluid, is the one which controls the nuclear protoplasmic portion of the cell, and governs the building of the body.

At this point let me quote part of an extremely able

résumé from the *Encyclopaedia Britannica* contributed by the British zoologist, Dr. Peter C. Mitchell.* After he outlines the general scheme of idants, ids, determinants, and biophores, which last, by the way, he says "become active by leaving the nucleus of the cell in which they lie, passing out into the general protoplasm of the cell and ruling its activities," he further elucidates Weismann's theory:

The reproductive cell gives rise to the new individual by continued absorption of food, by growth, cell-divisions and cell-specializations. . . . The germ-plasm has grown in bulk without altering its character in any respect, and, when it divides, each resulting mass is precisely alike. From these first divisions a chain of similar doubling divisions stretches along the "germ-tracks," so marshalling unaltered germ-plasm to the generative organs of the new individual, to be ready to form the germ-cells of the next generation. In this mode the continuity of the germ-plasm from individual to individual is maintained. This also is the immortality of the germ-cells, or rather of the germ-plasm, the part of the theory which has laid so large a hold on the popular imagination, . . .

With this also is connected the celebrated denial of the inheritance of acquired characters. It seemed a clear inference that, if the hereditary mass for the daughters were separated off from the hereditary mass that was to form the mother, at the very first, before the body of the mother was formed, the daughters were in all essentials the sisters of their mother, and could take from her nothing of any characters that might be impressed on her body in subsequent development. In the later elaboration of his theory Weismann has admitted the possibility of some direct modification of the germ-plasm within the body of the individual acting as its host.

The mass of germ-plasm which is not retained in unaltered form to provide for the generative cells is supposed to be employed for the elaboration of the individual body. It grows, dividing and multiplying, and forms the nuclear matter of the tissues of the individual, but the theory supposes this process to occur in a peculiar fashion.

---

*Article on "Heredity," XIth ed., vol. 13, p. 351.

The writer then proceeds to show that the disintegration of this part of the germ plasm takes place according to the historical or biological architecture of the plasm:

each division differentiating among the determinants and marshalling one set into one portion, another into another portion. . . . The theoretical conception is, that when the whole body is formed, the cells contain only their own kind of determinants, and it would follow from this that the cells of the tissues cannot give rise to structures containing germ-plasm less disintegrated than their own nuclear material, and least of all to reproductive cells which must contain the undisintegrated microcosms of the germ-plasm. Cases of bud-formation and of reconstructions of lost parts are regarded as special adaptations made possible by the provision of latent groups of accessory determinants, to become active only on emergency.

It is to be noticed that Weismann's conception of the processes of ontogeny is strictly evolutionary, . . . and from the theoretical point of view his theory remains strictly an unfolding, a becoming manifest of hidden complexity.

You have seen from what I have said previously that, whereas this theory may seem in some respects no different from that of the old materialism, it is different in one very significant way: the conception of the particular drive and urge behind each one of these inner faculties or powers of the cell which Weismann places in the idants, and individually and particularly in the ids. And to complete the doctrine, theosophy adds to the innate life working in the cell, which Weismann has outlined, what is called the astral fluid of the incarnating entity.

Each cell is a vital organ. It is connected with heaven knows how many possibilities of becoming the initial step in the growth of some entity seeking reincarnation. In former periods of geological time, when the human stock was still young and unsettled in its courses, each of the cells of the then physical body of a human entity could under certain circumstances produce not solely a human being, but if detached from the human dominant influence, might readily grow into some inferior creature. And here is the hint of the truth of what I have formerly spoken of when suggesting the manner in which the entire stocks of the beast world were produced from the human stock.

In our days this procedure can no longer take place. The cells are too tightly held in the dominant grip of the human astral fluid, and hence it is that a human cell will produce a human being, and a human being only. The reproductive cells of the various beasts will produce each one after its own kind, and only after its own kind; while in the vegetable kingdom the reproductive cells of a rose, for instance, will produce a rose and only a rose; and those of a lily will produce only lilies, and so forth.

It amounts to this: the reproductive germ or cell of any stock is the physical expression of an entity preparing or rather seeking reimbodiment, and the astral fluid of this incarnating entity, mixing with the vital activities of the cell, becomes the directing power. I have used the words "astral fluid," but in view of force and matter being fundamentally one, I might as readily and as accurately have said astral forces. They are forces to us on our plane; but on the plane of the reincarnating entity they are a fluid or fluids.

Therefore, this astral fluid mixing with the vital activity of the cells, becomes the dominant or directing power, carrying with it into the cell activity its own larger urge, and thus becoming, as it were, the directing intelligent power in each one of the many divisions in the multiplication of the cell as it grows in bulk and as it specializes. The resultant of these combined activities is that the astral fluid, working through and in conjunction with the vital capacities and potentialities of the cell, produces the body of man.

The building of the body of man is a mystery to the unthinking, and a wonder to the thoughtful; and yet, as already said, marvelous engine as our body is from the physical standpoint, it is as nothing in comparison with the supernal wonders belonging to the real man within and above that body, belonging to man's astral and emotional, and psychic, and intellectual natures. And still more sublime is the splendor of the spirit. Man links himself in his present life mostly with the astral and emotional and psychic parts of his nature, because his higher faculties, his higher powers, the intellectual and the spiritual, are not yet able fully to self-express themselves through more perfect vehicles than those he has up to the present evolved; but those more perfect vehicles will be formed in due time.

As time, that resistless river of events, flows on, our bodies will become more refined, more fit, more capable of self-expressing what is within; all our hopes and aspirations will then find fit and appropriate vehicles through which they may work. All this will come to pass, for the destiny of man on earth is a noble and beautiful one. So far as his physical body is concerned, he never was a beast, nor did he ever come from the beasts. On the contrary, they came from him as a primitive human physical form.

In his origin man was an unself-conscious god-spark, a spark, as it were, of the central Fire; but that spark, through its own inner drive and urge, seeking self-unfoldment in aeon following upon aeon, originated at various times bodies for itself through which it worked, in which it lived, learning life's lessons and thus training its powers for perfecting a better vehicle in the next and succeeding imbodiments.

Thus we are all children of the universe. Every one of us is an incarnate divinity in our inmost parts, having powers and faculties, potentialities seeking expression. How can we help ourselves in this most noble of adventures? What hinders us from doing this instinctively? Two things mainly. The first is selfishness which beclouds our vision; and thus we fail to cultivate the universal sympathy inherent in our souls. The second hindrance is self-identification with the lower vehicles — the psychic, emotional, and physical bodies in which we live and work. This latter defect of ours is perhaps the worse of the two, though the former, selfishness, is the root of the latter. The latter is the worse mistake in the sense that by identifying ourselves with our bodies, and by false emotional identification of the divine spiritual fire within us with the passional flames in which our physical bodies so often burn, we actually for the time being become one with these bodies.

This identification of our consciousness with the mortal vehicle causes the temporary loss of our self-consciousness at death, when that mortal vehicle disintegrates, and we fail to keep that consciousness from birth to birth or from death to death, as we could if we had trained ourselves to live wholly in our higher natures with their universal fields of thought. Instead, we live in our lower natures, and therefore falsely identify ourselves with those lower natures. Hence of necessity we participate in the vibrational rates of the emotions and of the feelings and of the lower physical fires that belong there.

This truth is so simple that a child can understand it: the choice between an alliance with the god within, or with the beast that the body is.

18

KARMA AND HEREDITY

KARMA IS A companion doctrine to reincarnation. The one
without the other is meaningless. It is the law of consequences, sometimes called the law of cause and effect; yet
more strictly speaking, it is the operation of effects or consequences, for *karman* is a Sanskrit word meaning "action"
— as cause plus effect.

The originating cause is the consciousness of the individual who acts upon nature; nature reacts against that action
upon it, and that reaction ensues immediately or at a later
date, or even in a future incarnation of the original actor,
or in a still more remote imbodiment of that actor in a garment of flesh. When the proper opening appears, when the
links, so to say, are ready, when the doors open to the
entrance of the forces of nature constituting that reaction,
then it comes. And the individual may say: "My God! What
have I done that I should suffer so? I know no reason for
it." Or, on the other hand, he may exclaim: "Immortal Gods!
What have I done that my destiny should be so great?
I remember nothing in my life causing it! There is no consciousness in me of meriting this, or of seeing my fellow

obtain that other destiny through demerit. Yet I recognize, since this is a universe of law and order, that it could have come to me not otherwise than as a reward for merit; nor the suffering of my unfortunate friend except as a just recompense for demeritorious action."

Our philosophic friend in this case would likewise readily recognize the fact that although his own karma is physically "good" it will not remain so if he selfishly live in it and take no thought of his brother's misery. The best karma that can possibly be made by any human being is that which follows on recognition, and consequent appropriate action, of the fact of his intrinsic kinship with all other men, this feeling and sense of unity urging him to work to alleviate suffering and sorrow wherever they are found.

Karma is in reality character. It is that which a man has made himself to become, not just in the one life, but throughout the succession of lives which the invisible entity, *the man himself*, undertakes in his progressive evolution. This process involves the working out of karmic effects and explains the problem of heredity as no modern biologic theory has been able to do.

Certain Western scientists in the last century have dealt vaguely with the exoteric Buddhist doctrines of reimbodiment and karma, believing them to be on all fours with the then latest teachings of biological science as regards man's physical nature and his destiny. This parallelism came about because they misunderstood just what the Buddhist doctrines were. Haeckel was chiefly responsible for this presentation, brought about as a result of one of his Oriental journeys and his contact with the Buddhist priest Sumangala, the head of the Southern school of Buddhism in Ceylon.

However, Haeckel gave to the Buddhist doctrine a meaning too limited, too restricted, applying its terms to man's physical body only; whereas these two noble old Buddhist doctrines of karma and reimbodiment apply to man's character, to his *skandhas,* which are his psychological, mental, emotional and physical attributes.

Again, Huxley, one of the greatest biologists of his time, perhaps one of the greatest that Britain has ever produced, in his book *Evolution and Ethics,* printed in London in 1894, appears to speak — champion of materialistic biology though he was — as a believer in reincarnation. But his words in no sense imply an acceptance of the doctrine of reimbodiment as theosophy outlines it. He says:

> Everyday experience familiarizes us with the facts which are grouped under the name of heredity. Every one of us bears upon him obvious marks of his parentage, perhaps of remoter relationships. More particularly, the sum of tendencies to act in a certain way, which we call "character," is often to be traced through a long series of progenitors and collaterals. So we may justly say that this 'character' — this moral and intellectual essence of a man — does veritably pass over from one fleshly tabernacle to another, and does really transmigrate from generation to generation.   — p. 61

Huxley is here speaking of the biological doctrine that a man passes on to his offspring his own characteristics, not merely of body but also his psychic tendencies, for these characteristics are supposed to lie latent in the germ plasm, in other words, in the reproductive cells which father and mother pass on to their children; and that it is in this something — what shall we call it? — in this "character" as Huxley calls it, in this purely materialistic aggregate of tendencies, that lie all that a man later becomes.

It is perfectly true that this aggregate of physical and psychical characteristics and tendencies actually does, as

Huxley said, transmigrate from the parent to the offspring; and "transmigrate" is exactly the proper term to use here. We say that it is the life-atoms, or rather a portion of the life-atoms in a lower state of evolution, which do transmigrate from parent to offspring, for these particular life-atoms are they *which inform and vitalize the transmitted* germ plasm.

Yet all this comprises not even a tithe of what is implied in the theosophical doctrine of reincarnation.

Huxley continues:

In the new-born infant, the character of the stock lies latent, and the Ego is little more than a bundle of potentialities. But, very early, these become actualities; from childhood to age they manifest themselves in dulness or brightness, weakness or strength, viciousness or uprightness; and with each feature modified by confluence with another character, if by nothing else, the character passes on to its incarnation in new bodies.   — Ibid., pp. 61–2

The biologists of Haeckel's and Huxley's day said, in effect: "We don't know how this transmission of physical and psychic tendencies is brought about, but we do know that it takes place; and this is what we call heredity. Heredity is a fact. The son and the daughter do resemble their parents to some extent at least, and even their parents still more remote than their immediate progenitors. This is what we know; and we must find out how this comes to pass."

Now the above is indeed a statement of a part of heredity, but only a subordinate part. It belongs to that aspect of it which involves the transmission of the vehicles preparing for incoming souls, and this is accomplished, as I have just said, by the passing of the atoms of life, the life-atoms of a lower grade, through their transmigration from parent to offspring.

Transmigration,* I may say in passing, covers a field of thought much wider than this. It has to do with the life-atoms composing the various vehicles in which man clothes himself — not merely his physical body. These vehicles are his sheaths of consciousness, the veils of his understanding; for remember that man possesses various bodies ranging from the spiritual to the physical, these bodies being on the different planes in which and on which he lives and moves and has his being and works out his destiny.

We are apt to think even in our day, on account of our continued subjection to the old materialistic doctrines of a bygone age, that when we speak of "man" the only mean-ing of the word is his physical encasement, his body alone. This body is a part of man truly, but the lowest, the most material part of him, the objective part. The real man is that spiritual entity, that sublime being, which is the root of his consciousness and which judges and intuits, has aspirations, and therefore aspires and has realization of things. In fact, it is his essential consciousness, what we call the spiritual soul.

To return to Huxley's comments: "The Indian philos-ophers called character, as thus defined, 'karma'" (ibid., p. 62). So they did; but Huxley's interpretation is but one small aspect of the great doctrine of karma.

The action of karma finds place on all the planes — most of them interior and invisible — with which man's inner constitution is linked: spiritual, intellectual, psychical, emo-tional, astral, prānic, and physical; including, in short, all the various encasements or vestures in which man lives on

---

*This subject is extensively dealt with by me in *The Esoteric Tradition,* chs. xxv and xxvi.

these various planes, and which ensheath the glory which man is in his spiritual nature. And of this glory, we in our physical brain-workings get but a faint reflection, somewhat as the moon gets a faint reflection of the glory of the sun and transmits it as moonlight to our earth.

Huxley, then, sets forth with graphic truth the biologic karma merely of the body, as transmitted as effect from parent to offspring, through the working of the aggregate of the lower life-atoms, in their preparing of vehicles for incoming souls *of similar tendencies, of similar character.*

Huxley adds the following note to his remark on karma quoted above:

> In the theory of evolution, the tendency of a germ to develop according to a certain specific type, *e.g.* of the kidney bean seed to grow into a plant having all the characters of *Phaseolus vulgaris,* is its 'Karma.' It is the "last inheritor and the last result" of all the conditions that have affected a line of ancestry which goes back for many millions of years to the time when life first appeared on the earth. . . . As Prof. Rhys Davids aptly says (in *Hibbert Lectures,* p. 114), the snowdrop "is a snowdrop and not an oak, and just that kind of snowdrop, because it is the outcome of the Karma of an endless series of past existences." — Ibid., p. 95

Just so; the teaching concerning this tendency of a germ to develop into a certain specific type is nothing new. It is an old, old conception. The school of the Stoics in Greece and Rome expressed it as being the operation of what they called the spermatic logos, the *logos spermatikos,* that is to say, the "seed-logos," what we may call the character-logos, the consciousness-logos; in other words, that particular and individual part of the constitution of any entity which is its specific character. It is this *logos spermatikos* which makes the rose produce a rose always, and nothing but a rose;

which makes the hen's egg bring forth a chick and nothing but a chick; which makes the kidney-bean seed grow into a kidney-bean plant.

Yet as Huxley interprets all these teachings, he is merely touching upon the heredity of the physical body; and true though his statements are they fail to take into account the astral directive matter-force of the incarnating entity. Taking this factor into account, we have as it were a thumbnail sketch of the whole doctrine of the process of reincarnation.

What then is heredity from the standpoint of the theosophical student? No clearheaded thinker will or indeed can feel satisfied with what the scientific theorists have written concerning it; and the proof of this statement lies in the fact that heredity is still under examination, and the question is still constantly asked: What, after all, *is* heredity? It is unquestionable that children take after parental and ancestral types. Nobody denies the fact. What we call heredity is simply the carrying on from generation to generation of certain traits or biases or peculiarities or deformities or symmetries from father to son to son to son. But when one examines all the scientific ideas about heredity one finds that the scientists are not giving any explanations; they are merely describing a procedure of nature. But what are the causes behind this procedure?

Admitting then that the studies of heredity have shown the coming together of similar types in a family milieu, the theosophist points out that such assemblings of similar individuals is brought about by psychomagnetic attraction. The facts of heredity as they exist are no mere fortuitous or chance happenings, nor are they merely a mechanical process, but they are the consequences of likes attracted to likes; and reincarnation is the means by which such aggregating similarities of character in a family are brought about. Thus ABC, GHI, XYZ, are all individuals with characters resembling each other, and consequently sympathy arises amongst these — what we call attraction. These egos, therefore, drawn by such psychomagnetic attraction to each other, incarnate or take imbodiment in the same family milieu; and thus we have a picture of what scientists call heredity passing on from generation to generation.

It is attraction which brings people together. When the entity is ready to reincarnate, it is drawn psychomagnetically, instinctually if you like, to the family, to the womb, most sympathetic to its vibrational rate. Thought and reflection, study and examination, will show you that the immense likelihood is that you will be attracted to the family milieu, to the family environment, which offers you the closest vibrational rate to your own. Your vibrational rate has less difficulty in synchronizing with the vibrational rate of that family than with some other. Characters, therefore, find imbodiment in families which are most like the character of the imbodying ego. And here we have the real reason for similarities of character types in families. It is not the parents who give the traits to the child. It is the child, *bearing these traits within himself,* that is attracted by sympathy of vibrational rates to the parents who will give him a body best fitted to express the character he already possesses *in potentia;* and thus the general family type of character is continued, though with constant modifying variations.

Thus it is the imbodiment in generation after generation of any single family strain, of egos already possessing similarities bringing these similarities into earth life, and carrying them in and through such family, which brings about the phenomenon called "heredity." And this is as true of physical heredity as of psychic heredity, the life-atoms in every case, under the dominant urge of the different imbodying egos possessing similarities, more or less slavishly following these communal egoic sympathies or character traits.

Being a bit more specific, one may point out that the psycho-astral fluid emanating from the ego of the reincarnating entity flows through, permeates, washes all the life-atoms which build the cells with the latter's stock of chromosomes, genes, etc. — to use the scientific terms at present in fashion. And the dominant psychic power of the reimbodying or already reimbodied ego forces these emanated cellular bodies in conformity with its dominant urges. Here we see what we may call the physical explanation of how it is that similar egos in a family will produce similar patterns on invisible planes, in their turn producing similar consequences or results in the developing ovum-plus-sperm, which in their turn transmit physically to their descendant these likenesses of type.

We have seen, now, that character is not something given to the child by the parents, but is carried over from life to life of an imbodying entity and brought with it into earth life. How is this carrying-over brought about? The answer is to be found in a study of the skandhas. When a man dies he takes with him into the invisible worlds the essence of that character which he had been building for himself in the life just ended and in other lives before that. These attributes are called his skandhas, and they remain as seeds of unfulfilled impulses lying latent until the time comes when they shall have an opportunity for further flowering in the field of another earth life. The reincarnating entity attracts them together again as it descends anew through the portals of birth, and as the child grows they gradually manifest themselves as his personality, his biases, his tendencies, his

strengths and his weaknesses, in other words, the sum total
of the character of his "personality," to use a technical theosophical term, which must not be confused, however, with
the immortal individuality, the essential self or fecund root
of himself on all planes.

Now then, if all the above is true, how is it that children
born of the same parents sometimes differ not merely in
small degree but even in very noteworthy degree? In every
case it is *character* from other lives, to be sure, that is manifesting itself. But why does an ego sometimes find itself
born into a family to which it is entirely antipathetic? It
sometimes happens — and this is a paradox — that strong
antipathies actually attract each other, it being an old saying
of philosophically minded observers of nature that hatred
has its attractions as well as love. So that in a single family
we may see two or more children developing on the one
hand most affectionate sympathies for each other, or on the
other hand even violent antipathies. This is a fact of common human experience, and in every case the attraction is
due to one or another type of vibrational rates set up in
other lives by former association, which links certain individuals together by ineluctable karmic bonds.

It is an undoubted fact that in the small centers of nature's biologic group which we call the family, there is sufficient biologic urge for the children to resemble their parents,
or it may be the grandparents, or the great-grandparents;
yet think of the enormous differences that so often take place
in one family — demonstrating the even more powerful individual biologic or hereditary lines of unfolding life!

This fact of the common human blood stream flowing in
us all accounts also for the cases of those individuals not belonging to the same family who not only have psychological

traits and emotional biases which cement them into a close friendship, but who may even look more like each other than either one of these with the members of his own family.

In the last analysis we see that man inherits *from himself*. Heredity is character and character is heredity. And even in the case of the purely physical heredity, it can be said that man makes his own body, the parents merely providing the workshop and to some extent the materials with which it is built. The incarnating entity is the directing power behind the scenes. And environment is simply the magnetic field that we have chosen in which we may best work out those aspects of character which are the "dominant" for that particular incarnation.

Man is an individuality. He has free will. He is changing from day to day, from year to year, from life to life. He is not static. He is building now what his character will be in his next incarnation, and when that next incarnation arrives he will bring *himself* with him into the new life. He is thus his own heredity, his own character, his own karma.

19

LOST PAGES OF EVOLUTIONARY HISTORY

IT IS THE TEACHING of theosophy that evolution — or the unfolding, unwrapping, self-expressing, progressive growth of an entity — proceeds in cycles both large and small. Each great cycle or tidal wave of life which sweeps over our earth lasts on this planet Terra for scores of millions of years; and each such globe-round, as we call such a tidal wave of manifestation, during the course of its activity gives new birth to numerous great stocks of beings, ranging from elemental beings to those quasi-divine entities beyond mankind.

Some of these stocks or kingdoms of nature below man are well known to everyone: the beast or animal kingdom, the vegetable kingdom, the mineral kingdom. Below these are the three kingdoms of the elementals. These last kingdoms, those of the three classes of elemental beings, modern knowledge knows nothing of except in this respect, that it recognizes certain forces in nature. These three elemental kingdoms are the channels through which these natural forces pour into our earth and work in it and on and through it and hold its component parts together, being, as it were, the vital cement or energies of coherence which bind together the hosts and multitudes of hosts of the conscious and semi-conscious beings composing our earth. These are the elementals.

There are likewise three other kingdoms of entities far more progressed than man is, which are above him in the scale of evolutionary advancement. These three superior kingdoms are the dhyān-chohanic. They consist of spiritual beings who were all once, in far past ages, men also as we now are. They had passed through humanity to attain their present stage or status of dhyān-chohanhood. And it is the destiny of humans similarly to follow this same path of upward progress, the destiny of every individual of the human stock — if it prevail over the down-pulling forces of matter along its evolutionary pathway upwards — in the future to become itself a member of these three nobler stocks above mankind.

The ancients called these three stocks superior to man, gods. In modern times, I suppose, they would be called spirits; not, if you please, excarnate human entities to whom the noble term "spirit" is often grossly misapplied. But they are truly developed spiritual entities which we call monads.

These three kingdoms higher than man, which he is destined to join in future time, form the three stages of progress preceding other still more advanced hierarchies of beings, all evolving, all on the upward march, all ascending higher and still higher, illimitably in eternal duration — both in the past as it will be in the future — and finding their ineffably beautiful destiny in the boundless fields of spiritual space.

Each of these great stocks of beings produces entities of

its own kind, of its own capacities, each one having its own inherent drive or urge or tendencies. Each stock, in other words, has its own individuality, just as man has, or a beast, or a tree, or a flower, or any other stock.

Here we shall discuss that great stock which we call the human kingdom. First it should be understood that the origin of man, according to theosophy, was not what most scientists are accustomed to call monogenetic, that is, the origination of man from a single point of departure. The archaic wisdom-tradition does not teach of a primitive Garden of Eden, or of a single couple, an Adam and Eve who gave birth to the human race. This old Biblical mythos was symbolic, as the Qabbalistic Jews well knew, and should not be taken in its surface meaning or in its literal construction. Man's origin was not monogenetic but polygenetic or, to be more accurate, a modified polygenesis; that is to say, the various stocks which form the human race as an entity did not derive from one couple, but arose from several contemporaneous zoologic centers or points of departure, from groups living on different zones of the earth's surface, aeons and aeons and aeons ago in the far bygone geologic past.

As nearly as we can give dates (due to the imperfection and uncertainty of interpretation of the geologic record) by studying the story of the rocks we may put back the origins of the human kind into the so-called Paleozoic or Primary era of geology.* And this first race, this primordial race, composed of a number of subordinate individual strains, produced the various stocks which have descended even to our own day, albeit more or less mixed. These we may very

---

*We are here using H. P. Blavatsky's time scale of geologic eras. [See Appendix I.]

roughly classify today as the pinkish-brown or white race, the black, the yellow, and the copper-colored races — the only four which remain of those seven primitive origins, those seven primitive biologic points of departure.*

During all those long periods of development, which run back for scores of millions of years into the past, in the present globe-round the human stock necessarily passed through many varying forms, retaining, however, even from the beginning of true humans, the general type-plan of the human frame, yet varying greatly as it progressed and evolved towards a wider perfection with the passage of time down to our own day.

The evolutionary history of man is characterized by the development of what are called in theosophy root-races. The root-races preceding our own were four in number. We are the fifth; and each of these root- or stock-races had its own physical characteristics or specific features.

The first of these great races which appeared on our earth during the present globe-round was in its beginning a race of astral entities, ethereal, invisible they would be to us in our present state of gross materiality.

This first great race was sexless, and propagated itself by fission; that is to say, it divided into two, each such fission producing a new individual. Consequently the daughter of

---

*With regard to the various theories as to the origins of mankind, whether such be monogenetic or polygenetic, we quote again the eminent English anatomist, Professor Wood Jones, who writes in *The Problem of Man's Ancestry* as follows:

"That all the races of mankind did not arise from one common point of departure [i.e., ancestor] is a view which has already been advocated (notably in more recent times by Klaatsch). It is one that carries high probability, and one which merits the expenditure of a great deal more patient research."   — p. 41

such a fission was likewise the sister of its mother. That first great stock-race lasted for millions of years.

As time passed, and as the cycling race circled downwards farther into matter, seeking self-expression in the material world, this first root-race grew more solid, but it remained ethereal even to its end. It had no human shape such as we now understand it. Each of the individuals composing it was an ovoid body of light, luminous, pellucid, translucent. These individuals had neither organs nor bones.

Have you ever considered the gelatinous structure of the jellyfish, a medusa for instance? It may be to you perhaps a hint of something still more ethereal, still more luminous and translucent, than it. Life builds houses for itself of many forms and kinds, nor are bones and organs necessary for the templing of the vital entity.

When millions of years had passed, the second root-race came into being. This second race was less ethereal than its predecessor, for the races following each other in time grew constantly more material, more solid, more opaque, down to the fourth root-race.

The second root-race was asexual and reproduced itself by a method which is still represented on earth among some of the lower creatures, that is by "budding" or gemmation. From a particular part of the individual a small portion of the parent entity broke off and left its parent body — the mother, if you can use the term "mother" of an individual which had no sex at all. The offspring or bud left it somewhat as a spore will leave a plant, or as an acorn leaves the oak, this bud or small portion of the parent entity growing into an individual in all respects like to the parent from which it had separated itself.

Even as the individuals of the first race had separated

off from themselves a large portion of their body — which was that race's method of reproduction, as said — this large portion growing to the size of its parent and duplicating it in all ways, so the second race reproduced itself by what zoology and botany call budding. A swelling appeared on the superficial or outer surface of the body of one of these entities; this swelling grew in size, and as it grew became constricted near the point of junction with the parent body, until at length the bond of union became a mere filament which finally broke, thus freeing the bud, which then grew into another entity in all ways like its parent.

The second race was more material in physical structure, and more humanoid in appearance, than was the first, but it still was more or less translucent, although growing more opaque because more dense with the passage of every one hundred thousand years of its long life cycle, which comprised many millions of years.

Towards the end of this second great stock-race, which by that time had become still more viscidly gelatinous and filamentoid in structure (although it was as yet more or less ovoid in form), this race even then began to show some vague approximation in shape to the present human form. Its filamentoid structure likewise covered and guarded deeply seated nuclei within it, which were condensations of the general cell substance, and destined to develop in the next race into the various organs of the body.

When this race had run its course, lasting for many millions of years, then the third stock-race came into existence, still more physical than were the first and the second, and constantly thickening, the gelatinous substance of the second race having become flesh, but flesh more delicate, thin, and fine even than our own of the present fifth race.

Let me add here also that, like the first race, the second had neither bones nor flesh (therefore no skeleton), nor organs (therefore no physiological functions of any kind). Its circulations, such as they were, and they did exist, were carried on by what may be called osmosis combined with magnetic attractions and repulsions — for lack of better words to express the process — working in this fashion in the body-substance.

With the incoming of the third stock-race, the filamentoid structure thickened or condensed itself, and became the different parts of what is now the human body: the muscular system, the reticulum or network of the nervous system, and also the system of the blood vessels. The inner filamentoid parts, becoming cartilaginous as the third race traveled along its cyclic period, finally became bones; while the nuclei, which existed in the body-structure of the second race as merely adumbrated or foreshadowed organs, became now the true organs of the body of the third race, such as the heart, the lungs, the brain, the liver, the spleen, and so forth.

The method of reproduction of this third root-race was in its beginning androgynous or double-sexed; but about the middle period of this great third stock-race, hermaphroditism died out, and our present method of reproduction ensued.

As regards the question of hermaphroditism or androgynism, it is already an established fact in physical science that the same condition exists in some of the lower classes of animate entities now on earth. Practically all antiquity taught it as a fact that early man must have been bisexual, if for no other reason than because of the rudiments of organs which even present-day human beings possess — I mean rudiments of organs in the one sex which are more or less fully developed in the opposite sex, and vice versa.*

Quaint and curious as the story may now seem to us, accustomed as we are to think that our present method of reproduction is the only possible one, those very ancient human individuals reproduced themselves by laying eggs. The human germ cell even today is an egg, albeit microscopic. But in those days these eggs, in which the infants incubated and from which they finally issued, were of much larger size than is the case today.

To recapitulate: mankind first reproduced itself by fission in the first race; then by budding in the second race; then, in the beginning of the third race reproduction was insured by an exudation of vital cells, issuing from the superficial parts of the body, and which, collecting together, formed huge ovoid aggregates or eggs.

This method of reproduction is alluded to in the archaic teachings by the term "sweat-born," meaning not that this race reproduced itself by sweat literally, but by an exudation of vital substance or cells which issued from the body in somewhat the same fashion that sweat issues from the

---

*In his *Descent of Man,* Charles Darwin had the following to say:

"There is one other point deserving a fuller notice. It has long been known that in the vertebrate kingdom one sex bears rudiments of various accessory parts, appertaining to the reproductive system, which properly belong to the opposite sex; and it has now been ascertained that at a very early embryonic period both sexes possessed true male and female glands. Hence some remote progenitor of the whole vertebrate kingdom appears to have been hermaphrodite or androgynous."

And Mr. Darwin added as a footnote:

"This is the conclusion of Prof. Gegenbaur, one of the highest authorities in comparative anatomy; . . . Similar views have long been held by some authors, though until recently without a firm basis."
                                                    — Part I, ch. vi, p. 161

sudoriferous glands, or as the oily substance of the skin and hair issues from the sebaceous glands.

As time passed and the condensation of the bodies of the individuals of the third root-race became greater and more pronounced, this exudation of vital cells slowly passed from the outward or superficial parts of the body into the inner parts, becoming localized in certain organs which the process of evolution had been slowly forming for that purpose.

This method of reproduction in its general line is nature's way even today in our own fifth race, only it now takes place within the protecting wall of solid flesh and hard bone, which wall nature has built about the reproductive functions of our race for its greater safety. But essentially the procedure is exactly the same as it was in the early middle of the third root-race.

As time went by, during the life cycle of this third race, reproduction by egg laying by the parent died out or passed away, as a method of propagation. Whereas formerly the drops of vital fluid were exuded from nearly all parts of the body, as was the case at the end of the second root-race, more and more as time passed they localized themselves in a functional part of the organism which was the root of the later reproductive organs. These vital drops collected together and became the egg in which the human infant incubated for a few years, and finally issued from it, and began life safely, walking and moving even from the opening of the shell, much as a chick does today among us — a still living example of the old method.

Such was the method of reproduction in the third root-race at about the midpoint of its evolutionary course.

Another point of interest that I might mention in passing is that each of these root-races had its own continental system and islands on the face of the earth, had its own long-enduring cycle of life, and likewise its own physical appearance, albeit all of them, beginning with the third, possessed the general type of the human frame even as we now know it, and of which each later race became a more perfect expression.

Then at the end of the third race, there followed the great stock-race which we call the fourth, which was the most material of all in its physical development — that race in which matter reached its climax of evolution, its highest point of unfolding. All the powers of matter were then functioning in every direction, but spirit was correspondingly in obscuration.

This fourth race lived its millions of years and produced some of the most brilliant civilizations of a purely material character that this globe has seen. Finally it passed away in its turn, giving birth to the fifth root-race: to us, who are still men of flesh and bones and organs, still retaining the old method of reproduction, which nevertheless is destined to pass away in its turn, giving place to a newer and a higher method. For sex is but a passing phase, and the next great race will see its end.

Towards the middle of the third race there occurred the most marvelous and epoch-making event in the history of humanity; and this was the infilling of the unself-conscious humanity with mind and its godlike powers. From the geologic standpoint, that awakening of mind occurred at about the middle point of the Mesozoic era, which we may perhaps put at the beginning of the Jurassic epoch, when the kings of the earth were the gigantic reptilian monsters whose fossilized skeletons are so frequently found in the rocks of that era.

It was then that began the opening acts of the human drama which we call civilization; and in those remote days, even as early as the end of the third race, civilizations of real brilliancy succeeded each other in time, and have so lasted down to our own period.

The first race, though physically conscious, was yet mindless in a sense, that is to say not self-conscious as we understand self-consciousness. Its consciousness was somewhat of the nature of a man in a deep daze or a profound daydream. The individuals of that race had, as yet, no mental or intellectual or spiritual self-consciousness. Similarly was it with the second race.

The beasts today have no mental self-consciousness. All spiritual, intellectual, or psychological faculties that human beings possess are latent in the animals, but in them they are still nonfunctioning. In man only, at the present time, has the godlike function of self-conscious thought been awakened. That awakening will come to the animals below man; but because the door into the human kingdom has been closed for many ages, this awakening by them to human consciousness can come no longer in this period of planetary evolution. The animals will attain to it only in the next planetary manvantara or evolutionary great cycle, hundreds and hundreds of millions of years hence.

Nevertheless in a few of the higher animals, that is to say in the anthropoid apes, the divine powers of self-conscious thought are beginning to function in very minor degree. The reason is that the anthropoid apes are an exception in the evolutionary development of the stocks below man, in that they have a strain of human blood in them, which like everything else is inevitably destined to work out its own inherent capacities. Their minds are dormant, but it is hoped that the monads now indwelling in the bodies of these apes will have developed a true human albeit imperfect psychological apparatus of self-expression, i.e., of self-consciousness, before the present planetary manvantara or great planetary evolutionary cycle is completed.

Please bear in mind, however, that when we call man of the first and second great races a mindless being, we do not mean that he was a beast. We mean only that the latent mind had not yet been aroused to function, through the partial incarnation in the waiting human individuals of godlike beings perfected in a preceding evolutionary period, billions of years before the present. The man of that early period, though mindless, possessed consciousness of a kind; he was, as said, in a sense like a man in a daze or in a daydream, deep, complete.

Towards the end of the third race there occurred the awakening of mind; and this happened very largely by the incarnation in these now ready human vehicles of godlike beings, who had run their race and had attained quasi-divinity in far past preceding planetary periods of cyclic evolution. These godlike beings projected, by hypostasis, sparks, as it were, of their own full self-consciousness into the childlike humanity of that time, thus awakening also the latent native mental powers that had lain dormant or sleeping in the recipient humanity.

Whence came mind? Have you ever thought of it, of its wondrous mystery, of its power, of its illimitable possibilities, of its inherent connection with self-consciousness? Does any sane man really believe that self-conscious mind comes from what the old school of materialists called dead, unvitalized, unimpulsed, unurged matter alone?

Very few of the thinking men of today have no conception of some kind or other of the nature of self-conscious mind. The conception may be perhaps vague and inchoate; but it does represent some striving towards a rational and satisfying explanation of this most wondrous part of the constitution of man. Their longing to reach some explanation of what is to them the problem — whence came mind and consciousness, whence came self-consciousness? — must in the very nature of things find an answer, because that longing is an intuition of reality.

With this coming of mind through the incarnation of these godlike beings into the intellectually senseless human vehicles of the middle third root-race, came likewise the main characteristic of self-conscious intelligence which is, briefly, the steadily growing sense of moral and intellectual responsibility. It was at this point of the incarnation of the "Sons of Mind" or *mānasaputras,* to use the Sanskrit term, that man first became on this earth the truly self-conscious, morally responsible being he now is; although indeed, it is of course true that mankind has evolved since that now far-distant epoch of the past.

Because of this incarnation of mind, men became conscious of their kinship not only with the hierarchies surrounding them in all nature, but they recognized their spiritual unity with the gods; and from then on they began to understand that the direction of their own future karma or destiny lay in their own hands. At first almost instinctively, but as time passed with ever-growing self-realization, they understood that they were thenceforth collaborators with the divinities, and the hierarchies of beings below the divinities, in the enormous cosmic labor.

What a picture such realization brought! What immense sense, thenceforth, of human dignity must have entered into their souls! For this greater sense of self-identity with the *paramātman* of the universe, with the cosmic spirit, provided vistas of future evolutionary grandeur which as of now man dreams of but has not yet even intellectually fully realized.

It was to this awakened humanity of the later third root-race that were given certain teachings which have been ever since in the guardianship of great men, true seers, who have penetrated behind the veil of physical matter and who, in addition, have received a body of teaching about man and the universe that today we call the ancient wisdom. This body of teaching stems back to those archaic days when spiritual beings from other and higher planes than ours consorted with the human race of that time; and it has descended in unbroken line from teacher to teacher even to our own day.

As we reflect over the evolutionary picture which we have thus far drawn in this and in preceding chapters, we realize that man is essentially composite of heaven and earth, as the ancient saying runs; and because he is a child of the universe, part spirit, part animal, therefore is he likewise a child of destiny — of that destiny which he himself is building with every breath that he draws.

Man is a child of nature. Nature has not so much "given" him his faculties by and in which he works, as he has them de facto as being a child of nature. They are not a gift; they are not a development of something outside himself which has come to him; nor are they merely produced by man's reaction upon something else in nature. They are innate in him. *They are he himself.* They form his destiny by evolving out.

And what is this destiny that man is slowly through the ages evolving? It is contained in those two noble sayings of the Christian scriptures: Know ye not that ye are gods, and that the spirit of the Divine dwelleth within you? For verily each one of you is a temple of the divinity (John 10:34; I Cor. 3:16).

These sayings to many have become a mere phraseology — pious ejaculations and little more — because the spiritual sense lying in the words has been forgotten. Yet they have become favorites on account of the intrinsic beauty of the imagery. When they are fully understood these sayings show the pathway to the student, so that he may truly become what they assure him he may become, and in fact *is* at the core of his being. They contain a promise of immense ethical value, as well as teaching the very essence of what evolution is; because it is man's destiny some day to become what he here is promised.

In future ages, aeons upon aeons hence, when the human race shall have run its course for this great planetary life cycle, it will have developed into full-grown divinities, gods, spiritual forces on earth. Then we shall become like those now ahead of us, the leaders and teachers of the race, and the inspirers and the invigorators of those who will then be below us as they are even now; we shall become to them the transmitter of the universal fire, the spiritual fire, the fire of pure self-consciousness, the noblest activity of the universal life.

That is what the gods are at the present time. These spiritual beings, these high messengers of the universal life and transmitters thereof to those below them, were once men in far bygone cosmic periods. Through past earnest endeavor, work and inner research, honesty and sincerity, universal love and compassion, these higher entities have allied themselves with the inner spheres along the pathway which each one of us *is,* and which they have trodden farther than we have as yet gone.

It is the higher, working with and in the inferior, who

stimulate the inferior, help them always, give them light, awaken them, lead them on. Thus we have even among mankind those superior ones who are our guides and helpers. They are the fine flowers of the human race, the noblest fruitage that the human race has produced; and for them we often use the Sanskrit word *mahātman* meaning "great soul," more accurately perhaps, "great self."

Such great souls are well known in the world. Nothing is so common to us as some knowledge of them. The Buddha was one; Jesus, called the Christ, was one; Śankarāchārya of India was one; Pythagoras was one; Empedocles of Sicily was one. They were and are relatively numerous — although not all are of the same degree or grade, for they vary among themselves, even as average men do. There are the greatest; the less great; the great; then in descending scale come the good and noble men; then average men; then inferior men — a hierarchy of intellect and mind and heart.

These greatest of men have developed to its highest point of self-expression the human soul, so that it has become a perfect transmitter or vehicle for the inner god. But every man has within himself the potentialities of this inner god. When Jesus said "I am the pathway and the Life," he did not refer to himself alone as that pathway. He meant that every human being likewise who strives towards and endeavors to live that cosmic life, thereby becomes the transmitter of that life and its many, many powers to those below him.

Every one of us is a potential savior of his fellows; and it is our destiny some day to become an actual savior and teacher, one who has trodden that inner pathway successfully. For each one of us is potentially a god, a divine being.

20

DIVINITY THE SOURCE OF ALL

ADEQUATELY TO understand the theosophical teaching of evolution requires the laying down of the general principle of the derivation of all entities whatsoever from a divine source, not in any sense as the children or creations of a personal deity, but as the emanational evolution of quasi-conscious sparks from the heart of our own particular universe. Theological thinkers in days preceding the Christian era considered this to be the divine hierarch of our own special universe.

In our inner hunting for "God" — to use the popular term — we may ask ourselves, where is deity? Where is the divine? Vain question! It is a specimen of the logical weakness of the human mind which, because itself is a limited thing, always seeks for limits and bounds, and has the greatest difficulty in translating into human words the godlike conceptions of the spirit indwelling in man.

We reject as unworthy of a spiritually-minded man, of a truly logically-minded man, any conception of the divine less in grandeur than man's inmost intuition of boundless infinitude; therefore we reject the idea usually passing under the term of a "personal God." Personality is limitation; even individuality is limitation. The divine is neither personal nor individual; and yet what can we call it? Assuredly it is not a he or a she. What can we call it but It — a term with us signifying the deepest reverence, and arising out of an instinctive refusal to attach personal pronouns to the profoundest and sublimest conception of the human spirit.

The question of the divine is a problem only so far as men have made it so. It is a matter of understanding causal spiritual — or rather divine — relations. We must all solve this problem for ourselves. The mere acceptance of the dicta of some other man will in itself lead us nowhere. It may possibly help us in the first steps of our studies as a mere rule of action, until we ourselves learn to enter within the arcana of our own spiritual being and thus know causal relations from individual experience. This can be done by anyone who will fulfill the conditions required. There is but one method of understanding the inner nature of the self and its links with the divine, and that is experiencing it by entering into it.

Show me a place where deity is confined and I will show you a limited entity! No, the divine is boundless, is subject to no places of limitation, is nowhere, because everywhere — nowhere in particular because everywhere generally. Therefore the search for the divine can take only one fcrm, follow one path alone; and that is inwards, along the pathway of the spirit, because this is the path of understanding, the path of conception, the path of inner realization, and the path of union and communion.

It is a vain and foolish imagining to suppose that the divine exists extracosmically, outside the bounds of anything. But when man searches the inmost recesses of his own nature, the deepest of the deeps of his own spirit-soul, then indeed does he come nearer and nearer as that search advances farther and farther, towards some realization of what that Light is which illumines the fields of space. He thus advances constantly towards an ever-growing conception of the divine, through endless fields of wisdom and expanding consciousness throughout all duration, which is boundless, beginningless, endless. That is the key to the theosophical teaching regarding the divine.

When the Christian intuits this, he speaks of it as the immanent Christos, and he speaks aright. The followers of all the great religious and philosophical systems — the Mahāyā- nists of Buddhism, the Taoists of their own classical period, the Neoplatonic thinkers and mystics of the Hither East, the followers of the profound Vedanta and other Hindu sys- tems — all have known the truth and practiced this inner communion. Why is it then that so many of the Christian scholars and researchers — more so in times preceding the advent of the theosophical philosophy, which has so largely elucidated these questions for the Western world — why is it, I say, that those old-fashioned thinkers have called the religious beliefs of other times and likewise of those more modern men who did not accept their particular brand of belief, godless or atheistic?

In the early days of Christianity, Christians were tried by pagan judges for disobedience to the laws, and not because they refused to acknowledge or follow the state religion. These Greek and Roman judges called the early Christians *atheoi* — "atheists" or "godless" in the etymological sense. Atheist at that time was no term of such reprobation as it is now. It then meant those only who refused to accept the gods of the popular state religion. The fact was that these ancients, in their broad-minded polytheism, cared little or nothing what the individual beliefs of the Christians were, and the term atheist was merely distinctive, perhaps ironical, scarcely derogatory. But they cared a great deal whether or not these Christians were obeying the laws of the state, quite apart from their religious beliefs.

When the Christians gained power with the downfall of the brilliant Mediterranean civilization, when Christianity grew by leaps and bounds and became the predominant faith, then the Christians in their turn called the still remaining adherents to the old religion atheists, because these latter accepted not the Hebraeo-Christian Jehovah. Yes, this term atheist merely means: "You don't accept my God; therefore you are an atheist." Very likely the 'atheist' in his turn could retaliate justly and say: "You don't accept my God; therefore *you* are the atheist."

In the Western world and nowhere else — and only because the real knowledge which Jesus gave to his followers was soon forgotten after their Master's passing — there are in religious thought three or four ideas as to how teaching concerning deity should be formulated. One is called *deism,* that is to say the doctrine accepted by those who believe that there is a personal God, but One who is apart from the world which He has created; that He takes no interest in it in particular; and that that universe which He created in some very mysterious manner runs itself.

The second theory, which fundamentally is the same in principle, is called *theism.* This is the doctrine of those who accept a personal God transcending the physical universe, yet a God who takes a most lively interest in the universe which He has created, and in the beings which He created to inhabit that universe.

The third specimen of belief, or disbelief, as regards deity is what is called *atheism,* which is the belief held by those who say that there is no God at all.

The fourth belief, which is misunderstood most deplorably, is called *pantheism.* This is the doctrine of those who say that the universe is inspirited with an impersonal life comprising universal consciousness and which exists in every particle, infinitesimal or cosmic, of that universe, and which universal life is the background of that universe; that this universal life is the source and also the ultimate destiny of every one of such infinitesimal or cosmic entities.

Theosophists may be called pantheists, provided that the word pantheism is used in the following way. We are pantheists in the sense that we recognize a universal life infilling, inspiriting everything, so that nothing is apart or separate or extra-vagrant, for such cannot be if this life be universal and boundless.

H. P. Blavatsky defines the position as follows: *

For to be one [a theosophist], one need not necessarily recognize the existence of any special God or a deity. One need but worship the spirit of living nature, and try to identify oneself with it. To revere that *Presence* the invisible Cause, which is yet ever manifesting itself in its incessant results; the intangible, omnipotent, and omnipresent Proteus: indivisible in its Essence, and eluding form, yet appearing under all and every form; who is here and there, and everywhere and nowhere; is ALL, and NOTHING; ubiquitous yet one; the Essence filling, binding, bounding, containing everything; contained in all.

If the divine is anything, it is boundless. Nothing can exist without it. It is everywhere, but nowhere in particular; for if it were it would be a limited thing. Therefore we say

---

The Theosophist, vol. I, no. 1, October 1879, p. 6.

that the divine is the All, and no thing — the All, because
otherwise it would be less than boundless; no thing, because
it has no limitations. It is not a thing, nor a being, nor an
entity, in the sense that these words usually have.

The English poet, Alexander Pope, when he says:

> Know then thyself, presume not God to scan,
> The proper study of Mankind is Man.

uttered a most astounding fallacy from the theosophical
standpoint. Man, "know thyself" — *gnōthi seauton* — was an
archaic Greek motto written over the portico of one of the
temples of the oracle of Apollo of Delphi. "Know thyself,"
is indeed the injunction; but why are we so enjoined? It is
because in knowing ourself, in looking within, in going farther and farther into the depths of our being, we come ever
closer and closer — but never can we fully attain it — to the
universal life.

The divine can be understood by looking within, along
the path of understanding, along the path of comprehension,
along the path of intuition; for the very root of man's spiritual nature is that divine itself, our spiritual origin, our
impersonal parent, the source of our essence. From it we
sprang in the far distant aeons of the illimitable past on our
cycling journey downwards into matter; and to it shall we
return in the far distant cycles of the future — but then as
full-grown spiritual adults, fully-developed spiritual monads.
Having left it in the morning of time as unself-conscious
god-sparks, we shall return to it as self-conscious divinities. It
is we, and we are it. It is the inmost self living at the core, at
the heart, of each one of us; at the heart of all that is, of all
entities that are, because fundamentally it is everything.

As a man thinks thoughts, which are ensouled things,

because they are matter and yet spring from a spiritual being, so, speaking in symbolic form, the divine sends forth from itself sparks of its own fire, and each one of these sparks contains in itself the root of self, selfhood, self-consciousness, growing ever greater, ever larger, ever expanding, never reaching an ultimate, but always marching towards it in constantly growing greatness of consciousness and beauty. Man, therefore, is the temple expressing as far as he may, by means of the building of the spiritual vehicle within, the vast and ineffable glories of the divine — of the Inexpressible. In man's inmost nature is the very heart of deity.

There is an old Sufi tale — and I quote it here on account of its beauty and aptness of application — which sets forth the story that a soul once came to the portals of the House of God, and knocked. And the voice of God issued therefrom in tones of reverberating thunder: "Who knocks?" And the soul answered, "I"; and the same thundering volume of sound again issued from the crypts of the House of God, saying "Who is I! I know thee not." And the soul turned sadly away and wandered for ages and ages, and finally, having learned its lesson through suffering and experience, it returned to the House of God, and again knocked. Again came the thunderous volume of sound, "Who knocks?" And the soul answered, "Thou knockest." And then a whisper, inaudible to the ears, yet filling all the spaces — the whispering of truth — issued forth from the Temple of God, and said: "Enter into thine own."

The moral here is that there is no longer separation, no longer division, no longer the contrast between the inmost and the outer, nor between "I" and "Thou," between the god within and the very imperfect vehicle which says, "I, I, I"; but a full recognition by the spiritual adult, by the spiritual monad, of its own self, its own source, answering in the voice of the silence, "Thou knockest!"

The divine exists everywhere, is everywhere, in "vessels of honor" and in "vessels of dishonor," to use the Christian expressions. "Vessels of dishonor" are such only because the evolving entity in which this god-spark is enshrined, is a living entity, learning its lessons, and having its modicum of free will, and temporarily having chosen a path branching off to the 'left-hand'; while the so-called "vessels of honor" are they which, exercising their free will and power of choice, have chosen the path branching to the 'right-hand.'

Every smallest spark, every infinitesimal particle or corpuscle which in their aggregate infill the universe — indeed, *are* that universe itself and existing therein in incomputable multitudes — every one of these living entities enshrines a spiritual monad, a spark of the universal life.

Monads are spiritual beings, self-conscious, self-motivated, self-impelled god-sparks, fully self-conscious for the manvantara, that is to say for this great cycle of planetary life; and such a monad exists at the core, at the heart, of every specific corpuscle or infinitesimal, and they are infinite in number literally. These infinitesimals, these atoms, these shrines of the monads, offspring each one of them from its parent monad, are elemental entities beginning each its upward march, as a thought will spring from the mind of man; for thoughts are things, and are ensouled.

These multitudes of living entities, following each one its own pathway of evolutionary development, begin any particular line of evolution in the heart of the divine hierarch of their own particular hierarchy, pass downwards through the manifold and various stages of matter, rise again when the turn of a particular cycle has been reached, and again reenter the bosom of the divine, from which each sprang in the beginnings of that period of evolutionary time. But the evolving entities along those particular waves of life have grown. They have advanced; they are farther along the path than they were.

Evolution is not a mere mechanical process of putting brick upon brick, of stone to stone. That alone would be but a piling up of substances. The procedure of evolution includes that in degree, but more than anything else it is the building of a manifesting vehicle capable of expressing the innate powers of the spiritual monad. It is the unwrapping or unfolding of latent or dormant or sleeping powers. It is the building of living temples of self-expression which grow nobler with every step taken forwards.

As Oliver Wendell Holmes puts it in his poem, "The Chambered Nautilus":

> Build thee more stately mansions, O my Soul,
> As the swift seasons roll!
> Leave thy low-vaulted past!
> Let each new temple, nobler than the last,
> Shut thee from heaven with a dome more vast,
> Till thou at length art free,
> Leaving thine outgrown shell by life's unresting sea!

This word *monad* is no new term to the Western world. It has been well known for ages. The Pythagoreans used it. Plato occasionally used it also, but he was a Pythagorean likewise in the substance of his teachings. Leibniz chose it as the term by which he designated his self-expressing centers of consciousness, mirrors of the macrocosm. Giordano Bruno, the unfortunate martyr, likewise taught of monads, for he was a Neoplatonist of the later times. With him the monads were the ultimate spiritual particles of all beings or things, each entity having a monad at its heart or core; in other words, being the offspring of that monad, the monad being its origin or source and manifesting through the various veils of matter which enshrouded it, these veils were its vehicles of expression built from itself, from its own substance.

Thus these various veils or vehicles through which the monad expresses itself, whether it be on higher planes or lower planes, are themselves entities on the upward path as offsprings of the life-giving and originating monad which they express, though of course inferior to it, their parent — inferior I mean in spiritual grandeur and evolutionary development.

Just as the mind of a man expresses itself through his physical brain, a part of his body, so do these various vehicles or veils express each according to its capacity the powers of the monad which they enfold or enshrine. As the physical body is composed of cells, in their turn composed of atoms, in their turn composed of still smaller particles, so these other veils, inferior to the monad, are themselves in their turn composed of entities inferior to the veil of which they are the infinitesimals. Thus there is no particle in all space that is not a living being.

A god manifests through the spiritual part of man, through his spiritual soul, and this god, this spiritual entity, this *jiva* or "life," to use the Sanskrit term, is the monad. On its own plane it is a self-conscious god. Not deity, but a god, a spiritual entity, a divinity as the ancients would have said, a spark of the universal life.

Next, the spiritual soul through which the monad manifests in the human economy, is also a living entity, built by the monad. It is the child of the monad, and is itself growing, destined in its turn to pursue nobler paths of evolutionary development, in time becoming a monad; in other words, reaching that state of sublime capacity and power when all the barriers of matter have been surmounted, so that the inner spiritual sun may shine forth through it in full splendor and glory.

This spiritual soul, again, possessing and manifesting its divinity — the monad — in its turn works similarly through another sheath inferior to it, through another soul which is another entity manifesting that spiritual soul, as the spiritual soul manifests the monad. This child of the spiritual soul is the human soul.

The human soul likewise is an entity on its upward way, growing, which means expanding, overcoming the barriers or dissolving the veils, so that the sunlight from above may stream through the open doors of the inner temple at the heart of its being, and thus manifest its transcendent powers and faculties. This process of self-expression and overcoming barriers is evolution.

The human soul in its turn is enshrined within another veil, a living entity still lower in the scale, but made necessary for the manifestation of the human soul by the more material world in which this still lower one, its vehicle, must work and function, if the human soul is to have communion with these stages of matter. This vehicle or sheath or veil, or soul — call it what you will — still lower than the human soul, is the vital-astral soul, or the animal soul. It is, likewise, a growing thing, born from the human soul, its parent, learning its lessons by its links with the human soul above and its connections with the more material world below.

This animal soul in its turn is enshrined in the vehicle or carrier or sheath or veil which it has built for itself and from itself, by evolving forth or unfolding its inherent tendencies or urges or capacities or faculties, in other words its character; and this last house or veil of all is the physical temple, the physical body.

Thus the monad or jīva, the cosmic life-center, is in the highest reaches of itself, the divine; and in its lowest reaches it is a body ultimately built from its own substance.

The human body should be considered as a holy thing, because it enshrines a spiritual entity, which in its ultimate reaches is a god, a divinity, which nothing can pollute or stain, or hinder in its workings or turn aside from its path of self-expression. Yet the physical vehicle can become so impure, the physical temple can be so soiled with stain, that it would seem to be more meet that it serve as a sty for swine than for the presence and dwelling of the inner splendor of the illuminating divinity within.

These are not poetical phrases. This is the teaching of the ancient wisdom, the meaning of which is to be taken literally; not the words, because words are treacherous often on account of ambiguity.

This physical temple of the living god within is composed of still smaller entities called cells, these cells in their turn being built of entities still more minute called atoms, and these in their turn are composed of corpuscles or of entities still smaller, the electrons and the protons, etc. And these electrons are themselves composite things, built of infinitesimal lives still smaller.

As every smallest atom or corpuscle of this vast organism of the cosmos, the universe, is the offspring of the cosmos, its child and therefore a part of its own being, the ineluctable laws of reason and intuition tell us that every such atom or corpuscle must have in itself everything that the All contains — not in bulk, but in capacity of development, in potency, in faculty, sleeping or dormant, in possibility of realization, in principle. Consequently, as man is likewise an intrinsic part of this organism, an inseparable portion thereof, no more able to free or separate himself from it or wander away from it than he can annihilate himself, we see that in the human heart abide all the issues of life.

Therefore if you want to know what the divine is, if you want to know something of the vastness of the fields of the spiritual spaces, then search earnestly within yourself. Treading these fields of space in thought, you will find that you can reach no ending; and in thus entering within yourself, striving steadily forward into your own being inwards, you will have set your feet upon the still, ancient, small path, which leads directly to the heart of the universe.

This is the only pathway by which human consciousness may forever approach the divine, without ever being able to reach it fully of course, and without ever being able to understand it in its infinite ranges. But there is an ever-expanding consciousness and comprehension of ever larger and larger fields of its action, and it is thus that the understanding of it grows ever more and more sublime.

Every one of us can do it if we will: we can enter these sublime spaces of our own inner spiritual being, because intrinsically each one is a pathway leading to the heart of the universe, from which flow out and forth all the forces governing the universe, and whose effects we are in the phenomenal appearances of that universe surrounding us — varied, manifold, multitudinous as they are.

When a man's heart and mind are penetrated with the conception of the fundamental and perfect unity of all things in the vast organism of the cosmos, then he will realize that this cosmos is the field of universal life, of universal consciousness, manifesting in every smallest particle of space;

and that it is also the field of an ineffable and boundless love — assuredly not love as we weak human beings understand it, but that intrinsic character of the Inexpressible, whose nature and functions we but vaguely conceive and hint at by our human word love. It manifests in the atom as attraction. It manifests in the cells and other smaller bodies as the force of coherence and cohesion. It manifests in the framework of the cosmos as that marvelous power which holds the universe in union, all parts in mutual sympathy and harmony, each to each, each to all, all to each; in human beings as spiritual love, and in beings higher than the human as something so beautiful that our human minds can but adumbrate it and call it self-sacrifice for others and for all.

These three, life, consciousness, and love — the Hindu expresses by his famous phrase, *Sat Chit Ānanda* — which in reality are but one, may give some idea of the nature of the Inexpressible, the all-encompassing divine origin, source, destiny, pathway and final aim of all beings, to which man raises both heart and mind in wordless reverence.

21

THE HIERARCHICAL STRUCTURE OF
THE UNIVERSE

WHEN WE SAY THAT the divine towards which we raise our hearts in deepest reverence is impersonal, we do not mean that the divine, which we recognize as containing the fundamental causal relations of the universe, whose phenomenal appearances surround us, is naught but an empty abstraction. No; we mean that it is the universal life, and that therefore it is impersonal, because personality of any kind is limitation; and the divine being boundless is bounded by nothing, and limitations are but phenomenal appearances.

But does the divine manifest immediately upon or rather in this universe? Is there no spacing between the divine and matter? Do they conjoin immediately? These queries contain their own answers.

Does the Infinite attend to the affairs of the finite? Does the general of an army brush the shoes of every private in his army corps? If so, then such a deity is responsible for everything that happens in the universe because it is his own direct doing; and the supposition, absurd as it is, like-wise forbids the existence of free will and self-initiative in any minutest degree in any entity.

Take the architect — to change our figure of speech — after he has drawn up the plans for some noble temple or palace, does he himself go out and quarry the stone for it, cut and shape it, and then cement it into place? No, he provides the plan, the idea, the spirit, of the thing; and then passes it on to the workmen who immediately become busy with the plan and build therefrom. And it is the interme-diate nature, both of the universe and of man, which is formed of these workmen, these builders, these transmitters of the divine idea; and as these builders are all as yet but learning entities, their work is characterized by imperfections.

Nature proclaims on every hand here on earth and in the spaces above and in our own nature within us, that imper-fection is the rule and that the action of multitudinous, free, but still imperfect wills is the cause of the contrarieties and differences so prevalent in our world. We see imperfection everywhere, in many degrees, and human nature manifests it as much as anything else. Nothing is perfect in this lower universe of limitations, which is the garment of divine per-fection, to use an old metaphor. Yet it is through and by these limitations that we learn, because these limitations arise out of the imperfect nature of the beings surrounding us — beings like ourselves living and learning and advancing towards that sublime goal which, paradoxically, recedes into greater distances the nearer we seem to approach to it.

We are indeed learning creatures, living for the present in our intermediate natures, in what we call our human soul, and thus linked to the spirit above and within us, which is the divine spark which we essentially are; and this human soul is again linked to and in the body which each one of us has, manifesting through it, and thus expressing itself on this plane and learning its lessons here.

The spirit within or rather above man, his essential self, can no more manifest directly upon matter and move it — although spirit and matter are in essence one — than, let us say, electricity can manifest immediately in and drive an electric car along the road without the proper mechanical apparatus as intermediary. There must be a machine, fit for, built for, proportionate to, its purpose, and of such a nature that it can transmit the electric power and turn it into mechanical work.

Similarly is it with the intermediate psychological nature of man, between the spirit above and the vital-astral-physical framework of this earthly body. Similarly is it as concerns the divine and the physical or material universe: there must be intermediate stages or grades of more or less ethereal substances between these, furnishing the links between them.

The divine in its essence is transcendent and above the material universe, even as the spirit of man is transcendent or above his intermediate and vital-astral-physical nature, and the forces flowing from his spiritual nature are transmitted to him more or less imperfectly, according to the degree of evolution that has been attained by the intermediate nature, the human soul.

It is the teaching of theosophy that between the divine and the phenomenal universe which we sense with our physical apparatus of understanding there is a vast congeries or collection or aggregate of hierarchies, in their turn composed of steps or degrees, or scales of beings and things, interconnecting, without disjunction or separation, indissolubly bound together. How could it be otherwise? Is any man insane enough to suppose that something can be separate from the All, from infinitude, and find a spot somewhere outside of infinity, outside of everything, where pure "nothing" is?

These hierarchies are not merely infilled with living entities, but are themselves composed of these living entities. Without them they would not be; because these living entities are they.

The modern theory of the cosmos, as outlined more particularly in astronomical science, gives us a good picture of the hierarchical structure of the cosmos from the standpoint of the physical plane. Our universe (that is the space comprised within our galaxy) is not the only universe. There are myriads of universes, similar in physical nature to our own, existing outside the bounds of the Milky Way. Each one of such universes we may call a cosmic molecule composed of the various solar systems which we may call cosmic atoms; while the planets which revolve around any central solar luminary are like cosmic electrons. Our earth is one of such cosmic electrons, so far as our own solar system is concerned. It is an atomic planet forming part of the aggregate of our solar system, which in its turn is one of the atoms of our own universe — a cosmic molecule.

The greater universe is thus a vast organism, a living entity, a quasi-infinitude of worlds, which together form the cosmic atoms, or the cosmic molecules if you will, of some vast entity surpassing human imagination. And just as in man the atoms which form his body are ensouled by the man himself and yet themselves are living entities, possessing in the minute all that man possesses, so the cosmic atoms and cosmic molecules — the "island-universes" which bestrew space — are ensouled by the life of the vast supergalactic entity, and yet are themselves living beings.

As music is perhaps the most spiritual of the arts, so astronomy doubtless may be called the most spiritual of the physical sciences; because, among other things, it deals with vast celestial spaces — not merely with spaces as these are conceived of in the sense of the mere extension of matter, but spaces which hint at and in some measure portray the vaster spaces of the inner worlds wherein the hierarchies of living beings are chiefly active.

The mind of man is elevated by such a study. He comes by analogy and suggestion into closer relationship with the spirit within himself, which likewise inhabits these wide spaces of the inner world, for indeed each spirit is a spark of the divine fire.

The physical body of the universe is but the united manifestation and effect of these hierarchies of invisible beings as we sense them in their work; and so in turn man's body is representative of such a hierarchy, composed of the multitudes of little lives which form that body. Subtract those little lives from that body, and what remains? There is no body. It is these little lives which are the body, which manifest the man; and he is the oversoul of these hosts of infinitesimals which form his vehicles or bodies, outer and inner. He in his higher self is also their divine inspiritor, invigorator, and vitalizer. The rule of unity is universal.

It is along any hierarchy, great or small as the case may be, in all its steps or grades or stages, that are transmitted the spiritual and divine powers flowing from within, which hold any universe in their grip, which govern its actions, which motivate its procedures, which actually form it and make it what it is; and each such hierarchy is the manifestation of an individuality, of the hierarch, the supernal entity at the head of any such scale or ladder of life or of being.

But is this hierarch "God"? If so, then there are many Gods, as the ancients truly said; because such hierarchies are numberless, as is obvious; interlocking, interwoven, interacting, and forming the vast fabric and web of life, which in its aggregate is the universal cosmos surrounding us. Of this we have but vague and indistinct glimpses, such as our physical senses can give to us, and such as our mind and heart and soul interpret, and more or less correctly in accordance as we are more or less illumined from above by the spirit within, our inner sun of consciousness.

I have sometimes been asked: Is there nothing in the Christian religion resembling this theory of hierarchies? Most decidedly there is. In fact, such a teaching is the very background of the Christian theological scheme, although today it has been largely abandoned, thereby robbing Christian believers of the very heart of their own religion.

About the fifth century of the Christian era there appeared in the Mediterranean world a series of three or four extremely interesting books, which passed under the name of Dionysius the Areopagite. These were acclaimed as having been written by that particular legendary individual of whom the New Testament speaks as being a member of the Council of Mars' Hill or of the Areopagus in Athens, and who was, so the legend runs, converted by Paul at the time when he preached as alleged on Mars' Hill.

It is unquestionable, however, that these writings are four or five hundred years later than the Dionysius alluded to in the New Testament. Therefore the actual writer of these particular mystical Christian books has in recent times been called the pseudo-Dionysius, for he was a writer whose identity is totally unknown, and who passed off his work as having been the work of the Dionysius mentioned in the

New Testament, and whom the Christians called the first Christian Bishop of Athens.

A careful scrutiny of these Dionysian works shows first that they were taken almost wholly in system and in structural form from Neoplatonic teachings, in other words from what the Christians call pagan teachings; and also that they contain certain allusions to some of the doctrines which belonged to the ancient Greek Mysteries.

These Dionysian works both in form and in content are expressed in the Christian vocabulary and religious thought of about the fourth or fifth centuries after the beginning of the so-called Christian era. Obviously, then, these books represent an attempt to import into the Christian religion of that time some of the mystical heart of the pagan philosophical doctrines and of the mystical spirit which gave the Neoplatonic teachings such immense vogue in the ancient nations surrounding the Mediterranean Sea. Included likewise in these teachings is a great deal of the Neopythagorean thought.

My point in alluding to these facts is this: these teachings were taken over wholly by the Christian church, and thus became essentially a part of the dogmatic structure of Christian theology for centuries afterwards, i.e., became fully orthodox. Yet, alas, the key to their origin, the real meaning which they had in the non-Christian systems from which they were taken, was lost. The mystical scheme remained, the philosophical system remained, somewhat of the religious spirit remained, the framework or house containing the thought remained; but the 'God,' the spirit, which had dwelt in that mystical framework of thought had long since departed.

In perhaps the most important one of these books, called

Concerning the Celestial Hierarchy, this pseudo-Dionysian writer teaches that Deity works through the intermediary worlds composed of three triads, that is to say three groups of beings which are intermediate between nature and man on the lower side, and the Deity on the superior side.

These three triads therefore form nine steps or stages or degrees in all, which the pseudo-Dionysius names as follows, beginning with the highest: Seraphim, Cherubim, Thrones, first triad and the highest; Dominions, Virtues, Powers, second triad and intermediate, interpreting and "stepping down" the spiritual forces from the first triad, as that first triad was the interpreter, so to say, the passer, of the forces flowing from the divine heart. Then came the third and lowest triad, composed of Principalities, Archangels, Angels; beneath these last were the physical universe and man.

This was a wholesale importation into the new faith from the original theosophy which had degenerated into the various religions surrounding the Mediterranean Sea and, as doctrines, were contained in the various religious beliefs of those peoples. It was a wholesale taking over of that part of the mystical thought of the ancient philosophy, and the expressing of it in new terms familiar to the new faith, as evidenced by the use of the words that Paul employed; for Paul of the Christians, when writing in the New Testament, speaks of Principalities, Thrones, and Powers, and of Archangels and Angels, and what not else.

One of the great difficulties that the protagonists of the new religion had in making some headway in the beginning for their particular brand of religion was this: they had to meet the objections of the trained minds and the alert consciousnesses of the non-Christian men, many of them extremely learned, who lived contemporaneously. And one of the first questions that these ancient philosophers asked the promulgators of the new faith was this: You say that God created the world in six days and rested on the seventh day, and that this creation included the origin of man. Did your God do this? Is your God perfect, eternal, infinite in power, as you say? Then we must ask: Can Infinity 'create' anything but an infinite work, and can an infinite work be created and thus have a beginning? Can Perfection produce an imperfect work? Does the Universal Life meddle with the details of the physical universe surrounding us, except in the general sense of the impersonal action of universal powers?

To these perfectly reasonable and logical objections no answer could be given, because the definite teaching of this new religious belief, as taken over from the Hebrew Old Testament, was that God had created the world in six days and rested on the seventh day, and that he is a "He" and lives in a particular part of supernal space which is called heaven — ideas, all of them, which are expressed in terms of limitation and bounds.

This was quite in line with the Hebraic ideas concerning Jehovah of the Jewish Bible, who smelled sweet savors and waxed wroth, and whose nature was moved in quite a human fashion by various human occurrences. Anger and love and preferences and hatred are things which are utterly impredicable of the Divine.

It was also quite in line with the old theories as held by the populace as regards Zeus of the Greeks, or Jupiter of the Romans, as expressed in the popular mythology of those peoples; but these mythological tales never were believed in literally by the philosophers and wise men of ancient times.

Now the theosophist says that all such expressions are

symbolic, and should be so understood, and this conception of the meaning of the literal teachings of the old religions was that held by all thinking men of antiquity. The wise men of those ancient days turned with disgust from all such figurative expressions limiting the divine. It was not the expressions themselves that they so much objected to, because these were definitely understood to be symbolic, but it was the danger that these mythological stories would be received by the unthinking masses as expressions of divine realities.

No, said they, between the Inexpressible and the expressible, between the Illimitable and the limited, between the Incomprehensible to man and the comprehensible, there is a scale of life endless in all directions, without width or length, which ranges neither up nor down, nor to the right or to the left, neither forwards nor backwards, nor within or without, but *is,* and is everywhere. It is symbolically called a "ladder" or a "scale" only because human words lack that with which the human consciousness may express, to some extent, its intuition of the Inexpressible, and hence it has to use metaphors. Yet, indeed, the human spirit may have some conception of the divine in proportion as that human spirit is enabled through inner visioning to transmit supernal illumination to the human mind or soul, which then can, in some degree at least, articulate it in symbolic words.

Now this universe, being an organism, being held together by unbreakable bonds of destiny, is infilled with all the potencies and capacities of the divine; but these potencies and capacities are of necessity unmanifest in their higher and larger reaches; for the finite never can comprehend nor express the infinite. As regards the universe, everything that it contains is finite and therefore is incapable of fully expressing all that the infinite is, yet containing everything in germ that is inherent in the infinite itself. But relative parts, so to say, appropriate forces and energies flowing from the heart of Being, infill every smaller or inferior entity, and drive it on by inward urge, give it birth, and will direct it and lead it on to the ultimate destiny which lies before it.

Whence, indeed, come the worlds which light up the spaces of heaven? Whence comes Man? From within. They come forth from the invisible outwards into the visible, manifesting the forces which they imbody, and which send them forth on their various and respective works and destinies. And remember that it is *spiritual beings* who, by and through one side of their nature which by analogy we may call the vegetative side, provide these various forces which play through the phenomenal seeming of the universe around us. Yes, all the forces which appear in nature spring from them, for in one sense we may say they are ultimately those forces themselves. For what are they? Are they separate or different from the universe which they inform? In no case whatsoever. It is these spiritual beings who ensoul the cosmos, the universe. It is they who are the inner worlds, actually composing them in their vegetative aspects, for these inner worlds are their inner vehicles for self-expression, even as man, the true man, ensouls his body, his physical encasement, as well as his inner bodies.

Worlds as well as men are built on inferiors, yet each one of these inferiors is not absolutely but relatively so. Each is in itself a learning entity, forming a part of the vehicle in which a living being manifests and which is in the process of building — for what? For becoming a fitter and nobler vehicle for self-expression, for the unfoldment of the spiritual self in the inmost of its nature.

Every world that comes into being is a living thing according to the ancient philosophies. Do you know that among the ancients the worlds were called "animals"? They meant by this that everything is alive or has an *anima*, as it is in the Latin tongue — a "vital soul," expressing what it can, according to its degree of development, of the inner and vivifying spirit. We are at once the children of this earth, our planet Terra, which is an "animal" or living being in that ancient sense, and likewise are we offsprings of the divine. Every world is the parent of many things, because itself is composite, and being a composite thing has roots of differentiation which this composition merely manifests, and these roots of differentiation of necessity follow out in various things and entities the inherent urge for self-expression.

The worlds and we sprang from the heart of Being; and we, in the inmost of the inmost, in the deepest depths of our natures, are that heart of the universe. In it are all things, all mysteries and the solutions of all mysteries, wisdom ineffable, because it is the eternal universal life, boundless, inexpressible, unknowable. An ultimate we may never reach; always are there veils to pass behind into the greater splendors.

What governs the coming forth into visibility of these worlds and of man; what governs their retreat or withdrawal again into the darkness when their courses have been run — darkness to us, but the light to them? (This retreat or withdrawal in the case of our human encasements, men call death.) What governs these various processes? — Random action? Chance?

These worlds, and man as well, are brought forth through the working of the self in its various vehicles on and in the various planes or spheres of the invisible universe. The self manifests in all these planes or spheres, passing, during the cycle of its progress, from the highest of our hierarchy through a graduated series of stages or degrees to the most inferior or lowest, and in each along its own particular cycle. Then, when the depth of progression into matter has been reached, we foolish men of the Occident, knowing no better, call the effects that we cognize the full splendor of material activity. Thus are we blinded by the māyā or illusion of things.

But when the "downward" cycle has run its course, when any cycle of any living entity during its evolutionary progress reaches its lowest point, then begins the "ascent" — not a retrogression in the sense of a turning back and a retracing of the old footmarks with new steps. No, the path ahead is inwards and back to the source whence we and the worlds — our mothers — originally came, but improved, grown, evolved.

When we finally reach the ultimate destiny for that particular cycle of manifestation, which is our return to the source spoken of, then the worlds and we both rest, each according to the effects produced during that cycle of evolution. When we have rested, slept, if you like, we begin anew another cycle of manifestation; we repeat what we did before, but on still higher and nobler pathways, because we ourselves, and the worlds in which we live and of which we are the children, are then more evolved than before. There is a beautiful old mystical saying, that the "sparks of Eternity," the worlds, are scattered anew with lavish hand by the universal Mother on the fields of space in order to run another course.

The whole course of evolution consists in one procedure fundamentally, and that is the building of ever-better vehicles for manifesting the inner light. That process of self-origination and self-building of fitter vehicles we call evolution.

After all, the building of vehicles is merely the effectual aspect. Evolution strictly in its etymological sense, as we have previously shown, means the unfolding of potencies which have been infolded in previous cycles of being and which await the appropriate times and fields for their expression. Evolution thus is the unpacking of inner faculties and powers and forces, and the finding a field for their manifestation.

Our modern physical sciences know very little of these inner and causal relations, but somewhat only of the physical phenomena of our universe; and in view of the circumstances that exist, what else can they know? What other pathway to truth have they than that of experimentation and patient research and waiting? These are good in their way, very good; but our scientists know scarcely anything of the wonders within man, or of the mysteries behind the veil of the phenomenal universe. They have lost two extremely important keys which the old wisdom always taught to its students. The first of these keys is: look within, if you would know the truth, for you are the only pathway to that truth.

The second key is equally important and its application follows upon the use of this first key. It is the consciousness and therefore the recognition that the universe is not merely an ensouled organism, but that this world of the outer seeming is the garment of Reality and that all things have their origin in invisible space and proceed therefrom in individual cyclic journeyings for self-development, outwards into the visible, finally to return into the worlds within, but as grander and nobler entities than they were before. And further that this cycling is carried on by means of a hierarchical unfolding of a series of vehicles on each and all the planes of being, each vehicle itself a living entity capable of expressing the powers and faculties of the hierarch which emanated it forth.

Think of the infinite around us, filled with its hosts of hierarchies; the infinite spaces in the large, and the infinitesimal spaces in the small! If a man's mind, if his soul and his spirit, be not raised in reverence to some understanding at least of the great principles that lie in the background of the universal life, he indeed must have a soul that is more asleep than awake.

An old and wise axiom of the Qabbālāh, the theosophy of the Jews, says: "Student, open wide thine eyes upon the visible, for in it thou shalt see the invisible." We should indeed so see the invisible had we only developed our inner eyes; and this we can do. For this faculty of seeing, this power of vision, comes from within, from a union of the inner part of the human constitution with its root, the divinity lying at the heart of things; which heart is the All if reduced to principles by rigorous analysis.

Every human being, as I have said so often, is a pathway leading to the divine, the only pathway that there is for each incarnate spirit to follow, his only pathway to utter truth. What we receive from others may be helpful, or indeed unhelpful, depending upon the way in which we take it and our understanding of what we take. But if we desire truth and truth alone, if we wish to know ourselves and the wondrous mysteries within us rather than the phenomena only of the outward world, then we must follow that still, small path, which leads inwards and onwards and upwards forever.

Thoughts such as these bring into the human spirit a sense of the marvelous power of our understanding when properly directed and used. Human dignity takes on new and worthier aspects. We grow too great for mean and

paltry things; for we recognize instinctively the working of
the god enshrined in the core of our being — the living
Christos within, the awakened Buddha, Īśvara "in the seven-
gated temple of Brahma," to follow the Hindu's own beautiful phraseology. Whatever the terms in which we express
this sublime truth, the conception is the same.

But while this conception gives us true intellectual and
spiritual dignity, while it raises our spirit in contemplation
of the vastness and the wonders of the cosmos that surround
us, it likewise teaches us modesty. We grow less critical of
our fellowmen and of their mistakes; we grow kindlier and
more charitable. Our hearts warm with the understanding
that all men — indeed all things, the vast hierarchy of our
cosmos — are fundamentally one, linked together for divine
purposes; not the purposes of a personal God, but the purposes of the infinite divinity in the hearts of all beings: a
principle of consciousness too great to be personal, in its
fullness incomprehensible to us, vast even beyond our imagination, and yet being that, as the Christian apostle Paul said,
in which "we live, and move, and have our being."

BIBLIOGRAPHY

Bateson, William, *Mendel's Principles of Heredity*, Cambridge University Press, Cambridge, 1909.

Blavatsky, Helena P., *The Secret Doctrine: The Synthesis of Science, Religion, and Philosophy*, 2 vols., Theosophical Publishing Co., London, New York, Madras, 1888; verbatim reprint, Theosophical University Press, Pasadena, 1974.

————, "What Are the Theosophists?" *The Theosophist*, vol. I, October 1879, 5-7.

Boule, Marcellin, "L'Homme fossile de la Chapelle-aux-Saints," *Ann. de Palæontologie*, 1912; quoted in Wood Jones' *The Problem of Man's Ancestry*, 34.

Browne, Sir Thomas, *Religio Medici*, 1643; J. M. Dent & Co., London, 1901.

Buffon, Georges Louis Leclerc, Comte de, *Histoire naturelle*, 1766; quoted in Wood Jones' *The Problem of Man's Ancestry*, 21.

Burroughs, E. A., Bishop of Ripon, in "Is Scientific Advance Impeding Human Welfare?", *Literary Digest*, vol. 95, October 1, 1927, 32.

Coulter, John M., "The History of Organic Evolution," *Science*, vol. 63, May 14, 1926, 487-91.

Cummings, Byron, "Problems of a Scientific Investigator," *Science*, vol. 63, March 26, 1926, 321-4.

Darwin, Charles, *The Descent of Man and Selection in Relation to Sex*, John Murray, London, 1877.

———, *On the Origin of Species*, 1859; facsimile of 1st edition, Harvard University Press, Cambridge, 1975.

Dionysius the Areopagite, *The Celestial Hierarchies*, Shrine of Wisdom, London, 1935.

Durant, Will, *The Story of Philosophy: The Lives and Opinions of the Greater Philosophers*, Simon & Schuster, New York, 1926.

Gregory, William King, "Dawn-Man or Ape?", *Scientific American*, vol. 137, September 1927, 230-32.

Haeckel, Ernst Heinrich, *The Last Link*, A. & C. Black, London, 1898.

Hegner, Robert W., *College Zoology*, 4th edition, Macmillan Co., New York, 1937.

Huxley, Thomas Henry, *Evolution and Ethics, and Other Essays*, Appleton & Co., New York, 1898.

———, *Man's Place in Nature and Other Anthropological Essays*, Appleton & Co., New York, 1898.

Keith, Sir Arthur, "The Evidence for Darwin is Summed Up," *New York Times*, September 4, 1927, sec. 8, p. 1.

Locke, John, *An Essay Concerning Human Understanding*, 1690; reprint, Dover Publications, New York, 1959.

Lodge, Sir Oliver, *My Philosophy: Representing My Views on the Many Functions of the Ether of Space*, Ernest Benn, London, 1933.

Lull, Richard Swan, *Organic Evolution*, Macmillan Co., New York, 1921.

Mitchell, Peter Chalmers, in *Encyclopaedia Britannica*, 11th ed., s.v. "Evolution" and "Heredity."

More, Louis Trenchard, "The Perennial Question of Man's Nature," *Hibbert Journal,* vol. 25, April 1927, 508-22.

Osborn, Henry Fairfield, in *Encyclopaedia Britannica,* 11th ed., s.v. "Palaeontology."

——, "Recent Discoveries relating to the Origin and Antiquity of Man," *Proceedings of the American Philosophical Society,* vol. 66, 1927, 373-89.

Patrick, G. W., "The Convergence of Evolution and Fundamentalism," *Scientific Monthly,* vol. 23, July 1926, 5-15.

Pelt, Gertrude W. van, *Archaic History of the Human Race as Recorded in "The Secret Doctrine" by H. P. Blavatsky,* Theosophical University Press, 1934 (pamphlet).

Purucker, Gottfried de, *The Esoteric Tradition,* 2nd edition, Theosophical University Press, 1940; facsimile reprint, 1973.

Snider, Luther C., *Earth History,* Century Co., New York, 1932.

Soddy, Frederick, *The Interpretation of Radium and the Structure of the Atom,* 4th edition, G. Putnam & Sons, New York, 1922.

Strömberg, Gustaf, *The Soul of the Universe,* David McKay Co., Philadelphia, 1940.

Thornton, W. M., "What Is Electricity?", *Journal of the Institution of Electrical Engineers,* vol. 65, July 1927, 674-80.

Weismann, August, *Evolution Theory,* 2 vols., translated by J. Arthur Thomson, Arnold, London, 1904.

Wood Jones, Frederic, *Arboreal Man,* Arnold, London, 1916.

——, *Man's Place among the Mammals,* Arnold, London, 1929.

——, *The Problem of Man's Ancestry,* Society for Promoting Christian Knowledge, London, 1918.

APPENDICES

APPENDIX — I

THE ANTIQUITY OF MAN AND THE GEOLOGICAL AGES

Charles J. Ryan

In response to requests to correlate the rounds and races of human evolution as given in the theosophical teachings, with the eras and periods of geology as estimated by modern science, the following suggestions have been prepared. They are the result of considerable study and comparison of the available evidence, but no claim to finality is made.

When we compare various modern scientific estimates of the duration of the geological eras since the first undisputed traces of life in the rocks, we are impressed by serious differences of opinion. Even the new method of measurement by the study of radioactive transformation in certain rocks has limitations and cannot be entirely depended on. The geological processes are not fully understood, and enormous gaps occur in the record.

When fossils of identical nature are found in strata thousands of miles apart geographically, we tend to assume that both series of rocks were deposited at the same time, but this may not be true. Development of certain species or associated groups may have advanced far more rapidly in some regions than in others, and the supposed parallelism of the time periods may be more apparent than real. This is by no means a fanciful notion and it is one factor which makes the exact chronology of the rocks uncertain. We must never forget that the geological record is very incomplete and difficult to decipher. Darwin himself compared it to a book in which whole chapters are missing; those that remain are imperfect; and few of the leaves are unmutilated. In regard to skeletal remains of man, the subject is highly controversial.

When H. P. Blavatsky was writing about the age of the earth in *The Secret Doctrine* she compared the teachings of the scientists of that time and found nothing but confusion and uncertainty as to geological figures. There was one scientist, however, Professor Lefèvre, who in his *Philosophy* adopted an original method of interpreting the data available. Instead of trying to reach exact figures in regard to the length of the entire fossil-bearing period of sedimentation from the Laurentian period to the present day, or of its subdivisions, he worked out the *relative* durations of the sedimentary deposits. With this for a background the actual duration of the eras and periods could easily be calculated when reliable evidence was found. Lefèvre's studies were based on the erosion of rocks and the deposition of sediments, and his conclusions have stood with little modification till now. H. P. Blavatsky noticed that his estimates of the *relative* duration of the geological ages agreed fairly well with the 'esoteric' information in her possession, and so by adapting her knowledge of the real figures to Lefèvre's proportional scale she constructed a time table which, she says, approximates the truth "in almost every particular." Her total of "320,000,000 years of sedimentation" is much less than that of modern geologists, even though she includes the Laurentian period in her table, which they omit.

A glance at the modern table alongside hers will show how greatly modern geologists have extended their time periods. Two reasons are given for this great extension: first, the supposedly known and constant rate of radioactive disintegration in certain minerals found in the rocks; second, the modern belief that biological evolution by natural selection, etc., required far more time than formerly seemed necessary or permissible.

In her 'Esoteric' table H. P. Blavatsky, following Lefèvre's arrangement, combines the three oldest periods, the Laurentian, Cambrian and Silurian, into her Primordial era. The two latter are now placed in the Paleozoic era, and the Laurentian and older rocks are included within the preceding Precambrian era, an enormously long complex of sedimentary, plutonic and metamorphosed rocks lying in tangled confusion below the Paleozoic strata, and in which forms of life are very scanty or altogether absent. The Precambrian era was longer than all the subsequent eras combined, and probably covers much of the "third round" evolution of life on this globe, for H. P. Blavatsky says that her 320,000,000 years of sedimentation, which approximates to the time elapsed since the Precambrian era, refers to this round (the fourth) of the human life-wave, for "it must be noted that even a greater time elapsed during the preparation of this globe for the Fourth Round *previous to stratification*" (*The Secret Doctrine*, II, 715). The tremendous cataclysms and the general transformations of the earth's crust that took place at the end of the third round (greater than any of the "revolutions" that have happened since) destroyed nearly all

H. P. Blavatsky's Table of Sedimentation (*The Secret Doctrine*, II, 710)			
ERA	PERIOD	DURATION IN YEARS	BEGAN YEARS B.P.
Quaternary		1,600,000°	1,600,000
Tertiary	Pliocene Miocene Eocene	7,360,000°	8,960,000
Secondary	Cretaceous Jurassic Triassic	36,800,000	45,760,000
Primary	Permian Coal Devonian	103,040,000	148,800,000
Primordial	Silurian Cambrian Laurentian	171,200,000	320,000,000

°Probably in excess

ERA	PERIOD	EPOCH	DURATION IN YEARS	BEGAN YEARS B.P.
		THE GEOLOGICAL COLUMN AS ESTIMATED BY CONTEMPORARY SCIENCE*		
Cenozoic	Quaternary	Recent Pleistocene	1-2,000,000	1-2,000,000
	Tertiary	Pliocene Miocene Oligocene Eocene Paleocene	58-68,000,000	60-70,000,000
Mesozoic	Cretaceous Jurassic Triassic		127-162,000,000	185-230,000,000
Paleozoic	Permian Carboniferous Devonian Silurian Ordovician Cambrian		315-370,000,000	
Precambrian	Late			500-600,000,000
	Early		1,500,000,000	2,000,000,000 +

*Figures are a reconciliation of several sources publishing geological time charts estimated in terms of duration and years before the present. Divisions in these tables are not strictly to scale.   — B. A. MOFFETT traces of the third round forms of life. A few living entities, mostly or entirely marine, managed to exist in and survive the great disturbances during the dawning of the opening drama of the fourth round. Their fossils are found in the earliest periods of the Paleozoic era associated with the rather more advanced forms which gradually superseded them (ibid., II, 712).

It is now necessary to explain the theosophical usage of the term *round* which is not found in geological textbooks.

THE ROUNDS AND THEIR SUBDIVISIONS

Before the "rounds" can be understood it is essential to have some idea of the entire scheme of terrestrial evolution from the standpoint of the ancient wisdom given in *The Secret Doctrine*. In a few words: the earth we see is the fourth of a sevenfold "chain" of globes which constitutes a single organism, as we may call it. The other six globes are not visible to our gross senses but the entire group is intimately connected. The vast stream of human monads circulates seven times round the earth planetary chain during the great cycle. We are now in the fourth circulation or *round* of the great pilgrimage on our globe and so this period is called the fourth round. While on our globe we pass through seven stages called "root-races," each lasting for millions of years. Each in its turn is subdivided into smaller septenary sections. Each succeeding root-race is shorter than its predecessor, and there is some overlapping. Great geological changes separate each root-race from its successor and only a comparatively few survivors remain to provide the seed for the next root-race.

The individualized life cycles in the rounds are associated with diversities in environment. Each round is a component part of a great serial order of evolution which may be summarized as the gradual descent of spirit into matter and the subsequent ascent. The first round, even on this globe, was highly spiritual and ethereal: the succeeding rounds are less so, until the middle of the fourth round is reached. After that axial period the process is reversed and by degrees the original state of ethereality is reassumed. A similar process takes place within each round, but on a minor scale — smaller cycles within a dominant one. The physical condition of the earth's substance is modified in a corresponding way. The amazing modern discoveries of the nature of the atom, of its transmutations, and of the transformation of 'matter' into energy have removed any prima facie objections to such a process.

In studying this subject we must remember that the word "man" is used in two distinct senses which must be clearly distinguished in order to avoid confusion. It may refer to the spiritual monad in the earlier stages of evolution before the appearance of mind, and which H. P. Blavatsky calls "the pre-human man"; or to the "human, Adamic man," thinking, rational, "seven-principled" man of the fourth and fifth root-races in this fourth round. In Hindu philosophy the latter is called "Vaivasvata's humanity." Vaivasvata is the Hindu Noah who allegorically saved the remnant of mankind after the Deluge and established a "new order of ages" on the earth (see *The Secret Doctrine*, II, pp. 69, 251, 309).

The first root-race of the fourth round was by far the longest of its seven root-races, because within it were included advanced monads from the third *round* or life-wave on this globe, called *śishtas*,* and other forerunners, who preceded by millions of years the main aggregation of monads that formed the first root-race properly so called.

The second root-race was not so long as the first, the third was considerably shorter, and so forth. We are now about halfway through the fifth root-race, and two-and-a-half root-races are still to come before the end of the fourth round on this globe. The fourth round contains the period of greatest materiality for the vehicles of the monad during the entire seven rounds, and during this middle round the ascent of the ladder of spiritual unfoldment begins.

Although the 'physical' conditions, if we may use the word, of the entire fourth round were denser than those of its predecessors, the early part of the fourth, which includes the first and second root-races and most of the third, was still quite ethereal and no material traces of man have been left for science to discover. The records remain, nonetheless, in the "astral light," the ethereal picture gallery of nature, the "Earth-Memory" as G. W. Russell (AE), the Irish poet and mystic, called it. In the fifth subrace of the third root-race, the monad began to build less ethereal embodiments for itself in preparation for the "descent of Mind," and after many long ages the physical and other characteristics of "man," as we understand the term, appeared and were gradually perfected. In the fourth root-race, the "Atlantean" man was fully physicalized, as the earth itself became hard and dense.

In regard to the dates and duration of the earlier root-races of the fourth round we are given but little information.

---

*A Sanskrit word meaning "remainders," those left behind to serve as "seeds of life" for the returning life-wave in the succeeding round.

We can, however, place the early root-races approximately side by side with the periods and dates given by H. P. Blavatsky in her 'Esoteric' table and reach a fairly close idea of their antiquity. From some casual hints contained in *The Secret Doctrine* it is clear that the first root-race began before the Mesozoic (Secondary) era, most probably in the Pennsylvanian (Carboniferous) period in the Paleozoic, but possibly earlier. According to the 'Esoteric' table this could even be almost 150,000,000 years ago. The ethereal first root-race, which did not know physical 'death,' gradually blended with the second root-race in the Permian period.

It is noteworthy that there is some parallelism between the root-races and the periods beginning with great geological, climatic and biological changes called by geologists "revolutions." This applies even to the earliest or ethereal races. At least four and possibly more have taken place, the most important and earth-shaking being that which ushered in the fourth round (about the end of the Precambrian era as already mentioned). As we are only in the fifth root-race no doubt we shall experience other cataclysmic changes during the closing period of this round on this globe. We read in *The Secret Doctrine:*

As land needs rest and renovation, new forces, and a change for its soil, so does water. Thence arises a periodical redistribution of land and water, change of climates, etc., all brought on by geological revolution, and ending in a final change in the axis.   — II, 726

The exact duration of the rounds or the root-races has never been given out; and the geologists are not inclined to commit themselves definitely in regard to the length of their eras and periods. But there is no doubt of the actuality of the serial events or cyclic repetitions and of the order in which they occur, irrespective of the number of years that may be assigned to them.

Nothing definite is revealed about the chronology of the four earlier *sub*races of the third root-race, but approximately exact figures are given for the first time when we reach the fifth subrace, and we learn that about 18,618,000 years have elapsed from that subrace to the present day. This period is called by H. P. Blavatsky that of "our humanity" because the characteristics of mankind as we understand it — physically, emotionally and mentally — showed their first indications in the fifth subrace. This period is the age of Vaivasvata's humanity* already mentioned. We have, however, so greatly changed since the monad emerged from the shadowy ethereal vestures or vehicles of "pre-human man" that as H. P. Blavatsky says:

that which Science — recognizing *only physical man* — has a right to regard as the *prehuman* period, may be conceded to have extended from the First Race down to the first half of the Atlantean [Fourth] race, since it is only then that man became the "complete *organic* being he is now." And this would make *Adamic* man no older than a few million of years.   — *The Secret Doctrine*, II, 315

As they grew more and more physical, the human em-

The Secret Doctrine, II, 312-13, says: "The History of the Races begins at the separation of the Sexes, . . . and the subsequent sub-races of the Third Root-Race appeared as an entirely new race *physiologically*. It is this 'destruction' which is called allegorically the great 'Vaivasvata Manu Deluge,' when the account shows Vaivasvata Manu (or 'Humanity') remaining alone on Earth in the Ark of Salvation towed by Vishnu in the shape of a monstrous fish, and the Seven Rishis 'with him.' The allegory is very plain: —

". . . . As to the Seven Rishis in the Ark, they symbolised the seven principles, which became complete in man only after he had separated, and become a *human,* and no longer a divine creature."

bodiments of the monad or immortal spirit in man in the latest period of the third root-race gradually became illuminated with the light of mind, the mānasic principle, which really marks the "new order" of Vaivasvata's humanity. The separation of nascent mankind into two distinct sexes took place about the same time. H. P. Blavatsky illustrates the transformation which changed the ethereal man into the physical by citing the materialization of 'spirits' in the séance room from invisible astral substance to physical in the manner investigated for the first time under scientific control by Sir William Crookes, the famous English physicist. At our present period of evolution the process is of course abnormal and very rare, only being produced by special and not particularly desirable means, but in the distant future the astral form now well hidden within man will be the outer body as it was in the early subraces. The importance of this knowledge is emphasized by H. P. Blavatsky on pages 174 and 737, volume II of *The Secret Doctrine*. On page 149 of the same volume she makes the following significant remark:

The whole issue of the quarrel between the profane and the esoteric sciences depends upon the belief in, and demonstration of, the existence of an astral body within the physical, the former independent of the latter.

According to the dating in the 'Esoteric' table the third root-race was at its peak in the Jurassic period, becoming denser in the Cretaceous period and ending in the early Cenozoic era. It overlapped the fourth root-race, commonly called the Atlantean, which reached its middle period 8-9,000,000 years ago, near the beginning of the earliest division of the Cenozoic era, the Paleocene. The disastrous breaking up of the main Atlantean continental area occurred in the Miocene period, but portions such as the great islands, Ruta and Daitya, lingered until much later, and Plato's small "island of Atlantis" perished only 11-12,000 years ago.

As Vaivasvata's humanity, in which we are particularly interested, began to develop 18-19,000,000 years ago, it is obviously far older than the Cenozoic era which, according to the 'Esoteric' table, began about 8,960,000 years ago, but here we find a striking unconformity between modern geology and the esoteric teaching. In several places H. P. Blavatsky envisages the possibility that the geologists might increase their estimate of the length of the Cenozoic era, and says that this would not be disturbing. She writes on page 693, volume II of *The Secret Doctrine:*

> It may make our position plainer if we state at once that we use Sir C. Lyell's nomenclature for the ages and periods, and that when we talk of the Secondary and Tertiary age, of the Eocene, Miocene and Pliocene periods — this is simply to make our facts more comprehensible. Since these ages and periods have not yet been allowed fixed and determined durations, 2½ and 15 million years being assigned at different times to one and the same age (the Tertiary) — and since no two geologists and naturalists seem to agree on this point — Esoteric teachings may remain quite indifferent to whether man is shown to appear in the Secondary or the Tertiary age. If the latter age may be allowed even so much as 15 million years' duration — well and good; for the Occult doctrine, jealously guarding its real and correct figures as far as concerns the First, Second, and two-thirds of the Third Root-Race — gives clear information upon one point only — the age of "Vaivasvata Manu's humanity."

Though Vaivasvata's humanity — our humanity — has existed for 18-19,000,000 years, and for less than half that time we have been complete organic beings, we may look forward to many more millions of years before any radical changes will take place in our physical structure. During the fourth root-race, the Atlantean, the lowest stage of materiality was reached, and we in the fifth root-race are now somewhat less physically dense. By the time we attain the seventh root-race of this fourth round, in the far distant future, our flesh will have become much more refined and almost translucent, and near the close of the manvantara or great life-period of planetary evolution in the seventh round we shall have risen so far above the lower cosmic plane in which our earth now functions that our highly ethereal bodies "will become self-luminous forms of light."

Theosophy and the New Science

Blair A. Moffett

The facts about man and cosmos enunciated by the ancient wisdom will stand, because they are derived from a matured vision not alone of the realm of physical matter and its transformations, but of the totality of being in all its multiple aspects and planes. Today scientists limit themselves largely to a method of inductive investigation, applied almost wholly to the phenomena of the physical universe. In the life sciences, research is concerned principally with our physical earth, considered as a single plane or sphere of life. The theosophist has an advantage in that he employs deductive thought to proceed from time-tested universals down to particulars and then, by reasoning from the known to the unknown, applies inductive analysis to test the axioms of theosophy by going from particulars back to universals.

The expectation is, however, that the findings of physical science, as these accrue over time, will corroborate and even verify elements of the more universal statements of theosophy, particularly those that concern earth-plane phenomena. And such has been the case, in abundance, since the late

1920s when Dr. G. de Purucker first presented the lectures that were later edited for this book. We now have a New Science — a New Physics, a New Biology, a New Astronomy, etc. — and there are fewer basic quarrels between theosophy and this new science. Unhappily, most scientists and many theosophists are not aware that this is so. The material in this Appendix is intended to help both become more cognizant of some of the more significant convergences between the two perspectives. Both kinds of thinkers are, if openminded, fellow searchers after truth; and truth must ultimately be one, not two.

THE NATURE OF MATTER

Little need be added to Dr. de Purucker's analysis showing modern science's dematerialization of the physical universe as a result of its own findings. Several developments in nuclear physics since the 1920s and '30s have more than confirmed the essential statements of theosophy regarding "matter." So illusive has the matter of science become that physicists now state that an electron is neither a particle nor a wave, "but an entity that defies every attempt at pictorial description."[*] The electron, or any other so-called material particle, can be studied solely by giving up the quest for a unified description of all of its properties and confining attention to a restricted range of experience. Only then can

---

[*] Arthur March and Ira M. Freeman, *The New World of Physics*, Vintage Books, Random House, New York, 1963; p. 133. This book is based on an essay written by Professor March, late professor of theoretical physics at the University of Innsbruck, Austria, and published in 1957 in Hamburg, Germany.

its behavior be understood as either a corpuscle or a wave, depending on how the boundaries of the field of interest are defined.

It is no longer legitimate to ascribe to such elementary particles the substantiality of pellets of matter: they are non-material structures, and in a very true sense the new physics has become *meta*physics because it deals with factors beyond visibility and seemingly beyond natural law, factors that can be coped with experimentally only by a statistical law. This is the famous "Principle of Indeterminacy," so named in 1927 by its formulator, the great German theoretical physicist, Werner Heisenberg. Individual atoms and electrons in their motions and actions are found to exhibit an element of un-predictability — a kind of free will or choice-making — so that even though they may be of the same kind or class, all do not do the same things. As a result, in atomic and sub-atomic phenomena strict causality, as this has been under-stood in classical physics, cannot really be applied. Predict-ability and determinism break down.*

So malleable and uncertain has the material aspect of the universe become in the vision of modern physicists that as recently as 1971 a book was published, titled *The Search for a Theory of Matter*,† which honestly acknowledges the in-

---

*Cf. J. W. N. Sullivan, *The Limitations of Science*, Viking Press, New York, 1933; p. 148 and passim. This is one of the most lucid and comprehensive summaries of the revolution that has taken place in science and in the thinking of the foremost scientists since the late 19th century when H. P. Blavatsky wrote. This British mathematician and interpreter of physics (who died about 1940) is still regarded as one of the most brilliant intellects of his time.

†Mendel Sachs, McGraw-Hill Book Co., New York. The author was then professor of physics and astronomy at the State University of New York in Buffalo.

ability of the new physics to devise a theory able to explain the phenomena it studies. We are indeed witnessing a revolution in science's view of the physical universe, one that has not yet reached its full course nor come anywhere near its destination. But the course has begun, and contemporary findings continue to shatter classical notions about the universe. Astrophysicists, for example, now realize that an evolution of the elements occurs within suns, beginning with the transformation or transmutation of hydrogen into helium, the next heavier element of matter; but they don't fully understand how this happens. In all the stars, processes are going on which build up the atoms one by one into more and more complex elements or material structures. Thus, as Jacob Bronowski put it: "Matter itself *evolves*. The word comes from Darwin and biology, but it is the word that changed physics in my lifetime."* That is a remarkable statement, reflecting as it does a dawning recognition by physical scientists of a definite evolutionary course in material substance. On the physical plane this very much resembles the more recondite process of emanation of substances and forces from inner or more ethereal and spiritual planes downward and outward to other, more material planes, as explained herein by Dr. de Purucker. The words of Bronowski epitomize perfectly how differently the new science views the universe, which in the 19th century was seen as simply a vast material machine in which every product was predetermined.

A good example is our sun, until recently regarded by science as a steady, well-ordered machine about which there remained little to be learned except the nature of the nuclear reactions believed to be going on in its heart. Now

---

The Ascent of Man, Little, Brown & Co., Boston, 1973; p. 344.

astrophysicists have been forced to rethink long-held theories about how the sun works, especially the notion that it is burning at exceedingly high temperatures. In 1974 Dr. Henry Hill of the University of Arizona, Tucson, trying to determine precisely the diameter of the sun, discovered that it is vibrating. Its limb or edge oscillates back and forth about every sixty minutes over a distance of about twenty kilometers. It is in fact breathing in and out in a natural vibration at various frequencies, a phenomenon that has been compared to the ringing of a bell.

Studies of the oscillating sun carried out at Birmingham University, England, suggest that the sun may be much less dense at its center than had been thought, and have only half the temperature assumed by current models: 7 instead of 15 million degrees. Many scientists do not believe such a low-temperature sun to be possible. Even the certainty of the eleven-year sunspot cycle has been upset. Carrying forward researches of the 19th century astronomers Gustav Spörer and E. W. Maunder, Dr. John Eddy of the High Altitude Observatory in Boulder, Colorado, finds that between 1650 and 1715 A.D. the sunspot cycle had disappeared.* Because our sun is a star, these findings have major implications for the study of any and all stars in the physical universe. Many other examples might be given, and we shall

---

*See Graham Massey, "What's Wrong with the Sun?", *The Listener,* June 17, 1976; pp. 762-4. Massey's article is based on a BBC2 "Horizon" television program, which he produced and directed, that examined these and related discoveries in some depth. See also the article "When the Sun Went Strangely Quiet," by Kenneth Frazier, *Science News,* vol. 109, March 6, 1976; pp. 154-6; and "Solar Variability: Is The Sun An Inconstant Star?" by Allen Hammond, *Science,* vol. 191, March 19, 1976; pp. 1159-60.

have more to say later on about contemporary scientific thought as *philosophy*.

Evolution and Darwinism

Turning now to the idea of evolution itself, we find this is regarded by most people as a process restricted to animate life forms and generally equated with Darwinism and neo-Darwinism. But "Darwinism" strictly speaking should more properly be used to mean Darwin's theory of the *factors* of evolution. There were many evolutionists before Darwin, some of whom also propounded theories about the constituents at work in the evolutionary process. Just which factors really apply in animate evolution is, however, a still-moot question for modern science. It happened that Darwin and his fellow worker, Alfred Russel Wallace, thought out a coherent theory about certain factors which at the time appeared to fit the known facts so well that their hypothesis won the conviction of a large body of naturalists. The essence of Darwin's theory is in the two words *variation* and *selection*, and not all the agents he believed produced those results are accepted as such today. As Dr. de Purucker points out, nobody denies that a process of evolution takes place on earth; the debate has to do with the causes and the mechanisms. Very soon after their joint presentation of the theory, Wallace found he could not agree with some of Darwin's determinants. He published several studies of his own which emphasized that Darwin's ideas were especially inapplicable in the case of man — and that other factors, particularly man's unique brain, became operative. In brief, Wallace contended that natural selection could have acted on man's body in any marked degree only *before* man acquired the intellectual capacities — the self-conscious awareness—which make him truly man. After that, this self-awareness became the principal and overriding determinant in his evolution, making him unique among all of earth's animate life forms. We shall discuss some of Wallace's arguments in more detail later.

With regard to *variation,* Darwin's teaching that acquired characters can be inherited had been disproved by biologists' studies and tests long before the 1950s. The findings of the new biology, well attested by all the available evidence, is that while a gene can make a protein, and a mutant gene a modified protein, the character of a protein cannot be communicated back to the genes. Genetics at a molecular level is a one-way street. Effects of the environment which alter the outward character of the animate life form cannot alter that organism's genes in any coherent way, as proposed by Darwin. Nevertheless, biologists recognize that a reciprocal influence between life forms and their environments takes place, but they admit their ignorance of the causes or exactly how the interaction works.

For want of any better theory most biologists still rely largely on Darwin's factor of natural selection as a broad description of the process of evolutionary change, some also continuing to maintain that it *explains* changes that arise in animate life forms. But in the late 1960s one school of evolutionary theory, led by certain Japanese molecular biologists, challenged the idea that natural selection offers any explanation at all of evolutionary change, because experimental results failed to show that a process of such selection could have any preference for this or that version of a molecule.

Since then, many molecular biologists have in fact begun to take it for granted that natural selection does not always apply.*

Mutations, which produce visible changes in life forms, arise in genes. Certain environmental factors appear to be responsible for certain mutations, but only for a very few, so far as biologists know. Moreover, not all mutations are found to conform to Mendel's laws, and there appears to be no explanation for what causes such mutants to arise in the DNA material. The situation at the current frontiers of the study of genetics and evolution is, then, that there are a number of theories in need of supporting facts! Having pursued to the atomic and molecular level the quest for the source and mechanisms of animation or "life," biologists find themselves reduced to chemical descriptions. They are back to a "random factor" — evolution governed by "chance," mutations which arise "spontaneously" — and most will acknowledge that these words when applied to the phenomena they study signify no more than that their actual *causes* remain unknown.

What this means in simple terms is that many if not all of the settled notions about the key factors affecting animate evolution, derived from Darwinism, are again at issue as a result of the new biology's observations and experiments. Thus a series of imposed theoretical conceptions that long dominated all consideration of those things which make man what he is, have been cleared away. This could result in some measure of serious attention being given to those inner

---

*Cf. Nigel Calder, *The Life Game,* Viking Press, New York, 1973; p. 65 and passim. The author is a former editor of *The New Scientist* and science correspondent for *The New Statesman.*

and spiritual factors *behind* the evolutionary phenomena —
especially of human beings — pointed to in this book. We
note in particular Dr. de Purucker's references to the powerful, indeed dominant, influence from within the entity of the
"dhyān-chohanic fluids,"* with their practically unlimited
individual potentials. Such potentials are, he says, checked
in physical manifestation by karmically originated electro-
and psychomagnetic conditions of the environment or field
of action.

SIMIANS STEM FROM MAN, A FAR OLDER LINE

This leads up to the theosophical teaching that man is
the *originant* of the simian stocks, rather than the reverse;
that man's origin was not monogenetic but took place through
a modified polygenesis; and, that man as a thinking being
is far older than modern anthropology has thus far allowed
him to be. Since Dr. de Purucker's book was issued, archaeology and anthropology have brought to light a wealth of
new information on prehistoric man and anthropoid. Much
of it upholds the theosophical material he discussed and
helps to restore man to man — no beast, but a higher being
poised between the animals and the gods, unlike any other
on the face of the earth.

Modern anthropology, however, takes no account of
man's spiritual ancestry nor of his ethereal beginnings on
this globe in this round as the *originant* of all mammalian
stocks, as discussed by Dr. de Purucker. Not all anthropol-

---

*Cf. ch. 16, "The Weismann Theory."

ogists are even in agreement as to which fossil forms of primates fall definitely within the family of the Hominidae. This Appendix uses the term Hominidae, or hominid, its Anglicized variant, for all of the forms man's *biological* ancestors have assumed here on earth – i.e., for the family of forms, both living and fossil, which are strictly human* – as opposed to the Pongidae, the primate family composed of the tailless anthropoid apes which resemble man anatomically: gibbon, gorilla, orangutan, and chimpanzee, and *their* ancestors. Such a usage has the advantage that it accords with the theosophical perspective of the primacy of the human line both biologically and spiritually with respect to the mammals.

Several years ago the respected contemporary Finnish anthropologist, Björn Kurtén, affirmed that the evidence of primate fossils themselves (in contrast with any theory) points unmistakably to the fact that man never descended from apes, but that it would be more correct to say that apes and monkeys descended from early ancestors of man.† Like Dr. de Purucker, this scientist maintains that in all the traits under comparative examination, man is the primitive while apes and monkeys are the specialized form. Space does not permit anything like a full recapitulation of Dr. Kurtén's

---

*The term genus *Homo* refers to the primate genus within the Hominidae that includes modern man *(Homo sapiens sapiens)* and a number of extinct species such as Neanderthal man. The term simian refers to both monkeys and apes in general. Not all scientists, however, not even the anthropologists themselves, use all these terms with equal precision. They should be regarded as no more than the best guidelines science has thus far devised for a relatively clear classification of the subject matter.

†Cf. his book, *Not from the Apes,* Pantheon Books, Random House, New York, 1972.

extensive, detailed anatomical comparisons in support of this thesis. Years of study have shown him that in all cases where sufficient fossil material is available to enable inspection of key skeletal features, there is no mistaking a hominid or early human form for a simian form. Dr. Kurtén observes that as far back as the earliest Australopithecines, which have been dated at some 4 to 6 millions of years before the present,* the anatomical evidence confirms an upright posture for man. This is not the case for the simians, whether fossil or living, no ape being a biped in the sense that man is. He considers it most unlikely that any human ancestor ever walked on all fours in ape-fashion, or knuckle-walked as do African chimpanzees and gorillas. The fossil record of the many specializations which all living apes exhibit (compared with man's unspecialized structure) shows these to have arisen independently. Dr. Kurtén recounts that a fossil upper jaw of a primate, unearthed in the Nagri formations of the Siwalik Hills of northern India in the early 1930s and regarded as that of an ancient ape, had been named *Rama-*

---

*References in this Appendix to the dating of fossil materials by means of their associated deposits are, unless specified otherwise, to the potassium-argon method, a radiometric technique that depends upon the slow decay of a potassium isotope (potassium-40) into argon-40, a gas. It is used to date materials having an age greater than about 60,000 years before the present, and is restricted to volcanic and plutonic rock formations. Like all other radiometric methods the potassium-argon cannot be regarded as a definitive measurement of time periods, because it depends upon a belief in the constant rate of decay of element-isotopes. There is no way to prove, for example, that 5 million years ago those isotopes were decaying at the same rate they are now, especially if the earth and matter itself are credited with an evolutional course of change. Although radiometric methods are those primarily employed by much of contemporary science, we should accept their results as provisional at best.

pithecus by G. E. Lewis. Noting some remarkably manlike traits in it, Lewis boldly classified *Ramapithecus* as a hominid. Shortly after, W. K. Gregory and M. Hellman, noted authorities on primate dentitions, corroborated Lewis's conclusions and the three published their findings. In spite of this, hardly anyone took notice and the fossil was virtually ignored until the late 1960s. Then Elwyn L. Simons, a leading paleontologist at Yale University, and David R. Pilbeam, a former student of Simons, carried out a careful analysis of it and of other similar fossils resting forgotten in museum cases in several parts of the world. Their study provided convincing evidence that *Ramapithecus* was not simian as the name implies, but hominid.

Meanwhile Louis B. Leakey, working in the Fort Ternan area of Kenya, East Africa, had found a fossil upper jaw of another type of *Ramapithecus*. The Nagri formations where the many Indian specimens were found are dated in a range of 8 to possibly 14 million years B.P.* Those at Fort Ternan are given a good 14 million years, making the African *Ramapithecus* the older. Other finds of this fossil hominid have since turned up also in Europe and China, but those of Africa remain the oldest so far discovered.

In Dr. Kurtén's view the significance of *Ramapithecus* is

---

*The letters B.P. after a date mean Before Present, "present" being considered for our purposes to be the present century. This system of dating has much greater utility for geological time than does the B.C.–A.D. system applied to our "local" time of recorded history. For the intent is to convey the total age of sites and fossil remains for instant contemporary understanding. Variations in the radiometric measurements of these can be as much as plus or minus several thousand years, making use of the local system almost meaningless. Use of the letters B.P. is becoming more widespread when referring to time measurements of millions of years.

that man had long been regarded as a descendant of *Dryo-pithecus* — that is, of a simian form possibly 6 or 7 million years old.* *Ramapithecus* then showed a true hominid form to have been in existence for at least as long as *Dryopith-ecus*! But the decisive contribution of *Ramapithecus* is the proof it affords that hominids show no convergence towards the simians as we go back from the most recent (around 7 million years) to the oldest (14 million years). Even those earliest forms of *Dryopithecus* have the specialized denti-tion — notably the peculiar premolars — characteristic of apes, whereas the hominid forms have a primitive premolar; and science knows of no case in which a comparable specializa-tion has been lost, once attained, by a reversal to the primi-tive condition.

This Finnish scientist extends his argument even further. More recent finds by Simons in 1966 of fossil primate re-mains in the Fayum badlands southwest of Cairo, Egypt, have been dated in a range of 25–30 million years B.P. Yet these remains exhibit the same distinct skeletal differences between simian and hominid forms† as do those dated mil-lions of years closer to the present, described above. All the simian fossils at Fayum are of very small creatures, the big-gest, *Aegyptopithecus,* being no larger than the present-day

---

*Dryopithecus is the name given an extensive group of very early anthropoid apes now regarded as the radical form of all the higher apes. Most fossil apes of the Miocene and Pliocene, with ages ranging from about 5 to 7 million years to about 20 million years B.P., are now classified within this single genus. Their earliest representatives ap-pear in Africa some 20 million years ago; those of Europe and Asia are dated considerably later, about 15 million years B.P.

†Specifically, *Oligopithecus* and *Aegyptopithecus* as distinctly ape-or monkey-like animals, and *Propliopithecus* as hominid-like.

gibbon. A clear lack of convergence between hominid and simian forms has thus been carried back as far as some 20 or more million years.

Dr. Kurtén sums up his cogent analysis of the meaning of this fossil record by concluding that "the most logical answer suggested by the fossil evidence is this: hominids are not descended from apes, but apes may be descended from hominids."* His conclusion, based not on any mere theory but on expert examination of "hard" evidence, closely parallels, as far as it goes, the theosophical view. Theosophy, or the ancient wisdom, avers that thinking, physical man as a distinct type has been in existence on earth for almost 19 million years. It is important, however, that such statements be properly understood when applying them to the anthropological record we are here considering. Theosophy does not say that *all* hominids gained self-consciousness at precisely the same period in far-past time. The process of lighting the fires of mind in man, which began between 18–19 million years ago among the karmically ready stocks, undoubtedly went on for millions of years thereafter for the less-ready, and cannot really be said to have utterly ceased until the 'door' into the human kingdom was 'closed' by nature at the midpoint of the fourth root-race, said to have been reached around 8 or 9 million years ago. Thus, a really enormous latitude is allowed for individual variation in development of the human mind and its physical focus — the brain — within the whole of the Hominidae, or *family* of man: that is to say, among its different genera.

Another fossil primate discussed by Dr. Kurtén, that of a creature named *Oreopithecus,* has been dated at about

---

*Op. cit., p. 42.

12–13 million years old — contemporary with forms of *Dryo-pithecus, Pliopithecus* (an ancestral gibbon) and *Ramapith-ecus*. All known *Oreopithecus* fossil remains come from coal strata in Italy, and fossil fragments of it have been known since 1871. A lucky find in 1958 of a complete skel-eton of this four-foot-tall creature, at Bacinello in Tuscany, showed it to have a number of curiously manlike traits in its teeth, jaws, skull and hipbone. *Oreopithecus* currently fascinates many anthropologists because it is perhaps the one kind of ancient primate — one of the oldest known, in fact — whose convergence with man appears to them to go further than any other. Another fossil discovery in 1957 consisting of very large jaws and isolated teeth, found only in Kwangsi Province in southern China, is that of *Giganto-pithecus*. Although regarded as a pongid, this form also displays several manlike traits including reduced canine teeth.

What significance has all this for our discussion? First, the farther back we go, the fossil record shows no evidence of any tendency for hominid forms to display apelike char-acters, while, on the other hand, some exceedingly ancient fossil ape-forms are found turning up with certain *hominid-*like anatomical characters. How can this be explained? It is certainly susceptible of an explanation under the theo-sophical view of the origin and evolution of the simians: (a) that the monkeys arose from fruitful unions between a "mindless" or unself-conscious hominid stock and a high beast stock — which we can tentatively date at some 20–26 million years before the present; and (b) that the anthro-poids resulted some 8 or 9 million years ago from fruitful unions of a degenerate human stock with descendants of the earlier miscegenations, quasi-beast stocks of types that have since died out.* In far past geological times both these simian stocks, says Dr. de Purucker, resembled their respective human half-parents in much fuller measure than do their present-day descendants, the living monkeys and apes. The earlier stocks were much nearer in time to the dominant human influence taking its rise within their heredity. The living simians show the effects of specialization away from that influence over the intervening millions of years. This may be seen in the embryos as well as in the infant members of present-day simian stocks – especially the ape stocks. Both the embryo and the infant are much more "human" in appearance than are the adults.

Moreover, contemporary anthropology does not consider the possibility that some of the earlier hominid-like fossil forms – such as perhaps *Oreopithecus* and some even of the Australopithecines or other so-called near-men – may well be examples of early miscegenations which brought into existence these stocks of beings intermediate between higher animals and man. These hybrids would be outside of the true human line and, as said, have become extinct. Only their more degenerated or animal-like descendants, the apes and monkeys, continue to survive in several parts of the world and to intrigue scientists because of their faint and blurred biological resemblances to true hominids.

The Hominidae Are Polygenetic

We see, then, that there is important scientific data which tends to substantiate man's great age as a form superior to

---

*Cf. *The Secret Doctrine*, II, 184, 191–2, 689; see also ch. 12 in the present volume.

that even of higher animals contemporaneous with him in time. What is of almost greater interest for our discussion is that some anthropologists are interpreting recent findings in a manner to suggest a polygenetic or polyphyletic human ancestry rather than the monogenesis of earlier theory. This new perspective, based upon study of actual fossil materials, deals so far with a period of some few millions of years only. Nevertheless it is suggestive of the far broader theosophical statement that man's first root-race — many, many millions of years B.P. — exhibited a modified polygenesis.

According to the teachings of the theosophical tradition, seven distinct human stocks — what could be called genera of Hominidae — took their contemporaneous rise in different localities on the earth. In their earlier expressions these groups closely resembled each other, certainly until the unfolding of self-consciousness began to take widespread effect among them during the latter part of the third root-race. Because of the differing rates and manners in which that new awareness made its impress upon the individual units, differentiation of form among the various hominid stocks became relatively accelerated. The maximum expression of such diversity among human genera was approached toward the close of the first half of the fourth root-race, about 8 or 9 million years ago. Then, this differentiation of form reached its acme, and radically distinctive types of human beings were to be found coexisting on the earth.*

Since that time, as the trend of nature downward into matter has begun to reverse itself on the upward arc, the human stocks have slowly tended to assume the same kind

---

*It is worth noting that traditional records the world over agree that very early man was generally of gigantic stature, while later stocks have steadily decreased in size to what we see today.

of form. Only four among the primitive seven stocks still remain, we are told, and as a result of intermingling even these now differ so little except in some superficial particulars that it is possible everywhere to distinguish immediately a human being – be it even abnormal in development – from any other animate life form on earth. Does the scientific picture tend to negate or to corroborate that offered in modern theosophy? To answer this question we must review the explosive changes that have taken place in anthropology since 40 and even 30 years ago.

In the 1940s the evolutionary line of man's direct ancestors – i.e., of the genus *Homo* – was generally thought by scientists to be not more than 500,000 years old at the very most. It was held to begin with the so-called Java and Peking man, now termed *Homo erectus*. In 1959, largely but certainly not exclusively as a result of discoveries made in East Africa by Louis and Mary Leakey, estimates for this ancestry were moved back dramatically to about 1.6 million years B.P. Then, in 1972 their son Richard Leakey found a fossil hominid skull and thighbones remarkably like those of modern man, in deposits dated at about 2.6 million years before the present. Anthropological notions of the age of our immediate ancestors were extended almost another million years. In October 1975 Mary Leakey announced discovery in Laetolil, Tanzania, at a site not far from those of earlier finds, of jaws and teeth of a type of the genus *Homo* in deposits that have been assigned a firm date of some 3.75 million years B.P. A year previously, in 1974, in Ethiopia's desolate Afar Triangle area to the north of the region worked by the Leakeys, Dr. Donald C. Johanson of Case Western Reserve University unearthed a near-complete female hominid skeleton provisionally dated at about 3.5 million years old. Other anthropologists working in East Africa have also found fossil remains of early hominid types that have been assigned comparable ages.

In their recent epochal fieldwork in Africa, Richard Leakey and Dr. Johanson have shared their findings and ideas all along the line. One result of their work has considerable importance for the ethical perspective de Purucker's book conveys as part and parcel of its scientific information: the absolute need of practical brotherhood among all men if we are to accomplish our evolutionary journey. Speaking at Pasadena City College in the spring of 1975, Richard Leakey presented film clips of life and work among the present native inhabitants along the shores of Lake Turkana (formerly Lake Rudolf) in East Africa. The films demonstrated how those people have learned to share among the whole community, without individual rivalry, what the surroundings offer for their survival.

Leakey then emphasized that his study of prehistoric men has shown him that they too must have lived together cooperatively, in a manner completely at variance with that of the "aggressive savage," as our forebears are so often stereotyped nowadays in some popularized anthropological books. The "stones and bones" of men more than a million years old, he said, have convinced him that within their own ecosystem early men must have displayed as much intelligence and as full a sense of human solidarity and compassion as do some modern men within their ecosystems which, though more highly structured and complex in material gadgetry, are not so different in terms of essential needs and interests. In other words, the need for brotherhood as a central force was just as vital for successful human evolution millions of years ago as it is today; and

further, that we — modern *Homo sapiens* — owe our existence not to our ancestors' "naked ape" aggressiveness but
rather to their ability to cooperate.

Just a year later, in the spring of 1976, Dr. Johanson and
his team announced discovery in the Afar Valley of about
150 bones from a group of two children and three to five
adults, all of whom were found together and are thought to
have been killed in a flash flood or similar catastrophe.
This is the first time that a group of fossilized individuals
closely related genetically has been found, and Dr. Johanson believes they can tell us much about the growth and
development of their species. Johanson has classified that
group as *Homo* or man, although not as advanced as *Homo
erectus*, and assigned them a date of at least 3 million and
probably 3.5 million years B.P. In a joint press conference
sponsored by the National Geographic Society in Washington, D.C., Johanson and Richard Leakey discussed their
newest finds and both emphasized that the evidence of the
fossil record is that "man is innately cooperative," for prehistoric men hunted in groups and did other things together
and "returned to a home base." Leakey said:

> One begins to see a picture of a social unit unlike that seen in
> any other animal. It's not just the old bones we're interested in. It's
> important to know if our earliest ancestors were decent, cooperative
> creatures instead of killer apes. I'm sure man was a predator. But to
> kill, to be like us, to kill out of being nasty — there's no evidence of
> that at all in the fossil record.*

The general view among anthropologists has been that
human social groups were a comparatively recent develop-

---

*As reported in *The Washington Post,* March 9, and *The National
Observer,* March 20, 1976.

ment, dating back little more than 60,000 years to the time of Neanderthal man!*

Contemporary paleoanthropological discovery has made it clearer that several types of hominids as well as "near-men" — such as *Australopithecus* — pursuing parallel but different lines of evolution must have shared the earth contemporaneously. Numbers of respected anthropologists, among them Alan Houghton Brodrick,† hold this view although it is by no means universally accepted. Johannes Hürzeler, director of the Basel Natural History Museum in Switzerland who received the 1958 *Oreopithecus* find at Bacinello, believes this creature to have been on a line of parallel evolution to that from which modern man descends, but that it

---

*The depiction of Neanderthal man of La Chapelle-aux-Saints as a kind of half-monster — ungainly, ugly, brutish and with head thrust forward between its shoulders as the anthropoids carry theirs — which persisted as recently as 1957, has been shown as altogether untrue. In that year the skeleton was examined by William Straus of Johns Hopkins University and Alec Cave of St. Bartholomew's Hospital Medical College in London. They found it was that of an atypical old man who had suffered from arthritis of the jaws, spine and perhaps the limbs; and that the reconstruction of the skull, especially at its base, was unsatisfactory. M. Boule, of the Institute of Human Paleontology in Paris, who had examined and reconstructed the skeleton between 1908–12, prepared the highly respected and highly misleading report about Neanderthal's apelike posture and gait. It is now known that Neanderthal — whose relatively extensive remains have since been uncovered in Africa and Asia as well as Europe — walked as upright as do we and, if he could be seen walking the streets of one of our cities, would attract no more attention than many of its modern denizens. Neanderthal man lived "side by side for long ages" with other types of *Homo sapiens*, and some of his remains have been dated at between 120-200 thousand years B.P., according to contemporary anthropological estimates.

†This well-known British anthropologist has assembled a great deal of evidence for such a prospect in his study, *Man and His Ancestry*, Premier Books, Fawcett World Library, New York, 1964.

was a "blind-alley" form which died out. At the joint press conference just mentioned, Leakey produced evidence for a 1.5 million year old *Homo erectus* in Africa, and said that the Peking and Java examples previously assigned an age of about 500,000 years are probably much older. He sees two other species as having coexisted with *Homo erectus* on the earth more than a million years ago, although these subsequently have disappeared as types. The perspective of parallel development, accompanied by the extinction of various early stocks, does much to explain why anthropologists cannot connect all existing fossils of manlike creatures into one straight line of succession leading to modern man.

With regard to the Hominidae — the much broader category of the family of man as a whole, and not solely *Homo sapiens* or our direct and immediate ancestors — there has unfolded the equally impressive extension into past time discussed above. As recently as the late 1940s anthropologists — still searching for a common link between pongid and hominid — were of the general opinion that these began separate courses of evolution from some common ancestor, mostly thought to be *Dryopithecus*, about 6 or 7 million years ago. Furthermore, reclassification in the late 1960s of *Ramapithecus* and its coordination with related fossil evidence in other parts of the world, showed that varieties of true hominids — of types naturally less evolved than those of our own genus *Homo* — existed as long ago as 15 and possibly as much as 20 or more million years B.P.

The 3 or 4 million years currently allowed our genus *Homo* shows man to have been man, and nothing less than man, pretty much as we know him anatomically and in terms of brain development, for a hitherto unsuspected antiquity. That period of time is, incidentally, just about the span of duration that modern theosophy assigns for the present or fifth root-race type of man since its earliest or *seeding* appearance as a variant or sport within and toward the middle of its parent fourth root-race. But as a race or stock exhibiting its own specific character completely distinct from that of its parent race, our fifth-race humanity is accorded an age of about one million years only. The emerging fossil record, nevertheless, appears to show that a *range* of hominid as well as near-hominid types overlapped with this early *Homo,* which itself displayed a number of differences within its own genus.

In order to avoid any misunderstanding, it must be pointed out that theosophy does not say that all of these fossil types of hominids formed part of the stream of human evolution that has led directly to *Homo sapiens sapiens* or the contemporary type of man. Which of them did is, of course, highly controversial. As one reviewer recently put it, "whoever makes assertions about human ancestry enters a minefield," because of the comparatively rapid accumulation of new fossil and associated evidence, as well as the changing ideas of scientists about how human biological evolution has proceeded from prehistory into the present.

The striking transformation in anthropology is still going on. It has far from convinced all anthropologists that hominids are not derived from some true pongid progenitor; however, it *has* shown that any such hypothetical divergence could have occurred only in an exceedingly remote past — an estimated 20 million or more years ago, to use a round figure. We would be making a mistake to infer from the argumentation in this Appendix that all anthropologists think alike about the wealth of fossil evidence that has been and is being amassed or even about the dates assigned it.

Scientists do not hold identical theories regarding the meaning of hominid and simian fossil features, nor even agree always as to which may be hominid and which simian. Nevertheless a picture is emerging that is a great deal clearer than that which confronted the anthropologist of fifty or sixty years ago. Incomplete as it may still be – and it is imperfect – overall it is found to support the anthropogenesis outlined in volume II of H. P. Blavatsky's *The Secret Doctrine.**

In brief, the distinction between anthropology and the ancient wisdom is mainly one of approach. The former seeks to develop a viable evolutionary theory on the basis of the physical changes that are known to have taken place in bodily forms; the latter regards man primarily as a monad of conscious energy which evolves a succession of material vehicles for the purpose of expressing ever more fully its inherent potential.

THE MYSTERY OF THE HUMAN BRAIN

In recent years increased scientific attention has been paid to a phenomenon in man that is truly remarkable if he is to be regarded as just a higher animal and nothing else. In terms of geological time and the terribly slow pace of evolutionary change and development required by Darwinian theory, the record of fossil Hominidae reveals a spectacularly

---

*For a full and interesting account of the growth of the idea of evolution from the time of the Greek philosophers until the early 19th century as seen by modern scholars, see *The Great Chain of Being* by Arthur O. Lovejoy, Harvard University Press, 1936 and 1964. This book is based on Lovejoy's delivery at Harvard University, 1933, of the William James Lectures on Philosophy and Psychology.

sudden increase in the size of the human braincase relative
to any other mammalian life form. Cranial expansion is centered largely upon the cerebrum or anterior portion of the
brain which in all higher mammals overlies the rest of the
brain. The human cerebrum consists of right and left hemi-
spheres and connecting structures and is held to be the seat
of the conscious mental processes, in contrast with the cerebellum or the lobes of the brain situated behind and beneath
the cerebrum. The cerebellum is the seat of involuntary control of the body's physical movements, translating the cerebrum's general instructions into precise commands. The
larger the cerebrum, generally speaking, the greater the area
of cortex or surface layer of convoluted pinky-grey matter.
The number of these cortical convolutions is held by science
to be a kind of index in man of comparative "brain-power"
or thinking capacity. The beasts show no cerebral or cortical
development comparable to man in terms of the so-called
"associational" or "interpretive" cortex of the frontal and
parietal lobes.* This is the brain area assumed to be responsible for thought and self-consciousness.

The human brain remains an enigma for scientific investigators. It actually is, in the conception of neuroscience, three
and perhaps four brains. The brainstem, known as the "old"
brain or "reptilian" brain, is at the top of the spinal cord.
Above and in front of it is the limbic brain or "old mammalian" brain. The limbic brain consists of the amygdala, pituitary and pineal glands, hippocampus, thalamus and hypo-
thalamus: a cluster of small, vitally important structures that

---

*Some researchers, notably Dr. John C. Lilly, maintain that dolphins
and some whales, such as the sperm whale, have well-developed associational areas of cerebral cortex, which they compare to that displayed
in the human brain.

scientists believe were left over from an earlier phase of mammalian evolution. These structures still regulate, monitor or censor much of the body's autonomic nervous system and emotions. They also affect what is going on in the cerebrum, the "cognitive" or third brain. This third or "new mammalian" brain envelops the others and dominates the brain's appearance. The cerebellum, the fourth major structure, lying under the "bump" at the back of the head, is usually considered as outside of the three-part brain.

Here, too, we find some links with the theosophical conception of the human brain as a whole and also in regard to the functions of the pineal and pituitary bodies (see chapter 15 of this book for further reference). As Dr. de Purucker tells us, the two structures of the limbic brain known as the pituitary and pineal glands receded from view during our early racial evolution in proportion as conscious mentation or reasoning – a function of *manas* or "mind" – became dominant as a human activity toward the end of the third root-race. But in distant future eras those glands – the bodily seat of man's spiritual intuition and cosmic vision of truth – will reemerge into conscious use and may well bring about some further physical transformation in the shape and size of the human braincase or skull.

Let us return to the puzzle of man's present braincase size. A well-known anthropologist, Dr. Loren Eiseley, has quoted the blunt statement of two scientists, M. R. A. Chance and A. P. Mead, that "no adequate explanation has been put forward to account for so large a cerebrum as that found in man."[*] This means, we infer, no *biological* or no *Darwinian*

---

[*]*Symposia of the Society for Experimental Biology,* VII, "Evolution," Academic Press, New York, 1953; p. 395.

explanation. Dr. Eiseley then states that while all other mammalian life forms exhibit particular *physical* specializations, man has a curious specialization of his own of a more abstract and generalized type: his brain. Man's brain is more than twice as large as that of a much bigger related creature (the gorilla), and trebles in size during the first year of life outside the womb, unlike anything else we know in the world of animate life forms. Inasmuch as the human brain is the acknowledged seat and focus of man's consciousness, and it is man's consciousness which makes him what he is compared with the beasts, Dr. Eiseley has here recorded the scientific complement of the time-honored axiom that man is not his body but the thinker within.

An imaginative scientist, Dr. Eiseley ponders the explosive suddenness with which man "escaped out of the eternal present of the animal world into a knowledge of past and future," and concludes that "the story of Eden is a greater allegory than man has ever guessed."

There is every reason to believe that whatever the nature of the forces involved in the production of the human brain, a long slow competition of human group with human group or race with race would not have resulted in such similar mental potentialities among all peoples everywhere. Something — some other factor — has escaped our scientific attention.*

The theosophist recognizes that just such a process, which is termed the "descent of the mānasaputras," is indeed the "factor" which sets man apart and above his companion species on earth. Through creative spiritual acts, evolutionally older beings senior in standing to our humankind, endowed the Hominidae with a portion of their own self-conscious-

---

*The Immense Journey, Random House, New York, 1946; p. 91.

ness. In other words, the allegory of the exit of Adam and Eve from a "Garden of Eden" depicts man's transformation from unself-consciousness into self-awareness. From this ensued our realization of time and space, of past and future, as well as nature's demand that we engage in self-reflective cognition as decision makers who have assumed full responsibility for our thoughts and acts.

As scientific analysis Dr. Eiseley's declaration implies the recognition that at some still undefined former time (for science) there took place a primordial linkage of bright *intelligence* with bone, muscle and nerve tissue in a manner that had never occurred before, and that dramatically and forever after revolutionized the development of our kind. He does not dogmatize, but leaves his readers to draw their own inferences from his presentation. Nevertheless, it is fair to conclude that Eiseley believes such an event or such a process is that "other factor" which has escaped attention.*

At this point several remarks are worth making about the findings of modern neuroscience concerning the human brain. Many brain investigators continue to believe that when matter is organized with sufficient complexity — as it is in the brain — it begins to manifest the qualities we associate with the mind. This of course is the orthodox stand of the reduc-

---

*For his part, Dr. Kurtén has also been struck by the inexplicably rapid expansion in brain size in certain hominid forms relative to others contemporaneous with them. He finds a strong probability that this took place two or three million years ago, but is unable to account for its occurrence:

"We can make guesses, and it is legitimate to do so, but we do not know for sure. We can only say that, based on the evidence at hand, it seems that the evolution of brain size was suddenly accelerated at least twice during Pleistocene times" (*Not from the Apes,* p. 136).

He estimates the Pleistocene epoch to have begun something more than three million years before the present.

tionists among scientists: those who attempt to explain all biological processes by the same explanations (as by physical laws) that chemists and physicists use to interpret so-called inanimate matter.

Brain research remained slow until just the past several decades, however, and of the five or six men regarded as foremost in this field several think differently from their reductionist colleagues; all of them in one way or another are described as having come to a religious or mystical feeling about the nature of human consciousness as a result of their own scientific work. In particular one of these leaders, Sir Charles Sherrington, after a long and brilliant career studying the human brain, could say no more than that "we have to regard the relation of mind to brain as not merely unsolved, but still devoid of a basis for its very beginning."* Sherrington concluded that man's being consists of "two fundamental elements" — brain *and* mind — and that brain action does not explain the mind. In 1975 his outstanding pupil, Dr. Wilder Penfield, after an equally long and successful career in brain research, came out emphatically with the same view, saying:†

Because it seems to me certain that it will always be quite impossible to explain the mind on the basis of neuronal action within the brain, and because it seems to me that the mind develops and matures independently throughout an individual's life as though it were a continuing element, and because a computer (which the brain is) must be programmed and operated by an agency capable of independent understanding, I am forced to choose the proposition that our being is to be explained on the basis of two fundamental elements. This, to my mind,

---

*"Wraparound," *Harper's,* vol. 251, December 1975; p. 6.
†*The Mystery of the Mind,* Princeton University Press, Princeton, 1975; p. 80.

offers the greatest likelihood of leading us to the final understanding toward which so many stalwart scientists strive.

So again we see a situation resulting from intensive recent research in one branch of the new science that has brought rigorously scientific, honest researchers — some of the foremost in the field — to recognize that the forces at work in man's mind are distinct from the biological operation of his brain. An even closer approach to the theosophical perspective in this connection is found in these words of Dr. Oliver Sacks, a neuropsychologist at Albert Einstein College of Medicine in the Bronx, New York, and the author of several books about human consciousness: *

> The entire organism is a functional unity: thus we are not conscious with our cortex alone; we are conscious with the whole of ourselves. . . . It cannot be supposed that the origination of consciousness lies in us alone. Our consciousness is like a flame or a fountain, rising up from infinite depths. We transmit and transfigure, but are not the first cause. We are vessels or funnels for what lies beyond us. Ultimately we mirror the nature which made us. Nature achieves self-consciousness through us.

The Contribution of Alfred Russel Wallace

For his part, Dr. Eiseley has done the cause of truth a real service by resuscitating some of the findings and conclusions of Alfred Russel Wallace, Darwin's great contemporary. It was Wallace, for example, who generously named their jointly-discovered theory "Darwinism." It was also Wallace who in 1913 protested that the Piltdown skull did not prove much, if anything, about human evolution. This famous cra-

---

* "Wraparound," December 1975; p. 5.

nium and jaw, forty years later shown to be a hoax, had seemed to many Darwinists to substantiate their notions of a "missing link" between pongid and hominid that would prove man's descent from a simian progenitor. But Wallace did not believe what the Piltdown skull *seemed* to reveal about the nature of the process by which the human brain had evolved.

Darwin had seen in the rise of man with his unique brain only the undirected play of such natural forces as he believed had produced the rest of the living world of plants and animals. Wallace, however, early abandoned this view and asserted instead a theory of a divinely directed control of the *human* evolutionary process. Darwinists in their desperate search for the required missing links between man and ape were depicting living aboriginal peoples as fulfilling that role! Wallace, on the basis of many years' experience among such tribes in tropical archipelagoes, refuted the Darwinists' contention that they were mentally inferior. He asserted that, to the contrary, the aborigines' mental powers were far in excess of what they needed to engage in the simple food-gathering activities by which they survived. Employing the Darwinists' own arguments as applied to man, he asked: "How, then, was an organ developed so far beyond the needs of its possessor? Natural selection could only have endowed the savage with a brain a little superior to that of an ape, whereas he actually possesses one but little inferior to that of the average member of our learned societies."*

---

*As quoted in Eiseley's *The Immense Journey*, pp. 83-4. For a fuller exposition of Wallace's views, see his *Contributions to the Theory of Natural Selection*, especially ch. 9-10; first printing, 1870; reprinted by AMS Press, New York, 1973. See also his *Darwinism*, especially ch. 15, "Darwinism Applied to Man," Macmillan & Co., New York & London, 1889.

Today it is a commonplace of scientific knowledge that no
race or people enjoys superior mental potential over others.
In essence, Wallace argued that proof of rapid brain development would imply a divinely directed force at work in
man. Once man's mental powers awoke, his success or fail-
ure in the evolutionary process would depend on mental and
moral qualities rather than on physical factors, and he would
continue with very little physical modification except insofar
as the development of intellectual capacity was reflected in
the shape and size of the cranium. Those stocks which did
not keep up that mental and moral progress would, said
Wallace, become extinct and give place to stocks that did.
All this is clearly theosophical. The Darwinians won the
stage, however, and Wallace's views, despite their logic and
clarity, were virtually ignored by later evolutionists. Wallace
had also contended, and from the same logical basis, that the
closer this research came to the starting point of the human
family the more varied would be the bodily structure of hominids, in conformance with the diverse effects mind or self-consciousness would produce in different units – a theory that
later anthropological discovery has done much to uphold.

Certain advances in science correlative to findings about
the human brain need mention here. It is a fact that most
contemporary anthropologists recognize that purely biological explanations of human behavioral adaptation are inadequate. While man, like all other animate life forms, must
adjust to environment, attempts to link human behavioral
systems to simple geographic or even genetic factors have
always failed. Today scientists group those major factors
which they find exhibited in human adaptation under one
word: *culture* – that is, an integrated pattern which includes
thought, speech, action and artifacts, and depends upon

man's capacity for learning and transmitting knowledge to succeeding generations. Man is not born with culture, but with a capacity to acquire culture. He does not, they affirm, merely react to environment: he consciously changes, transforms and modifies it. While in animals behavior is predominantly instinctual, in man it is almost entirely a product of culture, imparted by teaching and learning, and does not reflect a fixed set of drives as is the case with the beasts.

Writing in 1962, the leading geneticist of human evolution, Theodosius Dobzhansky, clearly endorsed this view by saying that from very early times "man has been adapting his environments to his genes more often than his genes to his environments."* In man, biological evolution is clearly subordinate to cultural evolution; the chief determinants of human behavior are neither anatomical nor genetical as they are in the beasts. Therefore human behavior is a function and result of the *inner* consciousness that works largely through the brain – that is, man's cerebrum.

Now, if we turn to modern theosophy we see that the origin of this distinctive human culture is found in the tremendous "mānasaputric event" already referred to, which rapidly brought latent human consciousness forth into activity. The awakened early human stocks of the latter part of the third root-race are described as building the first cities of lava and stone, cultivating the first crop plants, constructing the first implements and artifacts, etc. In this view, then, culture is a reflection on this earth-plane of the working of the distinctively human consciousness or monad to the degree that that consciousness has learned to manifest its creative

---

*In his *Mankind Evolving*, Yale University Press, New Haven, 1962; p. 319.

powers. Manifestations of human creative faculties display imperfection and error, as we all know — man often harming his environment as much as or more than he helpfully modifies it, and then nature reacts upon him. Although physical science and theosophy approach this topic from different angles or standpoints, there is nevertheless a clear convergence of thought about it, regardless of methods of analysis. This convergence has been aptly epitomized in the title of the contemporary book, *Man Makes Himself.** That study is only one example of what is in fact a growing literature devoted to the uniqueness of human culture that may fairly be said to have begun with the writings of Wallace. It is far too extensive for treatment here.

Some Discoveries of the New Biology

Remarkable advances in genetics and cell study made by the new biology have done much to substantiate Dr. de Purucker's statements that (a) what science calls the cell is an infinitesimal focus of cosmic forces through which these forces pour into physical manifestation; and (b) that there are uncounted and actually almost innumerable possibilities of development, locked up or latent potentialities, in a cell. These are all seeking expression, he said, and many have to bide their time for ages before the opportunity comes, if it

---

*By V. Gordon Childe, Watts, London, 1942. Examples of other works that discuss the scientific attitude toward human cultural evolution are *The Human Imperative* by Alexander Alland, Jr., Columbia University Press, New York, 1972; and *Naked Ape or Homo Sapiens?*, by John Lewis and Bernard Towers, Garnstone Press, London, 1969. Dr. Alland is an anthropologist, Dr. Towers an anatomist, and Dr. Lewis a scientific writer with university training in science and anthropology.

ever does: that is, until the appropriate karmic environment or "field" furnishes them with the open door to manifest. Of course, being a physical science, the new biology has no formal conception of the invisible divine-spiritual monad directing and urging the actions of those inner and *meta*-physical forces, and its evidence has to do with the chemistry of genetics at the molecular level only. But its testimony is nevertheless valid for our argument, because these findings at the physical level harmonize with and indeed reflect the implications of the broader theosophical statements. The latter encompass findings or data from several levels of being in addition to the physical.*

Since the 1940s biologists have conducted intensive in-vestigations of vital chemistry through what is known as molecular biology. This new field employs electron micro-scopes capable of seeing the complex molecules from which animate life is produced. Other equally remarkable tech-niques, such as X-ray crystallography, also help push research nearer to the very borders where physical life merges with astral life forces; biologists would not, as yet, employ such a term as this last, which has to do with a plane beyond their purview. To understand the findings of the new biology we must consider what it says about vegetable, beast and human cells — that is, cells of animate life forms, distinct from the life structures of the mineral and elemental king-doms, the latter being a theosophical term for the classes of

---

*But this distinction between the respective concerns of science and theosophy is crucial, philosophically speaking. So much is this so that we find H. P. Blavatsky saying that the only real quarrel between theosophy and science is that the latter does not recognize the exis-tence of an astral or etheric plane within the physical plane, through which inner and spiritual forces affect and shape the latter. (See *The Secret Doctrine*, II, 149.)

natural forces on earth which bind together the structures of all the planet's life forms.*

Every cell in animate life forms has the power of self-replication for the life term of the individual unit containing it. But sex cells are, in the words of Dobzhansky:

> potentially immortal; indeed, every sex cell is able, under favorable conditions, to give rise to a new individual with another crop of sex cells. The soma is mortal; it is the body which houses the sex cells, and which is cast off in every generation owing to death. Weismann's concepts of germplasm and soma were an important landmark in the process of understanding heredity and evolution.†

Isaac Asimov, a scientist writing more recently, after biological analysis had successfully isolated the essential chemical ingredients of the germ plasm, tells us:

> In theory, it is even possible that . . . there are polynucleotide strands that have persisted through countless generations, perhaps even from the very first appearance of life. . . . the possibility of a super-patriarch among the now-existing strands, straddling the eons since the earth was young, evokes a rather breathtaking picture of the unity and continuity of life.‡

It is within the chromosomal material (Weismann's germ plasm) in the nucleus of the sex cell that is found what the new biology terms the "genetic code": the information which, transmitted to every cell newly appearing in the growing life form, instructs it how to replicate. (The human body at full growth has an estimated fifty trillion or more cells, derived from one original cell.) The cell nucleus is

---

*Cf. ch. 18, p. 220, "Lost Pages of Evolutionary History."

†*Evolution, Genetics, and Man,* John Wiley & Sons, New York, 1955; p. 74.

‡*The Genetic Code,* Orion Press, New York, 1962; pp. 141-2.

composed of molecules of proteins and nucleic acids. These are chemical substances which are universally present in all animate life as nucleoproteins — large and highly-complex, energy-laden molecules. Protein molecules in the cell's nucleus are made of some 20 amino acids. The DNA and the RNA are the two types of nucleic acids which can be distinguished, each being built of only six chemical components; it is these nucleic acids which carry and transfer the genetic information. The DNA, but not the RNA, is the characteristic nucleic acid of the chromosomes and their component genes in the cell nucleus, and is the replicating material in cells. All cellular life, from the more complicated viruses (the simplest form of animate life known) up to and including man, is based upon DNA replication. (The RNA performs a messenger and transfer role in carrying DNA-originated information to all components of the cell.) DNA has been found to consist of two strands of what are called polynucleotides, which form a double helix that is held together by "crossbars" formed of four chemical bases joined together by weak hydrogen bonds. Biologists estimate that an individual gene may consist of a nucleic-acid molecule made up of a chain of between 200 and some 2,000 nucleotides. A human being may have as many as 150,000 genes altogether.

Intensive experimentation into the molecular and atomic complexities of DNA and its related materials is proceeding apace, and all the returns are not yet in, of course. Nevertheless a broad conception of the genetic mechanism governing cell formation and reproduction has already been arrived at, from which emerge several facts of paramount interest for us.

First, the number of kinds of proteins — that is, the essential building blocks of animate physical life — that can be built up out of the 20-odd amino acids acting on instructions from the DNA, is for all practical purposes *unlimited*. The question, then, is not where the body finds the variety of proteins it requires, but what *controls* the possible variety and keeps it within bounds. For, although the kinds of proteins required to form the vast array of specialized cells in a human body are very great indeed, they are nonetheless limited. Secondly and conversely, starting with only 250 genes (remember the estimate of 150,000 for a single human being), there may be produced as many particular kinds of sex cells having distinct combinations of genes as there are electrons and protons in the universe, according to current scientific estimates! Only a negligibly small fraction of all the potentially possible gene combinations in any one species is ever realized. In man a single ejaculation contains about 200 million spermatozoa. It is unlikely that any two spermatozoa, or any two ova in woman, will contain the same combination of genes. In all probability, except for cases of identical twins (which arise through division of a single fertilized ovum), no two persons alive carry the same genes. Every human being is, therefore, a carrier of a unique, unprecedented and probably unrepeatable gene complex!* The number of distinct individuals that can be composed by gene combinations in sexual reproduction is also, then, to all intents and purposes *unlimited*.

---

*While it is true that in the view of science identical twins carry the same genes, each is in actual fact a unique, separate individual, and this is well known even to laymen from simple observation. Here we have an example of the limitations of current scientific attempts to *explain* human individuality on the basis of genes alone; the cause and source of individuality is more recondite, although the bodies or factors we call genes may form an important part of the chemical mechanism that individuality uses for its physical expression.

One scientific writer* has summarized the lessons of contemporary molecular biology in this way: (1) the uniqueness of every individual; (2) the immense possibilities genetically latent in every group of individuals; and (3) the fallacy of any notion of genetic perfection. Thus, even at the level of the vital chemistry of animate life forms we see the findings of science affirming the principles of the ancient teaching, brought forward again in this book by Dr. de Purucker, that each entity is in essence a monad: a completely individual unit or life-consciousness-center, eternal as an essence. Every infinitesimal particle or point in the universe — an incomputable multitude — enshrines such a spiritual monad; and each such monad pursues or follows its own path or evolutionary course within broader categories or houses of life that are moving along *their* respective courses.

Molecular biology has also turned up some quite interesting facts about human, ape, and monkey blood-serum chemistry. Tests of their respective DNAs and three important blood constituents — hemoglobin, transferrin and albumen — have shown the structural differences of these to be small between man and pongids but much larger between man and monkeys. Within the pongids (including the gibbons) differences between man and gorillas and chimpanzees were quite small, but larger between man and orangutans and gibbons. A related kind of test, called the immunological, has yielded comparable results.† The table

---

*Calder, *The Life Game*, p. 135.

†See the article, "A Molecular Time Scale for Human Evolution," by A. C. Wilson and V. M. Sarich (biochemists at the University of California, Berkeley), in *Proceedings of the National Academy of Sciences*, vol. 63, September 1969; pp. 1088-93. For an informative overview of this subject, see the article, "The New Science of Human

which follows gives a graphic picture of these experimental
data. (Dots indicate no data available.)

Primate tested	DNA difference (relative thermo-stabilities)	Hemoglobin sequences	Amino acid sequence difference	Units of immunolog-ical distance
Man (the referent)	0	0	0	0
Chimpanzee	0.7	0	0	7
Gorilla	1.4	· 2	0	9
Orangutan	.....	....	2	12
Gibbon	2.7	....	3-5	15
Old World Monkeys	5.7	12	5-8	32
New World Monkeys	.....	....	9-10	58
Prosimians	.....	....	18	....

(Adapted with permission from the *1974 Yearbook of Science and
the Future,* copyright 1973, Encyclopaedia Britannica, Inc., Chicago.)

These measurements are valuable because they show
a taxonomic order among the primates: man is seen to be
related in a decreasing degree to the chimpanzee, gorilla,
orang, gibbon, Old World and then New World monkeys,
and finally the various prosimians, in terms of blood chemistry.

The test results have been employed by some molecular

Evolution," by S. L. Washburn and E. R. McCown (members of the
Anthropology Faculty at the University of California, Berkeley), in
the *1974 Yearbook of Science and the Future,* Encyclopaedia Britannica, Chicago, 1973; pp. 33-48. Kurtén, *Not from the Apes,* pp. 42-4,
discusses these blood-serum findings and says that comparative anatomy
tends to support them; but he has his own views about their meaning
and value.

biologists to project estimates as to how long ago man's evolutionary line separated from those of the monkeys on the
one hand, and the apes on the other, based on a theory that
at the time such divergences began all three life forms had
about the same type of hemoglobin. Sarich and others have
devised a fairly comprehensive phylogenetic tree of living
primates giving estimated times of divergence. This com-
pilation has gorillas and chimpanzees — the *African* pongids*
— splitting off from man about 5 million years ago, though
the researchers suggest that it happened "not more than" 10
and "not less than" 5 million years B.P. Certain kinds of
baboons are assigned a date of origin at about 7 million
years; gibbons and orangutans 12 million; some Old World
monkeys from 12 to 21 million years; and New World monkeys from 20 to 35 million years B.P. (Prosimians are estimated to have diverged as long ago as 75 million years.)
The scientists who constructed this phylogenetic tree emphasized that their concern is not so much with precise periods
of years as with general evolutionary relations, and they are
undertaking similar tests and projections with other mammalian stocks.

However, the student of theosophy does not necessarily
subscribe to all the inferences that various biologists are
making from these new data, nor does he accept all the details
of their theories about them. There are probably a number

---

*Gibbons and orangutans are found only in southeast Asia. The
fossil record causes anthropologists to believe the orang diverged from
man earlier than did the African apes, and the gibbon even earlier.
Gibbons are classified in a family called the Hylobates, sometimes held
to be distinct from the pongids, although they are regarded as anthropoids together with gorillas, orangutans and chimpanzees. Gibbons
obviously descend from a very ancient type of ape — possibly the oldest.

of significant inaccuracies attending their use as a dating technique, and this is recognized also by the scientists themselves. What is seen in the data – even when allowances are made for such inaccuracies and account is taken of the very general nature of theosophical dating of simian divergences – is the most interesting and suggestive "fit" that appears. The newer biological projections uphold the older theosophical statements. The general relation of the simian stocks to man is set out by Dr. de Purucker in chapter 7 of this book: monkeys have a "single dose" and the apes a "double dose" of human blood in their veins, but no human being has any simian blood in his or her veins. (The author employed, of course, a figure to make his point and did not engage in a precise chemical analysis of blood; that has now been supplied by science, at least in part.) Theosophy places the point when the monkey line arose from the human line as somewhat earlier than 19 million years ago, while the beginnings of the anthropoid ape line, on the other hand, are given as around 8, possibly 9, million years ago.

Modern Science is Becoming Philosophy

A salient feature of the new science is that it has become more philosophical. It is true that a number of outstanding scientists of the latter part of the 19th century were quite philosophical; but their work and conclusions were all too often smothered under the avalanche of materialistic thought which swept over and dominated the sciences and persisted well into this century, as the subject matter of its various disciplines became popularized. The growing realization by scientists of the limits of their capability to explain or even describe with any adequacy the full dynamism of life or the facts of being became apparent in a public way only in the 1930s and '40s. To a much greater extent it is humility which characterizes science in this last quarter of the 20th century; for, as Bronowski recently mused:

> One aim of the physical sciences has been to give an exact picture of the material world. One achievement of physics in the twentieth century has been to prove that that aim is unattainable . . . . The world is not a fixed, solid array of objects, out there, for it cannot be fully separated from our perception of it. It shifts under our gaze, it interacts with us, and the knowledge that it yields has to be interpreted by us. There is no way of exchanging information that does not demand an act of judgment. . . . And that requires, not calculation, but insight, imagination – if you like, metaphysics.
>
> — *The Ascent of Man*, pp. 353, 364

Thus has this brilliant scientific thinker tacitly assented to the theosophical proposition held by the entire ancient world that man *is part of* the universe surrounding him, inseparable from it. Other scientists have in their own way registered similar thoughts. In a series of essays questioning where modern science is going, the great theoretical physicist, Max Planck, titled one essay, "Is the External World Real?" That was in the early 1930s. Another German physicist, Max Born (1882-1970) in his autobiography said: "I am now convinced that theoretical physics is actual philosophy."

If we turn to astronomy, a field which Dr. de Purucker calls "the most spiritual of the physical sciences," a similar panorama unfolds. In 1940, for example, a well-known astronomer of the Mount Wilson Observatory in southern California, Gustav Strömberg, composed a scientifically thoughtful book entitled *The Soul of the Universe*. Much more recently Sir Bernard Lovell, professor of radio astronomy at the University of Manchester and director of Jodrell Bank, wrote: *

> Throughout the whole of recorded history a consistent thread has
> been the intellectual purpose of man to discover the nature of the uni-
> verse. Today we refer to this as the cosmological problem: That is,
> how did the universe come into existence, how did its current configu-
> rations — stars, solar systems, galaxies — evolve, and what is its fu-
> ture? . . . Is the answer transcendental or material?

Cosmology has in fact gained recognition as one of astronomy's three principal activities; it may fairly be called the
philosophical content of this particular field of science. Most
scientists would prefer using the term theoretical rather
than philosophical to describe the trend we are discussing.
But the word is not so important; the activity meant is
clear — that is, a rational search for the truths and principles
of being as these can be uncovered through the findings of
science, rather than a concentration upon the potential for
material application in those findings.

It is not altogether strange that this development is most
fully apparent in the scientific fields that are particularly
targeted at both extremes of the range of observation of
material phenomena open to man: the subatomic at one end,
and the galactic (or supergalactic) at the other. In both
directions the riddles — of subatomic particles and of the
light from celestial objects so distant that it has taken millions of years to reach us — are mental riddles, intellectual
riddles, spiritual riddles. Progress here can be made only as
scientists are willing to proceed with an open mind and an

---

*In an article in *The New York Times Magazine,* November 16,
1975, titled "Whence: We Are What We Know about Where We
Came From," based on his presidential address to the British Association.

active intuition, so as to be ready to accept new truth wherever and just as it is discovered, even though it contradict all their current theories.

It has been said that the history of inquiry into the ultimate questions can be analyzed as a succession of ages, each of which exhibits a certain dominant or favorite mode of investigation into the facts of being. This is the religious, which gives way to the scientific, and is in turn succeeded by the philosophical. Dr. de Purucker has referred to this in his writings, noting that what we call religion, science and philosophy — three aspects or ways of looking at truth — are but the natural working of the threefold operations of human consciousness. We cannot separate these fundamental operations of consciousness, he says; and only their unified vision proclaims the recondite facts of the whole of being. We see the dogmatic religious assertions of one era cast aside, as men take a fresh and unencumbered look at themselves and surrounding nature. Such prolonged, careful observation, steadily compiled and compared, gives rise to clearer perceptions into nature's meaning. These, eventually, lead to a new and fuller realization of the divine-spiritual heart beating within and behind physical nature, its vehicle. In that manner the cycle brings us again to religion; but with an improved and refined devotion, a deeper and truer recognition of our oneness with all life, and a wiser understanding of our role in the awesome procession of the universe.

INDEX

INDEX

356   INDEX

Man (cont.)
  resemblances between ape and,
    97-8, 107, 152
  structural simplicity of,
    explained, 132
  upright posture of, 89-90
Mānasaputras, 150. See Mind.
  awakened human mind, 242-3
Manvantara, 115, 254
  consciousness of animals in next,
    241
  consciousness of apes in this,
    241-2
  defined, 157
Marsupials
  appendix of, resembles human,
    84
Materialism, 162-3
  detrimental effect of, 6-7
  is unscientific, 15
Materialization
  of evolving worlds, 156, 167
  of forces, 159-60
  of original substance, 158-9
  reimbodying monad and, 173
Mathematical relationships
  in heredity, 135-8
Matter
  all, is radioactive, 16
  astral, 187
  etherealization of, 160-2, 167-8
  force and, are one, 159, 163, 191
  is consciousness, 43, 165
  is crystallized forces, 16, 159,
    163, 191
  is matters, 163
  is sleeping monads, 42, 164
  lifeless, 15, 119, 122-3
  nature of, unknown, 159
  original physical, 161-2
  spirit and, fundamentally one,
    160-1, 162-3, 168

was plastic in Mesozoic times,
  98-9
Māyā. See Illusion.
Mendel, Gregor
  work and theory of, 135-8
Mesozoic period, 90, 150
  awakening of mind in, 240
  mammalia originated in early,
    141
  matter plastic in, 98-9
  monkeys sprang from man in,
    98-9, 151
Metempsychosis, 58-9, 180
Metensomatosis, 179-80
Mind
  ancients reasoned from laws of,
    29
  awakening of, 150, 240-4
Mindless human races
  mammals sprang from, 150-1
  monkeys sprang from, 98-9, 151
  not beasts, 242
Miocene epoch
  ape sprang from man in, 92, 98,
    151-2
  Atlantis existed during, 152
Missing links, 121
  fossils of so-called, 128-9
  have not been found, 73-4
  invention of, 67-8, 106-7
  of Haeckel, 67-8, 107
  of Huxley, 70-1
  pictures of, misleading, 125-6
Mitchell, Dr. Peter Chalmers
  on Weismann theory, 205-6,
    215-16
Modes of motion
  explain nothing, 16
Modesty
  understanding brings, 7, 275
Molecule(s), 50
  cosmic, 46-7, 264

TEXAS A&M
UNIVERSITY-TEXARKANA

BP
565
P8
M36
1977

Purucker, Gottfried
  de, 1874-1942.

Man in evolution

DATE			
OCT 1 2 1994			
OCT 2 5 1994			
OCT 2 5 1994			
NOV 8 1994			
NOV 2 1 1994			

© THE BAKER & TAYLOR CO.